Foreword by Reuben Ezemadu

LEST WE FORGET

The life and times of the pioneer Christian missionaries to Ibadan, Nigeria
(1851 – 1868)

- David & Anna Hinderer

Edited by
Servant Robin

Lest We Forget

Lest We Forget

Copyright © 2006 Robin Jegede-Brimson

No part of this book may be reproduced of transmitted in any form or by any means, electronic, mechanical, photocopying and recording or by any information storage and retrieval system without the written permission from the author.

All scripture quotations are taken from the King James Version of the Holy Bible.

ISBN: 978-38325-0-6

Cover + Layout:
Femi Michael Adewoyin
+234(0)803-471-1471

Printed by
Mac Hamilton Inv. Ltd.
+234(0)803-368-1552

For additional copies of "LEST WE FORGET"
Contact: -
In Nigeria:
Henry Hamilton,
I.O.M.C., U. I P.O. Box 22974, Ibadan, Nigeria.
Tel 080 3368 1552.
E-mail hamiltonh78@hotmail.com

In England:
Robin Jegede-Brimson
C.A.G.A.,
7, Belton Close, Whitstable
CT5 4LG, UK
Tel 07745 591823
E-mail IOMCAfrica@aol.com

DEDICATION

To all my sons and daughters, both natural and spiritual.

I would gladly spend and be spent for you all. Go, Go! Go!!

FOREWORD

"LEST WE FORGET"

OYO State of Nigeria is nicknamed 'The Pace-Setter State' because of the many establishments, events and institutions in the State associated with Ibadan, the capital city of the State. Ibadan is honoured to have hosted the first University in Nigeria, the first and best Teaching Hospital in West Africa, the first Television station in Africa, the first parliamentary building in Nigeria; the first high rise building in Nigeria as well as various individuals who have distinguished themselves as pioneers in various fields of life, including the first indigenous traditional ruler who was a Bishop of a major denomination.

During the inauguration of International Outreach & Missions Centre ten years ago, a prophecy came to the effect that Ibadan would become a centre for missions in Nigeria. Already, some of the major denominations that are very committed to missions have their headquarters in Ibadan. The local Church that is regarded as supporting more missionaries per capita than any other local church or denomination in Nigeria and contributing the largest percentage of its budget to mission causes in Nigeria is located in Ibadan. A greater proportion of the leadership of the Nigeria evangelical missions movement has come (and still coming) from Ibadan.

Ibadan hosts the international headquarters of the two leading indigenous mission agencies in Nigeria as well as that of many members of the Nigeria Evangelical Missions Association (NEMA). In February 2005, four "pioneers of indigenous missions in Nigeria" were honoured with an honorary Doctor of Divinity here in Ibadan during the presentation of the first documentary on NIGERIAN INDIGENOUS MISSIONS: THE PIONEERS BEHIND THE SCENE, by another pioneer biographical research group in Nigeria (ARNI) also based in Ibadan. Many other significant missions' events and conferences have been hosted in Ibadan, all pointing to the fact that Ibadan soil has been 'mission-fertilized".

The story of Anna Hinderer (and her husband) offers us the secret of this 'fertilization'. I very much believe that the volume of the "tears" in prayer; coupled with the sacrifice and unfeigned love for Ibadan land and its people and the ultimate price paid by the Hinderers as revealed in the this presentation, truly 'fertilized' Ibadan land and put it in this privileged position that it occupies both in the secular and spiritual history of the nation.

"Lest We Forget" offers the current actors in the missionary scene of Ibadan and Nigeria indeed, both an inspiration and a challenge not to make any less sacrifice and commitment towards maintaining (if not exceeding) the standard already set up by the fore bearers of the missionary enterprise in Ibadan land. It is also a wake-up call to those Christians, church leaders, churches and ministries in Ibadan that have forgotten or ignored the very reason of the existence of the Church – MISSIONS! Anna (and her husband) have earned their rightful place in the annals of the history of the Church in Ibadan land and are among the assembly of saints watching how we play our own role. "Lest We Forget" will help us to focus on the only task the Lord of the Harvest has left for us to accomplish while we anticipate His return and joining with the Hinderers and other members of the Church triumphant! DON'T FORGET!

Rev. Reuben Ezemadu
International Director,
Christian Missionary Foundation Inc
January 5, 2006

CONTRIBUTIONS

"This book reveals the heart, the life, the struggles of a missionary. We must never forget that the missionary heart and missionary spirit finds its origin in the heart and will of God Himself. When we yield ourselves to do the Fathers will; His will must be to us what it was to Christ. As with Him, the salvation of men must be the main object of our lives, the one thing that we do. May this story serve to fire the reader's heart with that missionary vision which comes down from the very throne of God Himself!"

Martin Bentley, Kent
(Martin & Linda Bentley were (SUM) Sudan United Missionaries to the Kanuri tribe, North East Nigeria from 1976 – 1984)

"Lest We Forget" is inspiring, motivating and illuminating. As I read through this book, my heart was flooded with encouragement knowing the challenges these early missionaries faced to bring us the gospel, the joy with which they faced them and the results they got.

This is a must-read for every serious missionary. It will kindle a fresh passion for missions in the heart of every reader!

Debo Daniel,
Total Armour Intercessory Network (Missions to the Moslem World)

CONTENTS

Introduciton xx
Chapter I 1
    Early Years 1

Chapter II 19
    Voyage to West Africa Sojourn in Abeokuta 19

Chapter III 55
    The Gospel in Ibadan 55

Chapter IV 107
    Progress in The Work 107

Chapter V 165
    Visit to England & Return to Ibadan 165

Chapter VI 215
    Trials In Wartime 215

Chapter VII 285
    Second Visit to England Last Years in Ibadan 285

Chapter VIII 337
    Return to England Close of Life 337

INTRODUCTION TO THE ORIGINAL UNABRIDGED VERSION OF 1871

"SEVENTEEN YEARS IN THE YORUBA COUNTRY - MEMORIALS OF ANNA HINDERER, WIFE OF THE DAVID HINDERER, C.M.S. MISSIONARY IN WESTERN AFRICA."

These Memorials, which occupy the following pages, present before the reader a variety of vivid pictures of life in a mission-compound in the interior of Africa, in the first years of its existence; and place in the midst of the scene a remarkable instance of joyous devotedness to that interesting and important branch of Christ's service, and a bright example of trustfulness and constancy under severe and protracted trials.

With much confidence I anticipate that many readers will acknowledge a debt of gratitude to be due to my valued friend, the Rev. David Hinderer, for having consented, though with some reluctance, to the publication of a Memoir of his late beloved and admirable wife, derived chiefly from her own journals, letters, and other papers, nearly all of them intended only for the eye of personal friends, while some were even of a more private nature.

He was fearful lest by any means the human agency employed in the mission should be unduly magnified; and, with regard to her whose labours for Christ were so lovingly identified with his own, it was enough for him that her record was on high; he had no ambition to win for her the praise of man. But when he saw that his Lord and Master might be glorified, and His people edified, and stimulated to greater usefulness, by her example, he no longer withheld his consent, and permitted this earthly record to be prepared; in hope that the blessing of God might rest upon its circulation.

As soon as he had thus yielded to the wishes and advice of others, he at once desired that the work might be undertaken by the friends who now, to the best of their ability, have prepared this biography for publication. Their love for Mrs. Hinderer had only grown deeper and deeper, since first it was their happiness to know her; and to them, though more especially to one member of the family who now rejoices with her beloved friend in the presence of their Lord, she had for years freely opened the thoughts of her heart, in regular correspondence, and by occasional personal intercourse. For these reasons they appeared to possess peculiar qualifications for judging what portions of the materials to which they had access should be brought before the public, and what were in their nature too private or too sacred to go abroad.

The sources of information that the editors have used have been:

- Their own recollections of personal intercourse, amounting, when all put together, to as much as six or seven months of familiar conversation under the same roof, within the compass of the last thirteen years of her life.
- Uninterrupted confiding correspondence, spread over a yet longer space of time.
- A Journal, in the form of letters, transmitted regularly to her dearest then surviving friend on earth, the late Rev. F. Cunningham, vicar of Lowestoft, and under his direction carefully transcribed into a book, the use of which has been granted, for the present Memorials, by the kindness of a member of his family.
- Correspondence with other friends willingly placed at the disposal of the editors.
- A Journal kept, for about five years of her life in Africa, with considerable regularity, and afterwards continued by occasional entries till the beginning of 1862, when it abruptly ended without any written explanation.

- A few papers and letters that have appeared in periodical publications.

The subject of these Memorials was no ordinary person. I should wonder if any one who had spent only half an hour in her company would not have welcomed every subsequent opportunity of meeting her again. There was a charm in her vivacity and affability—in the ease with which she could draw graphic pictures of the scenes in which she had lived, sometimes touching and pathetic, sometimes singularly grotesque and ludicrous—in the readiness with which she had caught and could exhibit the salient points of her story—in the tone of kindness as well as truthfulness with which she noticed alike the faults and the virtues of the native character (which she always upheld, as having much in it to be admired and commended)—in the candour with which she took care to tell the tale of mission work without false or exaggerated colouring—in the vein of good-natured humour which ran through the histories of the adventures of her husband and herself—and withal in the entire forgetfulness of self; and the absence of all shadow of conceit, when she had been entertaining, instructing, and delighting a circle of listeners, rich or poor, it might be for hours together. **Above, all, there was her abiding love for Christ her Saviour, in whom she trusted with a faith which never failed, nor even wavered, in the dark and tedious hours of trial, and**

which kept her mind in peace, relying on His unchanging love for her, as one of His dear children. For His sake, and in His service, she had left comfort, security, and an eminently useful and happy sphere of duty at home, for peril, fatigue, privation, and special risk of death, in a climate noted for its destructiveness of the health and life of Europeans. Nor was it only the case that she braved the thought of those trials, while as yet they were only known to her through the testimony of others but, when fully initiated into them by painful personal experience, and borne down by their oppressive weight, she was firm, courageous, and persevering. **She never thought of leaving those scenes, even for a season, without reluctance and sorrow; nor actually quitted them, under a sense of duty, for the recovery of her health, without longing for the speedy arrival of the day of her return. Friends were loving and loved, home had its sweet attractions and congenial delights, but she yearned to be again at her post in Ibadan to serve the Lord Christ.**

Mrs. Hinderer necessarily fills nearly the whole space in the following Memorials; but an observant eye will perceive that she was always engaged in her own proper sphere.

Her husband was the Lord's chief instrument for gathering disciples, organizing the Church, and exercising discipline for its government. Besides ministering in the congregation, he preached in the open places in the town, planted and watched over new branches of the Church, instructed the converts privately, diffused a knowledge of the Gospel amongst the teachers, quickened their zeal, and cultivated amongst them firmness and consistency of character, introduced to the inhabitants the art of reading and writing their native language, and moreover conducted exploratory visits to towns more or less remote. On the other hand, her work, as will be seem, was chiefly within their own compound, amongst its few men and women, and frequent visitors, and still more amongst the happy children whom she was winning by her kindness and love, civilizing, training, and teaching, and for whom perhaps she was even doing still more by the silent influence of her Christian character. These Memorials must now be left to tell the story of her instructive life, and as far as possible in her own words. **They exhibit an example of thorough devotedness to the Lord's work which may confidently be recommended to the imitation of all who are called to labour in His vineyard, whether at home or abroad; while, as an illustration of the faithfulness with which God comforts and refreshes His servants, in their helplessness under overwhelming afflictions, it may give needful encouragement to many whose path of** duty constrains them to travel as she did, over rough and dangerous places.

May the blessings of the great Head of the Church, our gracious Lord and Master, accompany these pages wherever they may go.

RICHARD B. HONE, M.A.
Archdeacon of Worcester
HALESOWEN RECTORY
Feb. 17, 1872.

Lest We Forget

NOTE TO THE FOURTH EDITION OF 1877

THE Gospel of Christ having been first preached in Ibadan in 1852, and the good work having been faithfully prosecuted through the seventeen following years, the Church has been of necessity left, for the last eight years, to hold its ground, and to make progress, by God's blessing, without personal aid from Europeans, and with no other human help than that of men who were born in heathen darkness, but who, in God's good time, and by His grace, had been taught to rejoice in the light of His truth.

It has pleased God to bless and strengthen their faith and constancy. His word has taken root, and is fruitful. The Rev. Daniel Olubi, ordained in 1871 by the Bishop of Sierra Leone, is the native pastor; and he is assisted by two catechists at Ibadan, and by three other Christian men at Ilesa, Oyo, and Ogbomosho. In the latter place, the catechist is maintained at the cost of the church in Ibadan, so that by its zeal the Gospel of Salvation is being published "in the regions beyond."

The Rev. D. Hinderer visited this chief scene of his missionary labours last year, and rejoiced to witness the steadfastness of the people, and their growth in faith and in the fear of God.

Reports of later date are encouraging and hopeful. May the Lord be pleased to give increased prosperity to the work, which His grace has begun, and has thus far maintained, to the happiness of many.

Richard B. Hone

1877

Lest We Forget

EDITORS PREFACE TO THE ABRIDGED VERSION OF "17 YEARS IN THE YORUBA COUNTRY"

IT IS WITH GREAT pleasure that I introduce this touching and heart rending book. It's pages chronicle the adventures and hardships faced by the pioneer missionaries to Yorubaland and Western Africa, a region of the world then known as the "White mans grave."

Allow me to tell you now about how I first came in contact with the pages of this book through my mother.

In 1957, while still a young lady in London she met and fell in love with my father, a gentle and peaceable Yoruba man. My father was then a student on a government scholarship in England. They were married a year later. In 1960 Nigeria acquired independence from the UK and my father dutifully returned with his bride to help build the new nation.

They settled in a quiet area of Ibadan in south west Nigeria. Upon one of my mother's fortnightly excursions to the town centre she visited the local library where her eyes fell upon a certain book. The title of the book was "Seventeen years in Yorubaland; the Memorials of Anna Hinderer." This was 1962, the year in which I was born.

She was deeply touched by the book and in the decades that followed she acquired her own copy. Happily in 1985 through the witness of my brother, she came to know the Lord personally.

In 1996 I hosted a Missions Conference in the "International Church" and a burden for missions was sparked in my heart. Subsequently my mother introduced me to, "Seventeen years in Yorubaland; the Memorials of Anna Hinderer."

It has since been my desire to re-edit and republish these memoirs. I feel the book has a part to play in the calling forth of the emerging Joshua generation of missionaries; soldiers upon whom the task has fallen of completing the great commission. So may it be.

Contact has been made with the original publishers in order to pave the way for this edit and republication.

I have sparingly abridged the original manuscript for purposes of flow and clarity. Sub-titles have been added. The original language and sentence structure has been left untouched. Footnotes and sub-titles have been added.

Be ignited!

Robin Jegede-Brimson
Centre for African Gospel Advance, England
Dec. 22, 2005

INTRODUCITON

I AM HONOURED TO be asked to write this introduction for this highly significant work, "Lest we forget" which traces the earliest life and time of the first known white Christian missionaries to Ibadan Nigeria.

Robin Jegede-Brimson's passion and interest into the earliest research of this historic city Ibadan has been greatly achieved in tracing Rev. David and Anna Hinderer's Christian service in Oyo State (1851-1870).

This well researched book highlights the earliest Christian influence in Yorubaland with accurate and precise details of the Hinderer's personal journals and their letters to their friends.

Nigeria amongst other notable African nations with its strong Christian influence will increasingly impact the African continent and take centre stage in world missions in the next decade. I am convinced that Nigeria will "Fire the Gun" of global missions in an unprecedented manner, making waves in the advance of the gospel if only it obeys and fulfils its divine mandate that has been thrust upon her by the Lord. Scripture teaches that, "righteousness exalteth a nation: but sin is a reproach to any people."

Robin's book "Lest We Forget" is an urgent reminder to Africans of its great Christian heritage instilling hope for our great continent Africa, as we all combine our efforts, resources energies and finances to do missions in a more meaningful way.

I strongly recommend that African church leaders, prophetic intercessors and all who have missiological interest in the African continent do not miss reading this book.

Rev Richard Mitchell
Global Missions and Prayer Network
4th January 2006
London

Journey of the Hinderers to Ibadan

CHAPTER 1

Early Years

*"There is no little child too small
To work for God;
There is a mission for us all
From Christ the Lord.*

*Father, oh give us grace to see
A place for us,
Where in Thy vineyard, we for Thee
May labour thus."*

ANNA MARTIN WAS BORN at Hempnall, in Norfolk, on the 19th of March 1827. She retained through life a faint but sunny remembrance of her infancy, which was spent in a peaceful village home. But a shadow was early cast over her childhood by the death of the gentle mother who was the centre of its brightness, and who had left such an impression upon the heart of her little child, that thirty-six years later she wrote of the prospect of meeting her mother again as one of her most cherished anticipations of heaven. There is a touching simplicity in the words in which she gathered together the floating memories of her mother's last days, in a letter written in October 1868.

Anna's letter . . .

"I lost my dear mother when I was just five years old. I have just the remembrance of a form in bed, as white as a lily, with rather large bright blue eyes; and I know she taught me to sew; and when I was not by her bed-side, I used to sit on a low broad window-seat, and when I had done ten stitches, I was rewarded with a strawberry; and I used to say little tiny texts to her in the morning. I was only allowed to be in her room twice a day. But though I knew so little of her on earth, if God who is rich in mercy will have mercy on me, and admit me to His blest abode, I shall see her again, for she rejoiced in her God and Saviour, and I have been told that her last breath was spent in singing a few lines of a favourite hymn —

'I want, oh, I want to be there,
Where sorrow and sin bid adieu!'"

A happier period dawned upon her in 1839, when her father, who was affectionately attached to her, thought it good to accept the kind proposal of her grandfather and aunt that she should reside with them for a time at Lowestoft, for the benefit of her health. In this arrangement she afterwards gratefully acknowledged the

Early Years

"Providential leading guiding hand stretched out" for her future good. Her removal to Lowestoft formed the first link in a chain of circumstances which ended in her finding a home at the Vicarage, with the Rev. Francis and Mrs. Cunningham, whose affectionate care of her exercised a most blessed influence in the formation of her character, and on the whole tenor of her subsequent life.

Some additional details of this part of her life, with a further account of her youthful convictions and feelings, may be given in her own words:

"I loved Sunday above every day. I loved church, and was soon permitted to enter into the beauty and solemnity of the services. I felt I was in a holy place, and that holy words were being used. The whole service was frequently read through by me in the week, and I found fresh beauties in it, which I could comprehend. I felt there was something magnificent in it, and my mind would feed upon it, and soar away in imagination from many of its passages. The 'Te Deum' carried me to heaven. I longed to be a martyr, to be one of that 'noble army.' "Vouchsafe, O Lord, to keep me this day without sin," became a daily prayer; yet I did not entirely call upon Him who only can take away sin, the precious and only Saviour. 'Almighty God, unto whom all hearts be open.... from whom no secrets are hid,' made me afraid of sin, and when inclined to do wrong, and be

naughty, that passage would come into my mind, so that I feared; but it was not the fear of grieving my God and Saviour. However, I was graciously and gradually led on step by step. I cannot tell of times and seasons, but I became more and more happy. <u>I longed to do something. I had a strong desire to become a missionary, to give myself up to some Holy work, and I had a firm belief that such a calling would be mine. I think this was from a wish to be a martyr; but I wanted to do something then.</u>

"Dear Mr. and Mrs. Cunningham knew little of me then; they looked kindly at me often, as they did at every one, and he used often to ask me my name. I often thought if I might have a few little children in the Sunday school to teach, it would be an immense pleasure. I was, afraid to ask it, but having obtained my aunt's consent, when I was between twelve and thirteen, I ventured one Saturday, after passing dear Mrs. Cunningham three times, to make my request, fearing all the time that she would say I was too young, and too small; but what was my joy when she smiled so kindly upon me (I shall never forget that smile, I have the most vivid remembrance of it), and told me to go to the school at eight o'clock the next morning, and she would give me a class. I was up early enough; a heavy snow was upon the ground; but that was nothing. I went, and six little ones were committed to my care;

and thus commenced that intensely interesting work, to which, I may say, I more and more entirely devoted myself to the last Sunday of my time in that place. Oh, what a blessing has that been to me! How it filled my heart! How I loved the children, and gained their love!

"As I said before, I was seeking for something solid; I felt the want of something to make me happy, something that this world could not give; and I think, while talking to these little ones of Jesus, it entered my mind, 'Had I gone to Him myself? I went on seeking and desiring, and often said and felt, "Here's my heart, Lord, take and seal it; seal it for Thy courts above," and I was comforted in the sense that God would do it. This was doubtless the movement of the Blessed Spirit it in my soul; and amidst all my failings, my sins of thought, and word, and deed, the craving of my mind, was, that I might be the child of God. I saw my need of a Saviour, and in the Saviour I felt there was all I needed, and I was by degrees permitted to lay hold on eternal life. Notwithstanding all my sinfulness, and infirmities and shortcomings, the blessed hope of salvation in Christ Jesus, was mercifully given, with the secret assurance that I was adopted into the family of God, made nigh by the blood of the Cross, and sanctified by the Spirit. This has been my comfort, joy, and blessing, in sunshine or shade, prosperity or adversity, sickness or health. But grief, sorrow, and shame must fill my mind in the

remembrance of my sinfulness, the worldliness, the hastiness of temper, the pride, the evil that was within me, the temptation to run down the stream of life, whichever way it was going, and consequently denying my Saviour, not perhaps in word, but certainly in not confessing, as I ought to have done, Him whom I had promised to serve. I often had to walk in the dark for my punishment, and was not permitted to see the light; but my relief was in 'baring my heart before Him who its depths can understand.' I was very anxious to guard against any morbid melancholy feeling of distrust, and must say I was permitted to feel a great spring and glow in religion. It was all in all to me; it was all that I wanted to make me happy in this life, and in that which is to come. Joy and gladness were my association with it, that joy which is sown for those whom Christ hath redeemed, and the gladness that He promised. "I have mentioned my introduction to the Sunday school; this led to an introduction into the Vicarage.

It was a home of no common kind into which she was so cordially admitted. There was a charm in Mrs. Cunningham's character that gave her a strong hold upon all with whom she came in contact, and they were many. The benevolence which has endeared the memory of her sister, Elizabeth Fry, to all who are acquainted with her remarkable life, shone brightly also in her, and was exercised amongst other things in a large hospitality, which made Lowestoft Vicarage in a peculiar degree an "open house." Not only was it constantly filled with friends from a distance, but the parishioners and neighbours walked in and out at pleasure, and the beautiful garden, laid out in terraces along the cliff, was treated as public property. Amidst the visitors, of whom there was an unceasing stream,

Mrs. Cunningham moved with "sweet dignity," giving to each her unfailing welcome and sympathy. She and her venerable husband were endued with a heavenly-mindedness, which did not fail to attract and benefit many of those who enjoyed the privilege of their society. It was also a home in which idleness and 'self-indulgence found no encouragement, but where the example of Mrs. Cunningham's untiring energy stimulated the diligence of all who came within the range of her influence. Anna Martin also enjoyed the privilege of the society of Mr. Cunningham, in ways that were at once delightful and profitable. Among the duties, which were at the same time the pleasures of her life, were those involved in her acting as his secretary.

There were letters, journals, and extracts, to be copied daily, and for some years the parish registers, and other official records, were kept in her handwriting. It was the joy of her heart to be permitted thus to lighten in some measure the labours of his busy life, while she also took an increasingly active part in his unwearied and self-forgetting work of love, amongst the people of that large and important parish. None prized more intensely than she did his public ministrations in the church'; 'and more precious, if possible, to her, were the lessons of heavenly truth which she learned from his lips in private, when she sat at his feet in the retirement of his study, or walked beside him on his errands of love and mercy. 'Amid such associations the natural energy and nerve of her character were developed, and the wonderfully elastic temperament with which her friends in later years are familiar, was undoubtedly in part a result of her youthful training." She contributed in no small degree to the enjoyment of the guests at the Vicarage. With them she was a "general favourite," being "always ready and obliging, extremely bright and energetic, and remarkable for the power she had of adapting herself to different people and places, forgetting herself and throwing herself into the interests of others.' But to the service of God amongst the poor, her time and her talents were especially dedicated. She had the charge of one of the largest and most needy districts in the town, where, for her personal visitation, where, for her loving sympathy, she was received by all as a friend, and her beaming countenance testified to the happiness which might be found, as well as sought, in God.

Her love for children gave her a lively interest everything connected with the schools, and an important

Early Years

part was assigned to her the management and teaching at those at Lowestoft. A Sunday class ragged and neglected children, which she formed when she was only fourteen years of age, grew into a school of more than two hundred children, under her superintendence; and her occupations on Sunday included an hour which she devoted to the instruction of the boys in the workhouse.

One characteristic feature of her life at Lowestoft remains to be noticed.' The friend who has furnished many of 'the foregoing details writes

> *"Her face and voice are inseparably connected in my memory with the 'Sunday hymn-singings' at the 'Vicarage, a famous institution in those days. Between the five o'clock tea and the seven o'clock evening service; it was the custom to assemble the household, the pupil-teachers, and others who formed the choir, and any others who liked to attend the drawing-room; to sing hymns and anthems.'*

Mrs. Cunningham herself presided at the piano, and led the party with her clear high voice, her face beaming with faith and joy; a picture which must be treasured in memory by hundreds of hearts. She insisted upon every one joining, allowing no excuse whatever. In these 'hymn-singings' Aims Martin took the leading second, a part of some importance in such old-fashioned tunes as

'Calcutta' and 'Praise,' which were the great favourites in those pre-Gregonan days."

Anna's letter...

"Happy, happy years were those I spent with you," she wrote to Mr. Cunningham in 1853, "and entirely preparatory have they been for my work and calling."

CALL TO LAY DOWN THEIR LIVES FOR THE WORK IN AFRICA

What that "work and calling" were has now to be told. On the 14th of October, 1852, Anna Martin was married to the Rev. David Hinderer, of Schorudoff, in the kingdom of Wurtemberg, **who had been labouring since 1848, in connection with the Church Missionary Society, in the Yoruba country in West Africa.** The affairs of the Mission had compelled him to return to England for a season, but he was ready and anxious to hasten back to the service to which he had devoted his life and all his powers.

It has already been seen that the thought of such an enterprise was by no means new to her who was thenceforth to share with him its peculiar trials and blessings but she was animated by a higher and holier impulse than a child's vague longings for a martyr's crown. The desire which had first sprung from such longings bad taken deep root in her heart; the mission-field was still to her the most attractive department of Christ's service. To use her own words, she **"rejoiced in the thought of living and dying for Africa."**

A friend, whose recollections go back to the Lowestoft days, writes with reference to this period:

"Very distinctly I remember the time when, in full lire and spirits, she communicated the intelligence—' It's all settled; I am going to be married to Mr. Hinderer, and we are going to Ibadan.' Tie decision once made that she was to be a missionary's wife~ she furiously and trustfully went forth. I remember that time so well. She was wonderfully happy and bright in the prospect. She did not seem to see the difficulties before her. Her eye rested on the, work and its reward, and. her courage never failed her."

In her own review of her life at Lowestoft, Mrs. Hinderer recounted with thankfulness the way in which she had been prepared to obey the call with gladness, when it came in God's good time: —

"Notwithstanding all, my old desire for a missionary life would never leave me, and, though so much of my work at home was of a missionary character, yet I felt that to heathen lands I was to go, and that such would

be my calling some day, though I never saw the least shadow as to how it was to be accomplished.

"Yet often so near did it seem to be, that I suffered much in the thought of the cost it would be to give up all that I so tenderly loved. And in school, on a hot summer's day, when weary and dispirited, I would be roused and refreshed by the thought of the contrast between my present position and that of the missionary in other land~ under a burning sun, and other trials; and then the thought of how soon I might be called to one of those lands, and have to give up those dear children, then entrusted to my care, would bring a tear to my eye, and give me a fresh stimulus to make use of my present opportunities with them; and that text Jeremiah xii. 5 "if thou hast run with the footmen, and they have wearied thee, then how canst thou contend with horses and if in the land of peace, wherein thou trustedst, they wearied thee, then how wilt thou do in the swelling of Jordan?" has given me fresh 'vigour and power. Yet, although all this time no way in the smallest degree seemed to open for such a thing, He who only knoweth the future steps of His children was preparing me in a way I understood not."

It was a great satisfaction to her to have the full consent of those whom she truly called her "parental friends" both to her marriage and to her undertaking the

Early Years

work to which she was therewith called. She had also the happiness of receiving many cordial expressions of the sympathy and love of those amongst whom she lad lived and worked.

A friend' who was present at her marriage says, "The fine old church was thronged from end to end; the school-children, lining the path to the churchyard gate, scattered flowers before the bride and bridegroom. These are commonplace incidents, but the wedding breakfast was by no means common-place. 'Everybody' was there; it was regarded almost as a public festival... among the speeches was one from Mrs. Cunningham herself. To her with her hereditary connections to the Society of Friends, it was the most natural thing in the world to do; and well do I remember the breathless silence with which her affectionate and impressive words were listened to."

Mr. Cunningham's feelings on the occasion are beautifully expressed in, the. Inscription written in a book which was to be used as a journal given to Anna Martin, by the Roy. Francis Cunningham, the friend of her youth, and. the minister to her in maturer years, until she was called to devote herself to the blessed service of minions in Africa.

"This book is intended to record the working of Divine grace in her soul from the beginning, but especially during that period in which she dedicated herself to her

new calling; so that, in future years, if her life is spared, it may afford her a retrospect of the manifestation of her Heavenly Father's will in directing her to the duty she undertook, and a consoling assurance of His promised 'care' over her, as she desired, to cast all her care upon Him.

"May the covenant love of her Heavenly Father, purchased for her by the blood of Jesus Christ, and shed over her soul by the Holy Ghost, abide with her in her trials, her labours, and (if it may, as it will be) in her sufferings.

"May this book, too, serve to remind her of those who desire her continual remembrance at the Throne of grace, ~ho have loved her upon earth, who are separated from her with sorrow, but who hope to meet her again in a world where, without alloy, they shall re-unite to sing the songs of Zion, and dwell for ever in the presence of the Saviour, to whom be all the glory and thanksgiving."

The history of her early years, so far as it has been given here in her own language, was part of her first entry in that journal. Its introductory sentences provide a fit conclusion to this chapter.

Early Years

"I desire on this first opportunity to write a short sketch of my early life in this most valuable book, the precious gift of one so very, very, dear to me, who has indeed been the friend of my youth, my minister in the Gospel, and my kind faithful adviser and friend at all times. I never can say how much I feel I owe him, how I have loved him with the deepest respect, gratitude, and affection. I may truly say my great trial, in leaving this land for missionary work in Africa, is parting with this beloved father and friend. But this pang is softened by his own deep interest and consent in this matter, and the hope that after a few years we may meet again on this earth, to tell the tale of those past years, and of the loving-kindness and mercy of our covenant God. But in the midst of all the uncertainties, it is my joy and rejoicing to believe, tm-worthy as I am, that I shall, through the merits of my Saviour, be permitted to meet him in the better land above, where sin, sorrow, and parting shall never come; and also be among the number of whom he will say, 'Here am I, and the children whom Thou hast given me.'

"And in this separation how comforting is the thought of the mutual remembrance at the Throne of grace. My heart will cease to beat, ere I can fail to think of this beloved and honoured minister, of his precious wife, who has also been my dear friend, and who gave me the call to that dear Vicarage; of all near and dear to them

all in which they are so deeply interested ~ the parish, the people, the young who have also been of.

"The peace and blessing of Almighty God rest upon them all for ever and ever."

Yoruba Mother and Child

CHAPTER II

Voyage to West Africa
Sojourn in Abeokuta

"Oh, who else shall have our heart?
Shall we not with all things part
For the love of Christ our Lord?
Should it be a weary strife,
Should it cost no less than life,
Christ is our reward."

C.F. Richter.

THE YORUBA COUNTRY, WITH a population estimated at about three million[1], speaking one language, but comprising many separate tribes, occupies a region stretching inland from the Bight of Benin to within forty miles of the Niger, and bordered on the west by the kingdom of Dahomey[2]. The gradual suppression of the slave trade opened the way, in 1843, for the preaching of the Gospel to the inhabitants of this country, whose

---

[1] Present pop approx 60 million

[2] Present day Cameroon

religion is a system of idolatry, in which a multitude of orishas, or idols, above all, Ifa, the god of divinations, who is represented and consulted by means of palm-nuts, are worshipped as mediators between the people and the one Supreme God whom they acknowledge. Their religion is laden with foolish and cruel superstitions, even human sacrifices being offered to some of the gods on special occasions.

Abeokuta was the first, and, until the close of 1852, the only station of the Church Missionary Society in the interior of this country, with the exception of the neighbouring village of Oshielle. Thence Mr. Hinderer, during his first years in Africa, made exploring expeditions in many directions, seeking new openings for missionary enterprise. In 1851, availing himself of the protection of a caravan of traders, he penetrated to Ibadan, a vast city, fifty miles to the north-east of Abeokuta, on a spur of the Kong mountains, containing upwards of 100,000[3] inhabitants, noted for their warlike character. Great was the excitement caused by the arrival of the first white man who had ever been seen in Ibadan.

The chiefs expressed themselves as feeling 'highly honoured by his visit, and signified in council their willingness to receive Christian teachers for their people.

---

[3] Present pop 6.6 million

The words of one, "Now we have got a white man, we must hold him very tight," evidently expressed the feelings of many, and Mr. Hinderer's numerous visitors in private, both chiefs and people, eagerly entreated that he would come without delay to "sit down" amongst them.

After a sojourn of five months in Ibadan, he returned to Abeokuta, with the hope of finding there such help as might enable him to enter at once upon this new and promising field of labour. But as none could be spared, he proceeded to England, in order to represent to the Committee of the Church Missionary Society **the greatness of the work which invited him, and the importance of undertaking it at once, before the Mohammedans, who were seeking to gain a footing in Ibadan, had embittered the minds of the people against Christianity, and persuaded them to close what was now an open door for the preaching of the Gospel** The Committee entered cordially into his views, and promised him a fellow labourer, Mr. Kefer, who had nearly completed his term of study at the Church Missionary College, at Islington. The state of Mr. Hinderer's health rendered it desirable for him to remain some months in England, but immediately after his marriage he prepared to return to Africa. His heart yearned after a people whose need of the Gospel, and whose personal kindness to himself; had awakened his deepest sympathies, and he rejoiced in the near approach of the time when he should be able to respond to their invitation, which he regarded as the call of his Lord and Master.

On the 6th of December, 1852, Mr. and Mrs. Hinderer embarked at Plymouth for Africa, on board the *"Propontis"* Besides the Bishop of Sierra Leone and Mrs. Vidal the missionary party included the Rev. R. and Mrs. Paley, and Mr. Hensman, (a medical missionary), all proceeding to Abeokuta, and Messrs. Kefer, Gerst, and Maser; and though the roughness of the passage allowed of little opportunity for intercourse, it was cheering to all to realize their special bond of union in a common service, undertaken for their one Lord and Master.

A sketch of the voyage is given in Mrs. Hinderer's journal, in a passage which immediately follows the account of her last busy weeks in London, where she had parted from Mr. and Mrs. Cunningham. The subsequent letters show how acutely she felt her separation from those friends in their declining years; and the trial was increased by her knowledge of the delicate state of Mrs. Cunningham's health.

Anna's letter . . .

"Now came our parting on the 2nd of December. It made one sigh for the land where 'all partings are o'er.'

On the next day we went to Plymouth, expecting to sail on the Saturday, but such rough weather had been experienced in the Channel that no steamer made its appearance. We spent Saturday evening at Mr. Child's, and much enjoyed it. The next morning we went to Mr Hatchard's church. We were only there a few minutes, but I greatly valued those few minutes in my Father's earthly courts when it was announced that the vessel was in, and would start as soon as possible. We were all in a great bustle, but enjoyed prayer in the Paleys' rooms, and then, in a miserable drizzly rain, we went to the harbour.

"We could not be on deck, it was too windy and rainy; and as soon as we started the pitching and tossing made us prepare for our little berths, where I had to remain four days. To the end of the voyage I suffered, but there were a few days of enjoyment given us. We had a little service once on Sundays from the Bishop; the captain would not have more. We had a sad and godless set of officials on board, and were greatly tried by it, but we were not without comforts in all our trials, and when for ten entire days the wind blew a gale, it was blessed to feel 'He holdeth the wind in the hollow of His hand,' and has power to preserve His children; and the thought of our friends at home, in their constant remembrance and prayers for us, was very helpful and delightful"

On the 15th of December, when at length they were in comparatively still water, she began to write the first of the long series of journal-letters to Mr. and Mrs. Cunningham, which are the chief sources of information concerning the early years of her missionary life. Having described a refreshing day spent on shore at Madeira, she proceeded: –

Anna's letter . . .

"December 17th. - We are tossing about again on the wide waters, but we can scarcely believe now that we went through such horrors before. So it is, pleasure succeeds pain. Our God gives us such blessings, and sweetens our path where we could least expect it, and when prosperity is given, how soon we forget adversity. Well, days of trial, sorrow, and suffering, may be our portion during our stay in this lower world, but bye and bye we shall be taken to our rest above, when our deepest trial will appear but a light affliction. What a blessed time to look forward to! Now we will be glad to do God's will on earth, to do or to suffer, bye and bye to rest. Oh, that I may be able to be diligent and faithful in labour, as you, dearest friends, have been these many years. But I do feel that every remembrance of you will stir me up to the love of my Master's work, which I trust He has graciously given me. With His grace

Visit to West-Africa. Sojourn in Abeokuta

helping me, I may press on, and to the end endure hardness as a good soldier."

December 23rd, in the Gambia –

"Fancy the most lovely summer evening, our noble vessel at anchor in the stillest water possible, the little town of Bathurst[4] lying before us, the most glorious sunset just behind these little odd houses, the sweetest breeze that ever blew passing over us. Imagine all this, and then you will have a picture of me; but to complete it, I am half lying on a mattress on deck, with my desk on one of the seats, and my dear husband close by. Very few people are on board, for they are gone to spend the evening in the town."

"Christmas Eve, 1852. On board the Propontis,' in the Gambia –

"I have really touched the African shore now! And seen and talked with Yoruba people. Yesterday we visited the little sandy town of Bathurst, where there is a mixture of people. My husband knew his own 'kith and kin' by the marks on their faces, and saluted them in their own tongue, which delighted them immensely, they crowded round him, and laughed, and shouted. When I was

---

[4] Present day Banjul, The Gambia

> *introduced as his wife, and they learned that I was going with him to Ibadan, their delight seemed to know no bounds; and they came and shook hands most heartily. I feel so happy to have touched African ground, and rejoice to think my little services are to be given for that land; but my heart turns to my friends in England with a deeper and more tender feeling than ever, and the tears will come, when I think of tomorrow away from you. I think of last Christmas Day, and am thankful that I was so much with you: How little we then imagined what the next Christmas Day would be! How much dearest Mrs Cunningham will mind being away from you, and you will feel it so much. I long to hear how she is. Oh, I never shall forget tearing myself away from her, and shutting that door, and my last look at you from the omnibus. Those moments of agony are only known to Him who knoweth the secrets of the heart; and what a comfort that He looks on with tender sympathy, and has balm for that wound also."*

On the 27th of December they touched at Sierra Leone[5]. The arrival of the first Bishop made it an eventful day to the colony, and the missionaries who accompanied him shared in the joyful welcome which be

---

[5] An African Colony originally founded for the resettlement of freed slaves

received. Mrs. Hinderer was interested in seeing many servants of Christ whose names and work had long been familiar to her, and the hours flew only too quickly till the evening of the 28th, when the missionaries for the Yoruba country sailed away. This time they were favoured with a quick and prosperous voyage, though the heat made the days wearisome. The dawn of the New Year carried Mrs Hinderer's thoughts into the midst of the old familiar scenes at Lowestoft, and she wrote: -

From Anna's letter ...

"3rd January 1853. At anchor in Cape Coast Castle Bay

"Can it be possible that 1852 has passed away; and 1853 arrived?' Yet so it is. I felt very unwilling to let the old year go, but it would go in spite of me. I rose very early on Saturday morning (New Year's Day) on account of the heat, and I went and sat by myself at the end of the vessel, where I could see no one, and no one could see me. I imagined you rising early in the dark and cold to go to the schoolroom; it is strange to feel such intense heat, and to know how cold you are. How I could have longed to be with you; I did feel really homesick; but at such moments comfort is only to be found in looking up, and I did, from the depths of my heart, desire every good and blessing for you, and all whom

you love, and in whom you take so deep an interest. For myself, I cannot say what I felt my need was. How sweet 'it was to be assured that you remembered me, and. that many kind friends, in seeking a New Year's blessing for themselves, had not forgotten the missionaries, whether on land or water. How delightful is the thought that, though separated by so many miles, we are brought together in spirit at the Throne of grace, where we may tell our deepest thoughts, and breathe our largest petitions, and not be sent empty away. I do indeed live with you, my beloved friends; I have never slept yet without dreaming of Lowestoft."

On the 5th of January the missionary party landed at Lagos, and were hospitably welcomed by the Rev. C. A. and Mrs. Gollmer. Two days later Mrs. Hinderer rejoiced in receiving her first letter from Mr. Cunningham, which had in fact been conveyed by the same mail-steamer in which she had been a passenger; and gratefully did she appreciate the thoughtful kindness which had prepared this unexpected pleasure for her so soon after her landing in Africa. Among all the treasures which each mail conveyed to her from that time forward, none were more eagerly awaited than the unfailing packet from Lowestoft Vicarage. Besides giving her tidings of the beloved friends, whose every joy and sorrow and care found an answering chord in her heart, and details of the work in which she had long borne a part, it often contained precious words of sympathy and loving counsels, which were no less valued by her husband than by herself.

FIRST ILLNESS

On the 18th Mrs. Hinderer was seized with the fever from which Europeans invariably suffer upon their arrival in West Africa, and to which, should they survive its early attacks, they continue to be liable so long as they remain in the country. This fever, which is caused by malaria, varies in form and degree from ague to the worst type of yellow fever; and where it does not prove fatal, it undermines the constitution, and leaves it a prey to many other painful and trying diseases, peculiar to, or aggravated by, a tropical climate. Upon her recovery, Mrs. Hinderer wrote to her aunt: —

25th January Lagos - I had a very sharp attack of fever indeed, but, through the mercy of our tender Father, on the eighth day I was able to get up a little. I suppose few people ever had the first fever last so short a time, but when I got up I felt my weakness. My poor limbs tottered and, trembled fearfully. I am still weak, and expect to be so for some time yet. Indeed, I daresay I shall never regain the same strength I had before. I believe no one does, but one will soon forget it, and go on by slow degrees. I feel thankful to have got on so far, and do from my heart desire that the life so mercifully spared may be afresh and more entirely devoted to my Master's service."

The next letters tell of their three days' journey to Abeokuta, whither Mr. and Mrs. Paley had preceded them: -

From Anna's letter ...

"We left Lagos on the 26th of January, and went up the River Ogun in canoes. There was much to enjoy; the scenery was magnificent; such banks, foliage, flowers, scented shrubs, exquisite little birds — red, purple, orange, yellow, green — besides plenty of chattering monkeys and parrots. The nights were the time of trial, yet we had the moon, and a most brilliant one it was, to cheer us. The first night we had to stop at a little town, and were allowed to pitch our tents in a small market place. Our men made a fire on the ground, and boiled some water and we had tea, which refreshed us greatly. Hundreds of people sat round to look at us, and clapped their hands and shouted to see us eat. They were kind enough to retire about eleven, and, though surrounded by goats, fowls, and. dogs, I slept soundly in our tent, on a mattress on the ground. We were off by six the next morning, with all the people to watch our departure. The morning air was delicious, the water

Visit to West Africa. Sojourn in Abeokuta

lilies most fragrant and lovely. The next two nights we pitched our tents on sand-banks close by the river, and had several large fires to keep off the wild animals; nevertheless, a baboon and some foxes had a great desire to make our acquaintance, but a man fired a gun and sent them flying. Still there were many things that made a queer noise all night. The insects were my worst enemies; I could not close my eyes, so I sat at the opening of the tent, watching the moon, and our black men sleeping close to the fires. We left at two o'clock on the third morning, the moon gave us the opportunity of leaving at this early hour; and we parted with our canoes at a place called Agbamaya, in the middle of the day, where Mr. Crowther[6], his son[7], and several people were kind enough to come and meet us. The Chief of Oshielle sent a horse for my husband; I was put in a hammock, and did not wake till put down on the, ground outside the town wall. I could hardly believe that I really opened my eyes upon Abeokuta[8], the past has seemed so much like a dream. We had still to go two miles further to a house vacated by missionaries now in England, not very inviting in its appearance. The white

---

[6] Later the renowned freed African slave, Bishop Ajayi Crowther

[7] Crowther's son was to follow him into church leadership

[8] The first town in present day Nigeria to have a church settlement

ants had eaten holes in the floor and walls, and insects of various kinds haunted it, spiders as large as the palm of your hand, and many others. We arrived in the last rays of daylight. My husband began to unpack the stores and things he could put his hand upon; our good boy Olubi helped him, and the cook killed a fowl, and boiled eggs, which happily were to be had close by our gate. I had to get out sheets for our bed. Then we sat down to tea, laughing heartily at our first attempt at housekeeping. "We went early to rest, tired enough, and I slept till the ringing of a bell awoke me a little before six, to usher in the blessed Sabbath morning, and to call the people to prayer, which they conduct among themselves. The school met at nine: a most interesting sight, young and old assembled together, and as earnest as possible over their books. I thought of my own dear children at home, and tears flowed abundantly. I went to both the services, and though I could hardy understand one word, yet I greatly enjoyed it, and felt that I was in God's house, and that He was there.

They sing, while the people are going out of church, English hymns, and that afternoon they sang,

'One there is above all others;'

"...That was too much for me, and I sat down and wept. The children looked mysteriously, and one little thing,

Visit to West Africa. Sojourn in Abeokuta

about four years old, came quite close to me, and looked as if she would say something if she could; her countenance was full of sympathy, it overcame me the more. As I walked home she still clung to me, and then put her little black hand into mine, and ran away. The next day she saw me, and looked up saying 'Missis no cry to-day, Missis cry no more.'"

Shortly after reaching Abeokuta, Mrs. Hinderer had a new and more trying experience than the first, of African fever: -

From Anna's letter ...

"February 18. — I shall be glad; indeed, when the time comes that I can do something regularly, and talk with these people and children. I find it true, indeed, that one must go 'softly, softly,' in this country; it is every one's word to me here. I have been very ill again, from a little too much exertion on arriving at Abeokuta, so soon after the fever at Lagos; it brought on a relapse which was far worse than the first attack. I thought it impossible to recover, and looked upon myself as passing away from this world, but God in mercy has raised me again, and I get stronger every day, and believe I have learned to 'sit still,' and I find I am gaining by it. For the present my dearest husband was taken ill too, when I could hardly lift my hand to my head, from weakness; we were quite alone, and he was delirious all day. The boys did their best to keep order outside, and to bring what I asked for, which was little more than cold water. Oh, it was a sad day, but our Father helped us in our distress. What a mercy to be able now to say we have recovered, and are both feeling pretty strong.

"I had a little walk this morning early, and a ride this evening, and am teaching the children not to be afraid of me, encouraging them to come near to me, that is, children who do not belong to the school; they cling close enough, but heathen children run away in the most ludicrous manner, as if I were a serpent; yet they like to look at me, and come creeping; but if I look, they run; if I stoop to gather a flower they think I am going to catch them, and then they fly; yet this evening when they saw it was only for a flower, with which I seemed very pleased, one was encouraged to gather some like it, and then venture to bring it to me, but she held it out to the full extent of her arm. I then persuaded her to come quite close, by holding out a few cowries, after which she lay prostrate on the ground to thank me, with her face in the dust, 'Mo-dup'—"Thank-you!' Poor little things—such slavish fear. One quite sees the effect of slavery through everything, their countenances speak it, but oh, what a difference there is in the countenances of the converts: it is most striking to look at them in church, it is wonderful, such relief and ease and peace, which tell loudly of a hope beyond the grave.

"*February 23*. —The harmonium [Mrs. Cunningham's gift] arrived safely. You would have liked the sight of my first black singing-class on Saturday, and the delight and amazement of these children would have amused you; such a thing has never been heard. The people gather round the house in numbers, with eyes and mouths wide open. On Sunday evening our room was full, and we sang for an hour and a half. We did enjoy it: I only longed for the power of painting, to give you some idea of the scene—the black beaming faces. I kept looking up at your dear pictures, and it made my eyes swim with tears to think how entirely it was a scene you would have liked and approved.

"Ogubonna, the great war-chief, who often comes to see me, wanted to play, but of course he could not bring out a sound, so he says it is only white people who can do anything great, and only the 'Iya.' (mother, as they call me) who can make wood and ivory speak, with her fingers."

PERILS OF FIRE

From Anna's letter ...

"*The promise of help and deliverance from all evil was again verified a few days since. A fearful fire broke out in the town, about two miles from us. Two hundred native houses were burned in no time. It speedily came near to us before we were aware of it; we saw little hope of our house being spared, as it has also a thatched roof We turned out a few boxes but all the men and boys we could get were obliged to be on the roof with water and boughs of trees to ward off the sparks. I gathered together a few of my treasures, the pictures, journal-book, and bible, and then with a deep heart-ache resigned everything else, fearing I should never see them again, and had to make my escape on account of the smoke. My husband led me far away, and put me under the care of a native woman; we sat under a tree, and he went back to see the end. But before dark he came to tell the joyful tidings that the fire was out, and our house untouched. Oh, what shall we render for these preserving mercies? Ourselves, to Thy service, gracious God.*"

A few days later, Mr. and Mrs. Hinderer visited Oshielle, where a native catechist was at this time

Visit to West Africa. Sojourn in Abeokuta

carrying on the work which Mr. Hinderer had begun in 1849.

From Anna's letter . . .

> "On the 26th of February we went to Oshielle; it was most interesting going with D. over the same ground which he had traversed, through some opposition, to establish & missionary station in that place. It is about eight miles distant a most pleasant but narrow path. We had to ride one behind the other, our boys walking, and two or three men carrying loads, for a mattress had to go, and food, and anything we wanted to make use of, so that we formed quite a cavalcade, partly through bush, partly through cotton-fields, and palm trees, and bushes of every description. We set off, not as soon as we hoped, for a little storm came, and thus we were benighted; but Olubi carried a lantern before me, and our horses are so sure-footed that I was not in the least afraid. When we entered the town, people came out of their little huts, but were disappointed they could not see us, numbers of them had come on the road to meet us, but as we were not to be seen by six o'clock, they gave up all hope of our coming that night: a multitude of salutations were roared out from the houses -' Okabo[9]

---

[9] Yoruba – literally 'welcome'

!' 'I salute you for returning,' salutations for having brought a wife, and all sorts of things. In the house where the schoolmaster lives, there is one room left on purpose for any European visitor: in this there is one little table, and a wooden bench, something like a sofa, which we sat upon by day, and slept on by night; so you see the necessity for taking a mattress.

"Happily there is no more furniture, or we could not very easily have turned ourselves round, but we were very happy, and much amused. The chief came directly he heard we were there, and greeted us heartily: and early the next morning, our habitation was more than surrounded by people, and they were all pleased to think me a wonderful sight I have a colour, as you know, in my cheeks, and this is such a novelty in Africa, that I might be made a little vain with the great and grand expressions of 'very fine, good, beautiful!' were it not that I would give all the colour I possess to be able to talk a little Yoruba, and tell them of something else. At nine we went to Sunday school for a little while, and then to church, that mud church of which my husband was chief builder. It was extremely interesting going over these old scenes with him. He had been here, and I had read of it, and now we were in that spot together. He took both services, and our little room was full all day of visitors, and hundreds outside;

many to look at the wonders of a white woman! We left very early the next morning amid sorrowful farewells."

On the 9th of March, Mr. Hinderer went to Ibadan, to make final arrangements with the chiefs for the commencement of the mission. He had also to provide, as far as might be, for the comfort of his wife, in what was to be the first home of her married life. During his absence, she remained at the Ake mission station in Abeokuta, to which she and Mr. Hinderer had lately removed, when Mr. Paley entered upon the work at the Ikeja station, where they had spent their first weeks. Thus she had the comfort of being near to the Rev. H. and Mrs. Townsend, from whom she received much kindness. She occupied herself in studying the Yoruba language, and gladly availed herself of every opportunity of making friends with the natives. It was but natural, however, that her letters at this time should express some sense of loneliness, mingled with various thoughts on the path which lay before her.

From Anna's letter ...

> *"'March 3rd.*—*My husband leaves me, if all is well, on Monday, for his first journey to Ibadan, to make preparations. We have had the warmest messages from chiefs there, and I trust that by the good hand of our God, we shall all be there in less than three months. We*

are now, I am thankful to say, both well again, but I am obliged to be careful; the heat is so intense, and I think this is one of the hottest days we have had. No day has the thermometer been under ninety degrees."

A Journal Entry –

" On Wednesday, March 9th, my dearest left me before six in the morning, we both felt it much. God bless and prosper him! We have had such miserable noises in the night, wind and storms, and people with their country fashions, that I have not had much rest, and do feel it is the last time we must be separated, if possible, but must share together whatever comes. I have occupied myself as much as possible with reading, writing, work, and children.

"*March 12th* — I heard from my dearest husband; he does not seem to have many external comforts, but is content and happy: I take care of his little notes, which are a great comfort to me."

From Anna's letter . . . .

"*March. 12th* —A messenger from the chief met my husband on the road to salute him: he sent him on to see me, and to tell me how he was getting on. I told Olubi to ask him what the chief's words were to the white man; they were very good indeed, full of delight at the *thought of seeing us, and if we want to send anything at once, there was a room in his house which we should have to put them in as long as we liked; so that I am sending off things. Five loads went yesterday, others will go next week; and if all is well, in two months from this time, we and all our goods and belongings will be settled there, and by next January, or February, we hope to be in our own house. I am so glad to look forward to getting there so soon, it will be such a relief to my dear husband, whose calling is there, when the moving and unpacking are over, and he is free to go about his Master's work. It is an immense interest going to such a place, and such a people; it is a stronghold of the enemy, of war, and slavery. It is a great cause for thankfulness to have such a welcome, but as my dear husband says, this is not all we want, we far more want that they should receive the Messiah, the Saviour of sinners, who lived and died and rose again for them. Oh, that the Holy Spirit of God may open their hearts to receive the message of salvation. You, my beloved friends, and others, do and will unite with us in earnest prayer to God that it may be so. How great is the work! But it is God's. May we all only be faithful in the different portions of work appointed us, whether it be to preach, or teach, — 'hewers of wood, or drawers of water.' 'I only pray God make me holy.'*

"I am very well now, I am thankful to say, and feel the climate not unlikely to suit me. I am looked upon as somebody wonderful, being so much stronger than any white woman has been who has been here. From five to six I enjoy a good game with the school children at ball, and all sorts of things; but you must know my play is not half so energetic as in England; still I am so thankful to be able to do this, and the dear children are delighted. This is a great encouragement for Ibadan, where the children will be frightened enough at first, never having seen a white woman, and, as slaves, having a horror of white people.

"God grant we may meet again in this lower world; I do intensely feel my separation from you, which nothing but the belief that I am where my God would have me to be will ever alleviate."

The feelings expressed in these last words were poured forth more fully to another friend, in a letter of about the same date: -

"March 18th. — Hundreds of times has the query, if not uttered, been asked within, 'How could I leave this and these? How could I? And how can I bear it now?' and only the assurance that 'He ordereth our goings,' that He said, 'Go,' and then led me by His own hand, and that He, our Father, our Guide, our Leader, can do

nothing wrong, but that 'He doeth all things well,' could comfort me often in moments of depression, and times of pining for the sight of those so beloved. Thus have I been made to see the pillar and the cloud. And this makes me rejoice, and give thanks, that in the preparation for moving, I only felt the guiding hand, and no doubts or misgivings were permitted to disturb me at the time. And now, when I see what is the need, I feel that if I had twenty lives I would gladly give them to be the means of a little good to these poor but affectionate and well-meaning people, who, though black enough their skins may be, have never-dying souls, which need to be led to the Saviour, to be washed clean in the blood of the Lamb. But then, again, I have been led to feel, of what use am I? Nothing can I do; I can scarcely even speak to the little children, except by signs. But here is the lesson to learn: 'wait, sit still, be patient.' Thus I hope I may be preparing for the future, and if I am able to be any help or comfort to my dear husband, who is bearing the burden and heat of the day, I may be thankful. And what a comfort it is to feel that those whom I so dearly love, and who also love me, have their hearts' desires so much in and for this work that we are about, and that we are thus united in a stronger tie, a tighter bond."

Letter to her aunt...

"**March 19th**—*My dear husband has been away just a fortnight in Ibadan. Before the letters go, I hope to tell you of his return; glad enough shall I be to see him again. It has been so strange to have only three young black servants in the house; but altogether I have been very happy, quite well, and very busy; but I shall be much more happy when I have him to speak to, and won't he be glad to get home, too? Mr. Kefer will arrive, we hope, from Sierra Leone, by the next packet; and as soon as possible we all go. It is extremely interesting thus going forth on an entirely new mission, but it is with a solemn feeling, into such a country, among such a people, and for such a work. Who is sufficient for these things? Not we alone in our own strength. We go not for ourselves, or of ourselves: we go not to tell our own words, but the words of God, so that gives us courage, and we seem to hear the words that were long ago spoken to Joshua— "Have not I sent thee? Be strong and very courageous, for behold I go before thee;' and then our Saviour's confirming words, 'Lo, I am with you alway, even unto the end of the world.' such a Commander and Leader, what have we to fear? Only God grant that we may he found faithful, enduring to the end, like good soldiers and servants, and oh! That the Blessed Spirit from on high may be abundantly poured out upon us and the people; that* their hearts may be opened to receive the good tidings of salvation through Jesus Christ!

"Good Friday is approaching we shall all think much of each other on that solemn day. It is one of my great comforts to know that I did value and enjoy the services of God's house at home, for nothing now do I feel the lack of so much. Home comforts, or anything, I can resign, and I feel the loss of them less than Sunday services, the feeding in God's house. I go, of course, and enjoy in a measure being there, to look on and see so many bright beaming black countenances enjoying to the full the blessing of the Gospel of peace: yet its being in a strange tongue prevents my benefiting, and I travel in thought to dear St Peter's [Lowestoft], look at my Bible, and see marks when such and such a text was preached from; and try to think of what I heard then. - In church I shed as many quiet tears as anywhere, tears of varied emotions, tears of a little home sickness, a longing to see the beloved ones, and hear their voices, tears of thankfulness, and tears of joy and hope.

"I have already a great many friends among the Africans: people come to see me, and say wonderful things, through my interpreter. I let them look at my things, and touch them, which delights them much; and boys and girls come in numbers to sing with the music, listen to the clock, look at pictures, turn over my *workbasket, and laugh and shout at some of the mysteries. Their black skin makes no difference to me; to have them come to me, to see them pleased, makes me quite happy. I often saunter out for a little walk among the hills and rocks, and a nice little party surround me, and there is a famous rush which shall take my hand, to help me up or down in a difficult place; I have sometimes gone back again to brighten the tearful eye of some little girl who thought she had almost possession of Missis's hand. I take a ball or two, and set them running vigorously with their naked feet; really I almost think shoes are an inconvenience, they trip along so nimbly without them!"*

"Easter Sunday, March. 27th. *—Oh, how much do I feel this day, my heart is so full. I do indeed desire to rise above things temporal, and press onward to the things eternal; to be risen with Christ, seeking more and more the things above. How many and mingled were my feelings on waking this morning, but very very thankful to have my own dear husband at home, though I grieve to say he is in bed with fever, from his exertions in Ibadan. On Monday I heard from him, giving no hope of his return till next week. Great indeed was my joy to see him return unexpectedly on Thursday evening."*

All was now ready for their removal to Ibadan. A native house had been prepared for their temporary habitation, and the chiefs had promised protection to the missionaries, and liberty of conscience to their own subjects.

FIRST DEATHS DUE TO SICKNESS

But, before they could leave Abeokuta, they were to witness striking and melancholy instances of the fatal power of the African climate. **Some of those who had gone forth with them into the mission-field were called away when they had scarcely put their hands to the work.** Mr. and Mrs. Paley had already been so exhausted by fever and dysentery as to cause serious anxiety to their friends, and the only remaining hope of their recovery rested on a change of climate. In Mr. Paley's case, however, this hope was quickly dispelled by a new attack of fever, under which he sank on the 1st of April.

Mr. and Mrs. Hinderer shared with the other missionaries in watching and ministering to him in his dying hours; and when all was over, they took the young widow to their own house, where Mrs. Hinderer tenderly soothed and nursed her, and helped her to prepare for her voyage, though perceiving that there was but a faint hope of her living to reach England. She accomplished the journey to Lagos, and embarked on board the steamer, accompanied by Ellen Apthorpe, an infant-school teacher, who had gone out to Africa with her, and was now ordered to return home on account of serious illness. **The missionary band at Abeokuta was yet further reduced by the sudden death of Mr. Hensman, on the 10th of April.**

Mrs. Hinderer was deeply affected by the removal of these friends at the commencement of their career. She regarded their death as solemn witnesses to the special uncertainty of her own life in that climate, and as urgently calling upon her to work diligently while it was "yet day." These and other like thoughts were expressed in her letters

"March 31st. — We are both, thank God, well, but we are in deep sorrow. Mr. Paley has been taken ill, and oh, how I shrink from saying it, I fear he has not many days to linger here. We hope and trust a change may be granted, that he may be able to go home by the next mail, but he appears to us to be sinking. The doctor is most attentive, kind, and skilful; but alas! Our hearts are sorrowful. Dear Louisa does not seem to take it in, but I think it is because she is too ill herself. Your valued letters are a double comfort in this sorrowful time."

April 2nd. — I begin my writing very early, but the work before us for this month is great, and life and

health so uncertain. We have this day laid in an African grave the mortal remains of our dear friend Mr. Paley. He got worse and worse, and gently fell asleep after two days of light delirium.

We did indeed feel he was entering upon his eternal rest. His poor wife was wonderfully supported. I stayed with her today while the solemn ceremony was being performed; it was a painful time, but help was near. I read to her or rather repeated little bits of the exquisite burial service (for she could not bear reading), and texts of Scripture, and... We all feel very sensible of having sustained a loss, but his God has taken him from earth to serve Him in heaven. How inscrutable are His judgments, and His ways past finding out! I could not but exclaim, 'Thou didst well that it was in thy heart,' as I gazed on his lifeless form. **Though only permitted to see the land he loved, God has accepted the service at his hand, and has given him his full reward in His kingdom above.** *It behoves us who remain to look well to our goings, to be upon our watchtower, our loins girt, and our lamps burning. Oh, that grace may be given for this, but our evil, cold, and dead hearts come with us to Africa. We have double need for watchfulness and cultivation of diligence, for this enervating climate is indeed liable to damp our zeal; and we may hang our hands down, unless the same grace and help are given us that we need at home. Pray for us, that our God may do His own work; that His servants may be found faithful; that we may all of us, in our different capacities, only seek to do our Father's* *will; that we may live to Him, and serve Him, and so cling to Him that we need not so much these sharp strokes of the rod, which He sees are needful for us now. We must now help the poor dear widow to prepare for her homeward journey, and make ready for our own removal to Ibadan, which, if all is well, we expect to accomplish at the end of this month."*

*"**14th April**—Much indeed has transpired since I began this letter, scenes of various kinds we have been called to pass through. Our doctor, Mr. Hensman, was of a poor and shattered constitution, but I little thought I should so soon have to record his departure from amongst us. Suddenly and unexpectedly to us all, he died on Sunday, about two o'clock. This week he was going to teach me so much for my benefit in Ibadan, how to mix my medicines, etc. but how entirely passing away is everything in this life; it is well said, 'Boast not thyself of tomorrow.' What a break up of all our party! **So many in one vessel a short time since; now two in their graves, some in Sierra Leone, Mr. Gerst in Lagos, Mr. Kefer going with us to Ibadan, Mrs. Palsy and Ellen about to return home, only Mr. Maser remaining in Abeokuta.***

Before this letter was closed, Mr. Kefer, Mr. Hinderer's appointed fellow-labourer in Ibadan, who had lately arrived from Sierra Leone, after his ordination, was struck down by fever. Mr. Maser also, the other newly arrived missionary, fell ill, and required Mrs. Hinderer's nursing care. Thus there was much, besides the removal of their little possessions, to occupy them both during their last days at Abeokuta, as the next extract shows: -

April 15th. —*Our house is looking very desolate; much is packed, and now we must finish. I am sorry to find Mr. Kefer has fever; if he goes on well, we shall still, please God, start next week, leaving him here, to prevent the danger of a relapse. We are nursing and doctoring him to the best of our ability, but we miss our doctor very much. Yet we must hope for the best. He can give wisdom and skill to the unwise and unskilful. We have indeed had to dwell among solemn scenes and thoughts. ... Do not be over-anxious about us, dear friends. He who has helped us hitherto will still vouchsafe to be our Guide.*

"*It is now Monday. Mr. Maser has fever, as well as Mr. Kefer, so that my hands are full; they are going on well. We must go away now, to make room for them, and we shall have seen them over the worst. Mr. Kefer will not join us for some few weeks. How interesting it will be to write to you from Ibadan. If it pleases God that I have health and strength, and get a few people and children about me, I shall be very happy; and then nothing shall I have to desire but that we may meet again in this life, before we are taken to dwell together in heaven."*

On the eve of the journey, she wrote as follows: -

"April 24th, 1853. - This is our last Sunday night in Abeokuta My heart is full in 'the remembrance of all God's mercy to us while we have sojourned here, and of all the events that have befallen us. I have been comforted by the collect for the day (Fourth Sunday after Easter) in the prospect before us. May God order the unruly wills and affections of sinful men; and oh, may He grant that our hearts may be surely fixed on true joys! The text for the day, too, is so appropriate - 'Our sufficiency is of God.'"

Preaching in a Yoruba Village

CHAPTER III

The Gospel in Ibadan

"It is Thine own, O Lord,
Who toil while others sleep:
Who sow with loving care,
What other hands shall reap:
They lean on Thee entranced,
In calm and perfect rest:
Give us that peace, O Lord,
Divine and blest,
Thou keepest for those hearts who love
Thee best."

A. A. PROCTER

ON THE 25TH OF April, a few hours after Mrs. Paley and Ellen, accompanied by the Rev. S. (now Bishop) Crowther, had begun their journey to the coast, Mr. and Mrs. Hinderer left Abeokuta for Ibadan. The account of their journey and arrival there is now to be added in the words of Mrs. Hinderer.

Lest We Forget

Anna's letter...

"We journeyed on and on, one behind the other, very quietly, with our long train of attendant carriers, full of thought of the past and future. There was something to admire around, good pasture and beautiful cattle. Our silence was broken, and we talked of the goodness and mercy which had so surrounded our path in the midst of our sorrow and trials, during our short sojourn in Abeokuta, and we could look forward with confiding hope and trust, and take comfort and courage in that we were following the leading of a gracious Providence. **And now we were on our way to this long-talked-of town, to attack, in the name of the Lord of Hosts, this stronghold of sin and Satan.** I tried in the stillness of the bush to draw near to the Living Fountain, to seek help, comfort, and protection in our great undertaking, and I had some precious hours. I soon left my little horse to Olubi's care, and got into my hammock, for I was tired. I certainly may say that I have had no little to do the last month or six weeks, so that I did enjoy the rest of this hammock, with its cradle-like motion; and a little refreshing breeze sprang up. 'We did not reach our resting-place till quite dusk, but the tent was quickly up, and we had bright lanterns, comfortable tea, and prayers, and our people were soon fast asleep on their mats. We walked about by moonlight, we were within reach of the dwellings of man, and people were passing backwards and forwards from and to their farms, the greater part of the night. We slept some hours, and after a nice breakfast in gypsy-like style, the next morning we pursued our journey. After an hour, we were quite in the bush. I did enjoy that day's journey; such nice cool air, trees and scented bushes twining together so thickly that even the African sun could not penetrate. Now and then we stopped to refresh ourselves, and to change my carriers, and then sometimes we sang and sometimes talked. Many, many times we wished our dear good friends could take a peep at us. We halted for the night, about five o'clock, on a rock which seems spread out on purpose for weary travellers, but alas there was no water. We had some in a bottle for our tea, but our poor attendants got none. However, with their usual easy nature, they each spread a mat on the hard rock, down they threw their weary bodies, and in less than five minutes were that asleep, except those who kept up the fires. I could not sleep; the whole scene and circumstances were so novel. About eight o'clock the moon again rose majestically, and a wonderful sight it was.

"We were now in the midst of an African bush, no human dwelling near us, but how different to what it once was, when the kidnappers haunted almost every bush, and wild animals were near. Now all our people were sleeping away, with their guns by their side truly, but only in case any kind of animal should be troublesome. Monkeys, foxes, parrots, owls, now and then made a little noise. I often listened with all earnestness for any sound, and I am sure I heard strange ones far, far away, and have no doubt they were creatures we should not have liked very near. No harm however reached us, not even a drop of rain. With all there was to amuse in the night watches, I was very glad to see the morning light, to start quite early, and to sleep without any nervous apprehension in my hammock. When l awoke l found myself on another rock, with our fellow travellers watching my sweet repose; and they enjoyed a good laugh when I opened my eyes.

"In the middle of this rock was most delicious water, and very deep; it made us think of the provision God made for the children of Israel from a stony rock. Our people drank heartily, and we had, a delicious cup of tea under a mangrove tree, and finding a nice little brook close by, we washed, and put on tidy clothes, that we might make a respectable appearance in Ibadan, which we expected to reach in a few hours. I now mounted my horse, but certainly it was not so easy jumping over big trees. **At the next halting-place we saw large tracts of land covered with Indian corn and cotton trees, and the immense town of Ibadan appearing at about two miles distance.** It was a beautiful sight, *and now my faithful affectionate men, for so I must call them, nearly began to quarrel as to who should carry me into the town, for be carried in my hammock I must, according to their desire."*

EXCITED WELCOME INTO IBADAN

"We waited at the town wall, and heard that the chief was out of town at one of his farms, so we went in and through it, to our little dwelling, which is quite out of it at the other side. But as soon as we touched the town there was such a scene, men, women, and children shouting and screaming, "The white man is come!" — "Oyinbo 'de!' and 'The white mother is come!' and then their thousands of salutations, everybody opening eyes and mouth at me. All seemed pleased, but many frightened too when I spoke; they followed us to our own dwelling with the most curious shouts, noises, and exclamations.

"All seemed perfectly bewildered; horses, sheep, goats, did not know where or which way to go, even the pigeons looked ready to exclaim, 'What is happening?' The people were good and kind enough to let us enter our house by ourselves, but many, many of them stood round about till sunset, just to catch a glimpse of the wonderful white woman; and every time I appeared,

down they went on the ground, rubbing their hands, and saying, 'Alafia, alafia,' — 'peace, peace.' We could but let them enjoy the treat, though we were not sorry when daylight fading warned them to depart, for with all our comforts and alleviations we were tired enough. We soon unpacked things sufficient for present necessity, and a good night's rest was very refreshing.

THE MISSION HOUSE IN IBADAN

"We have all this day had people surrounding our dwelling, and we have put our room in order and already feel at home. Chiefs' messengers have come to inquire after our welfare, and the Chief himself intends visiting us on Saturday. The harmonium has arrived quite safely, and, we have unpacked all we shall really want while in this abode. I wish you could see it, quite by itself, far from the filth and bustle of the town a few dwellings here and there and plenty of trees. From the back we look out upon a forest of feathery palm-trees, and I am half inclined to think it a pity to have the trouble of building."

This little native dwelling continued to be their home till the end of their first year in Ibadan. It had no upper floor; indeed such a thing was unknown in the town, even in the abodes of the chiefs. It comprised what may be called their own apartment, thirty feet long by six wide, which occupied the whole length of the building, and two wings, each consisting of two rooms, appropriated to Mr. Kefer, their missionary fellow-labourer, to the schoolmaster and catechist, and to the purposes of kitchen and store-room. Attached to this curious house, at the inner side of the quadrangle, was a piazza, which, besides affording shelter from the burning rays of the sun, served for various useful purposes, such as receiving visitors by day, and being the sleeping-place of the servants at night.

Their own narrow room, with its dismal bare mud walls, mud floor, and thatched roof, had to serve for sitting room and bedroom. With cheerful hearts, ever looking on the bright side of everything, and *with* much ingenuity in contriving, they at once framed a partition, and divided the shallow strip into two small rooms, which were soon made not only habitable, but home-like.

The house had neither doors nor windows, a curtain alone serving for a screen at its entrance. But the inhabitants felt perfectly secure. A robber would be far too much afraid of the white man to approach the house in the dark. They were, however, liable to other troubles.

FLOODING AND INSECTS

The whole town was exposed to injury from periodical hurricanes, and in the rainy season torrents of water would make their way through the roof of this dwelling, producing great discomfort, and doing much damage to their scanty but precious possessions. At all times the grass roof, which had no ceiling under it, harboured spiders, and other unwelcome insects, which would not be dislodged; and to these must be added creatures of a more noxious kind. One night Mr. Hinderer heard a rustling noise, proceeding, as he supposed, from the compound; wishing to ascertain the cause, he rose hastily from his bed and his foot alighted on a venomous serpent, whose bite might have caused his death had the creature turned upon him. Dr. Irving, R.N., who visited the missionaries, from Lagos, some months later, gives the following description of their habitation: -

> "Mr. and Mrs. Hinderer at present live in such a funny little place, quite a primitive mud dwelling, where no two persons can walk abreast at one time and yet there is an air of quiet domestic comfort -and happiness about it, that makes it a little palace in my eyes. It is unfortunate, however, for my temples, for in screwing in at one door and out at the other, forgetting to stoop at the proper time, my head gets many a knock. At one

end, six feet square, is the bed-room, separated from the dining-room by a standing book-case; my bed-room is at one end of this, formed by a sofa, and my privacy established by a white sheet, put across for a screen at bed-time."

This native dwelling, and the more solid **mission-house**, which was built in the course of the year, **stood** in the south-western quarter of Ibadan, on the Kudeti hill, which commands an extensive view of the town, beginning with closely-packed houses, low, and thatched, spreading over the slopes of the hill on which the old town was built, and continuing into the plain below, where the houses are less crowded together, and are interspersed with gardens, in which flourish the orange, plantain, banana, and other kinds of trees and shrubs. The whole is enclosed by mud walls, eighteen miles in circumference, beyond which there is a broad belt of cultivated land, five or six miles in breadth, reclaimed from the bush. The outlying country has been described by Dr. Irving as

> "Very beautiful, undulating, watered by numerous clear running streams, marked, in their course through cultivated fields, by the more luxuriant vegetation. Everywhere graceful palms rear their tall straight stems and crowning summits of leafy fronds in flue relief against the sky; and wherever the higher grounds

> *command a more extended view, we behold the same lovely country reaching far in the distance, till lost in the faint blue of the horizon."*

Ibadan has the characteristic features common to the Yoruba towns. The houses are all of one pattern, being a square, enclosing a court open to the sky. The apartments occupied by the family are low dark rooms, without windows, covered by a sloping roof of grass or *agidi*[10] leaves, projecting beyond the building, so as to form a piazza, supported by posts. Here visitors are received, and business is transacted. There are also sheds for the horses, goats, sheep, and poultry, which throng the court by day. A doorway leads into the street, forming the only break in its monotonous face of blank mud wall. The streets however are diversified by sheds, which serve the purpose of shops, and here and there by *orisha*[11] or idol houses; and at intervals there are open spaces, shaded by trees, and used as markets. Here, amidst a merry hum of voices, above which are heard shrill sounds, which may remind an English listener of the cries in the streets of London, a lively traffic is carried on in the produce of the farms and native manufactures. Of the latter there is a great variety, for in Ibadan there are numerous weavers,

---

[10] A staple African food made from corn starch

[11] Yoruba prefix meaning 'idol'

tailors, blacksmiths, carpenters, tanners, leather-dressers, saddlers, potters, and dyers; others are employed in extracting palm-oil and nut-oil, and in making soap. But the principal occupation of the people is farming, in which everyone is engaged, whatever other calling he follows, each having a right to such land as he chooses to occupy outside the walls, provided only that it be not already appropriated.

"GOD OWNS THE LAND"

When Mr. Hinderer, on first settling at Ibadan, asked what price he must pay for some land which he wished to cultivate, the chief said, laughing, "Pay! Who pays for the ground? All the ground belongs to God; you cannot pay for it!"

The soil is extremely fertile. Indian corn and yams, the staple articles of food, form the principal produce of the farms, but Guinea corn, beans, ground-nuts, and cassava, are also cultivated, as well as cotton, which is grown both for home use and for exportation.

NATIVE ADMINISTRATION

Ibadan, like other Yoruba towns, while nominally subject to a king who resides at Oyo[12], is in fact an independent state, governed by its own chiefs, and claiming tribute and military service from many smaller towns, in virtue of the protection which it affords them. Highest among its rulers is the Bale, or civil chief, who conducts the affairs of the government. Next to him, and almost his equal, is the head war-chief[13]; and these together sit in judgment on criminals charged with grave offences, and likewise settle important cases of dispute between man and man. Below these are a number of inferior chiefs, who, besides having rank in the army, act as magistrates in their respective districts of the town, and decide all except the most weighty matters for their people. Their services are rewarded by fees, to which they do not scruple to add bribes; and by tribute money, paid by the subject towns. The chiefs have extensive farms, which are cultivated by their slaves, whom they sometimes number by hundreds, but who are generally treated with kindness, and often possess little plots of ground adjoining their master's property, on which they work when the comparatively light day's task is done.

---

[12] The capital city of what was once a huge empire
[13] **Yoruba - Balogun**

Thus in course of time many are enabled to redeem themselves. Others of the slaves are employed by their masters in trading, and they are so implicitly trusted, that they are sent out on expeditions which involve an absence of several months at a time, and return when their commission has been fulfilled. Others, again, are "war-boys," on whose ready service the chiefs can rely in any of their schemes of pillage or kidnapping.

Mrs. Hinderer's letters and journal give a lively description of their first settling in Ibadan, and express the thoughts and feelings with which she regarded that important event in her life.

Anna's letter...

> **"May 1st, Sunday.** — *A very interesting day. Many people came, as on every other day. Many thoughts of dear ones at home, but very full of the present scene. Olumloy (a young warrior) interests me much, and said, with many others, 'The words were sweet,.' On what has this day been sown here, and everywhere, Thy blessing, Lord, bestow!"*

> **"May 5th,** *Ascension Day - I have been comforted to-day by Keble's[14] words,*

---

[14] A noted poet of the time

'He to earth's lowest cares is still awake,'

"*for at times I do intensely feel my separation from you all, my beloved friends. On such days as these I seem to be among you in thought, and partaking with you in service, as in days of* **yore**; *and then such a feeling of being very, very far away comes over me, and the thought, 'Shall we ever meet again?' As to this world it must be uncertain, but oh, that I may be permitted to meet you in heaven! A glimmering hope of this dries the eye, and cheers the heart.*"

"**May 8th. - Another blessed Sabbath-day; people remarkably attentive. They heard of Jesus for the first time, and seem much struck with the message of salvation.** *The past week has been one of much occupation, putting things to rights, and receiving no end of visitors from morning till evening. It requires a little tact and patience to meet the whole thing. I have had some nice little presents of yams, fowls, and fruit. Oh, for wisdom and patience to deal rightly and wisely with these people; to be willing to amuse and give myself up cheerfully to little things, if by any means I may win some. My dear husband is well, always occupied, and much interested in everything around him.* **We do enjoy finding ourselves in Ibadan, and a work, a great, a holy work, commenced. O God, give Thy blessing!**"

"Whit – Sunday, May 15th. - I think you might not have been uninterested if you could have seen a certain Anna to-day, with a large mixed-up class of men and women on the ground, with her four little boys, who are with her every day, clinging to he; each trying to be nearest at this afternoon school. You must remember they are cramped for room. As I sat on my chair, one little black fellow had clasped my hand with both his hands, another every now and then nearly resting his chin on my shoulder, the other two sitting close at my feet; and then such a burst of voices after me repeated the Lord's Prayer in Yoruba, and then two of the Commandments. The affection of these people is very great, and in these four boys it is remarkable; if a fly comes near me they push it away. I have had a little fever in the week, so did not come out of my room all day. They were wandering about quite disconsolate, and one of them went in the evening to Olubi, with tearful eyes, saying he could not "find Missis all day;" and when I came out the next day they were so delighted."

FIRST NEWS FROM HOME

On the 23rd May the first mail arrived in Ibadan. It is easy to imagine the excitement and eagerness with which the missionaries awaited the arrival of their letters. Mrs.

Hinderer tells how they watched for "the easy smiling African, who might be seen some time before he reached our dwelling, he so entirely unconscious of the treasures he then held in his possession."

By the next mail she described the sensations with which these letters were received, and then gave further particulars of their new home, and of the arrangements by which she had endeavoured to make it cheerful and comfortable.

DEATH OF LOVED ONES

*"But oh! What mingled hope and fear, in opening these treasures, takes possession of one's heart, sad tidings my eye fell first upon, in a note from Mr. Townsend. I told you in my last that poor **Mrs. Paley left the same morning we did, but before the vessel reached Sierra Leone she had joined her husband in heaven!***

"Indeed we have been dwelling amid solemn scenes; the tale of these few months is certainly beyond description! Oh, if we could not repose in our Father, and commit the keeping of our souls and bodies to Him, believing that He doeth all things well, where could be our hope? Where could we find rest? But what inexpressible comfort there is in knowing that we are in such hands,

such keeping! My precious home letters tell a tale of joy and sorrow. You can hardly think what the sight even of a kind friend's handwriting is, in this far-off land. Newspapers certainly will be a great treat; one feels the lack of those things, and the multitude of publications we have had in such abundance in England. **The whole world is so full of movement and interests; it is a trial not to know what is going on. Only one newspaper have I seen since I have been in Africa!**

AN AFRICAN SCENE

"I do wish some of you could just look at us this evening. A bright lamp, French moderator, now lightens our dwelling; our various boys, with some of their friends, sitting in the piazza with their country lamps, teaching each other to read, some Yoruba, some English. We have a nice table, not mahogany, nor rosewood, but covered with a bright cheerful-looking cloth, with some beautiful green oranges of delicious flavour, one of the many little offerings of my African friends. Now and then a frog hops in to take a survey, but being taken by surprise it is generally glad to hop out again, after a little scream from me; and some long worm-like looking things, with at least a hundred legs; but my greatest enemies are the mosquitoes. We are

very near the bush, which accounts for their constant visitation; but they are, after all, far better than the dirt, noise, and dangers of the town. Our own house, when we can build it, will be sufficiently away from native dwellings to make us fearless for ours, even if the whole town were in a blaze. But these fires are not usual in Ibadan; there is a law that, if the person who has been the means of producing such a calamity is found out, all that he possesses is to be taken from him, and he put in prison; and this, not because it was felonious, but accidental. This seems cruel, but the result has been that not a fire has happened here in five years."

"May 26ᵗʰ *— I have had many visitors this week, particularly women. Their tenderness over me is touching; if they see me hot, they will fan me; if I look tired, they want me to lie down. I have had much talk with them, through my little maid Susanna; they do indeed receive us with joy and gladness, and we have many regular attendants on Sunday. They are quite beginning to understand that it is a holy day with us, and I feel sure some are trying to give up Sunday occupation. One woman, who is very fond of me, was missing last Sunday; she came on Monday, and with tears in her eyes told me, 'Too much work live in her house on Sunday; her hands were too full, and she could not get them out.' I was just talking to some new visitors about Sunday; she sat down, and told them of* all she had seen and heard, and begged them to come also. They promised, and left; and I lay down in my hammock in the back piazza, very tired. The above-mentioned woman, on her way home, met four of her friends, and came back with them; they found me out in my resting-place. After talking a little with them, I rather wished them to go, when my old friend said she wished me not to speak another word, but rest; yet if they might sit down quietly and look at me, they should like it. I mention this to show their kind and respectful and really polite way of speaking, and to describe their tender and affectionate feeling towards me, which must be seen to be fully known. I am still somewhat of a curiosity, the novelty has not yet worn off, and our house is pretty well surrounded all day long. I like to feel that, though they have come to look at me and my possessions, they go away having heard the good tidings we have come here to bring; and we only long and pray that they may receive that blessed message of salvation into their hearts. **But we are on uncultivated ground, and our work at present, by God's help, is to 'break up the fallow ground.'**

"It has been a lovely cool day, after rain nearly all night, and some hours this morning. The sun has not peeped out once, so that at about three o'clock we went out, Mr. Kefer too, all on horseback. The town is built on a tremendous hill; we wanted to get to the top, to see its extent, and a wonderful sight it is, myriads of houses on every side. A queer and rugged pathway we had often to travel, but I have no fear now with my good little horse. We went also through different parts of the town, to various markets; they are a pretty sight, with their native productions, but oh, the noise! We were surrounded all the way by hundreds, with open eyes and mouths. Some made music, after their fashion, and sang and shouted. Many who had visited us at our house were prepared with an extra welcome. Kola-nuts were given me, and I might have had many things."

"May 29th. — Another Sabbath day hath reached its close. We have had nice services, many people, and very attentive; and some having come for several Sundays, bringing new ones with them, is very encouraging. We have now a nice little day-school. Some having come very regularly, I gave them blue shirts yesterday, and it was a pretty sight this morning to be greeted by nine blue boys. I have also now four children given me, but as our house is small, and they like to go home at the end of the day, we let them. They are here early enough in the morning; a little boy and girl of Olumloyo's; a boy whose father had been quite an enemy of ours; and a little boy without parents, the brother of our schoolmaster. Though he is so young he has been nicely taught, and is quite a help in the school. **I feel I have indeed a little charge, but a precious one, and**

desire that a blessing may be given, that I may have grace and strength to train them up for God, and that they may walk in the right way. I only wish you could take a peep at my little group."

FEARS OF CHILDREN

The children of the chief Olumloyo were the first whom Mr. Hinderer received into the house. These were Akielle[15], a boy four years of age, and Yejide[16], a little girl who was about two years older. Their first day in the mission compound passed happily enough, so long as the light lasted, but towards sunset, the little girl did her best to persuade Akielle to return home, which he showed himself most unwilling to do. She grew more and more earnest in her entreaties, and was overheard pleading, **"Akielle, you must not stay, don't you know that when it gets dark the white people kill and eat the black?"** This terrible suspicion prevailed, and away they both ran, intending, however, to return to their teacher in the morning. It was not long before Akielle ventured to remain for the night, much to the alarm of his sister, who left him, with a trembling heart, to the mercies of the

---

[15] Probably spelt – Akinyele. Meaning 'courage befits a man'

[16] a common Yoruba name, literally 'Grandmother has returned'

white people, and returned at the first dawn of day, anxious to know what had befallen him. From this time forward, Akielle, trusting himself to the care of his good friends, was glad to make his home in the mission house.

TRIALS IN SICKNESS

More particulars of this new life are now to be added.

Anna's letter . . .

"June 8. — Last week I had to doctor and nurse both my dear husband and Mr. Kefer; they were quite down with fever. It is such a curious malady with them, and comes so frequently; they get ill quickly, and are very ill for a few days, and then suddenly they are up again, and enjoying food. I do not mean to say that I am exempted altogether, but it seems to be different. I get hot and languid, lie down, and keep quite still, and as cool as I can, take quinine, and am soon up again: but they are so cold, they want blankets, and no one knows what, and are far more ill, and much oftener. I cannot say how thankful I am to be so well; tired enough I am by night. My children and housekeeping and visitors keep me going all day. I almost fear for writing, drawing seems out of the question; however, as I get more and more used to it, I shall more cleverly manage my time. We know children are a great care and trouble

at home, and can imagine that they would be rather more so in this country, having been under no control, and coming all at once into such a different Life. Washing every morning, for instance, is passing strange to them; once or twice a week is the outside of what they think necessary, and why we want them ever to be quiet and silent is equally strange. They are beginning to comprehend that they muse be quiet at family prayers. Nothing composes them so much as music. We always sing a hymn with the harmonium at prayers, with which they are delighted. But though decidedly a care, and no slight trouble, I would not for anything be without them; they will lose their wildness in time, and they are so affectionate. Akielle is very high-spirited, but has a most loving heart. He often comes and throws his little arms round me, exclaiming: 'My mother thou art!' But he is also extremely passionate. The other day he was beating a boy bigger than himself tremendously. I interfered, and he lifted up his hand at me; then I had to punish him. He only said he would go home. I said, Very well, Akielle, go; good-bye for ever.' He burst into tears: '0 no! O no! I will never leave my Iya[17]!' and he was quite inconsolable till received into favour. They are all happy enough, and

---

[17] *Yoruba* - Mother

are a real pleasure to us, and often rouse us a little, if we are inclined to be flat or weary.

"My needle comes into constant requisition, for if strings or buttons are not needing it, a ball bursts.

"We have erected a large shed, and covered it with palm leaves, as a temporary church, till we can get a better one. In it we have the day school, and services on Sunday. It was very full both times last Sunday. The people sit on the ground, and are very attentive on the whole, at least quiet, sometimes they ask questions in the middle of the discourse, and appear much interested; another time, if you ask them what they have heard, 'they don't know, they did not understand.'"

"June 16. —

'Mercies, multiplied each hour
    Through the day, our praise demands

"I had a fall from my horse on Monday last, it was accidentally pushed from a narrow pathway, by a boy, down a half-filled hole. I was thrown under it, and I quite expected broken limbs, yet, thanks to our gracious Preserver, no harm came near me."

"Though at the time when it happened, this accident seemed to be of little importance, a few days later it was *found to be of a much more serious character, and Mrs. Hinderer felt the effects of it more or less to the end of her life."*

AT DEATH'S DOOR

Weeks of sore trial and anxiety speedily followed. Scarcely had she recovered from the consequences of her fall, before Mr. Hinderer was taken ill. Night and day she watched and nursed him, often filled with most serious apprehensions.

Of her feelings in those days of intense anxiety she gave the following account in one of her letters

"July 1st. —Sometimes the sunshine of prosperity is our portion, and a gracious God very near; but we are often in trial and difficulty of some shape or other, or sickness is our portion. My husband has had the sharpest attack of fever he ever had, with the addition of inflammation. **Last night was the worst; I was up with him all night; in the middle of it I feared I should soon be left alone in a strange land. He told me he thought he was dying, and if such an event were at hand, expressed what he wished me to do. It was a solemn time, one I shall never forget."**

"Mr. Kefer was at the same time disabled by fever, which deprived Mrs. Hinderer of his assistance; but, with heavy hearts, she and their faithful servant Olubi spent the night in watching, and administering such relief as was possible; and in those silent hours God gave to His tried servant a submissive heart, calmly resting on His wisdom and goodness.

"I could only lift up my heart unto God," she wrote, "and I am sure the black African boy by my side lifted up his in all earnestness. The sentence in Exodus iii. 7, 'I know their sorrows,' has been very comforting to me; and the hope which my dearest husband has many times expressed today, 'that this will draw us nearer to our God and Saviour.' Our house and garden have been as quiet as possible, an anxious look on every face, and not a sound from the dear children."

FEARS FOR THE FUTURE

The narrative, gathered from her journal and letters, is continued by the following extracts: -

"*July 2nd.* — We have had a grievous night, sickness I have every hour. All night, and this morning, I had agonizing doubts and apprehensions of what is before me; tonight I am a little cheered and hopeful; the dear patient sleeping, and much less sickness. I know what it *is to wish for the morning; the darkness and solemnity of night are painful; I know 'the darkness and the light are both alike' to our God; but the body gets weary, and then nervous. Yet I am wonderfully well through God's mercy, not even a headache, which is an unspeakable comfort, for I have for two or three months suffered intensely from headache. But so our gracious God 'tempers the wind to the shorn lamb, and gives abundantly the needful strength in every trying hour."*

SICKNESS & RECOVERY

*"**July 6th.** —Since I last wrote I have been very ill; a sharp attack of fever, brought on, doubtless, from anxiety and want of rest; but I am thankful to be about again, though weak. The good hand of my God hath been over me, and I have had the tenderest care from my still suffering husband. He is, I trust, recovering, but very, very slowly; the alarming symptoms have passed over, but he is intensely weak; it is such a comfort to hear him speak this evening a little above a whisper. He has* indeed been brought to the edge of the grave, and is so altered; I think you would hardly know him. I have sometimes almost been inclined to ask, 'Can it be he?' It must be long before he quite recovers; but I am so thankful that there is a prospect of this blessing. The interest

and sympathy of the people have been very touching; coming with a light step, and asking in a whisper, 'Baba o **sandi**e?' —' Is our father better?' Our young warrior, Olumloyo, has come every day, and has been truly heart-broken; he told me 'I must pray much for my husband.'

KINDNESS FROM LOCALS

"The orange season is just over, we could not get one in the market; I mentioned it to Olumloyo, when he sent his servants to the farms, but they came back without any. He was very sorry, 'Yet I must have some,' he said; and he mounted his horse and galloped off to several farms, and brought back eleven, with great delight. He sat by the bed and saw the dear patient devour one almost greedily; the young chief was so pleased that tear filled his eyes. My husband tried to thank him, Olumloyo lifted up his hand, exclaiming, 'don't speak: I am too glad.' He came this afternoon and saw my husband on the sofa; he was very much pleased, and told Olubi that many people would be so glad to have the white man well again, that there would be much rejoicing when he could once more get out; they would fire many guns, he himself would give a whole cask of powder."

"*July 10th, Sunday.* —*I must close this day with a few words with my friends. I have been at school twice, and at one service; during the other service, I stayed with my husband; he had a comfortable morning, though rather a trying afternoon; but after tea he revived much, and said he should like our usual singing. So now for the gathering, I only wish you could have seen it. Mr. Hinderer on the sofa, Mr. Kefer near him, our Christian visitor on a chair; in the wide door-way, on the ground, his daughter Martha, a girl of ten years, our two men Simon and Jacob, our horseman, cook's wife, and one or two of Mr. Kefer's servants; I at the harmonium, with two little lamps fixed in wine glasses for convenience sake; on a long bench, close behind me, Olubi, Benjamin, Susanna, schoolmaster, carpenter, and cook. Two of my boys, who are very fond of singing, and could keep their eyes open, stood one on each side of me, sometimes listening, and sometimes putting in a few sounds; and then we had a hearty singing truly. These people have the art of catching an air quickly, and are able to follow music; and they sang the collect for the day, the 7th Sunday after Trinity, beautifully; then we had the Lowestoft hymn-book box, and sang 'Comfort,' 'Lydia,' 'Arabia,' and we finished with*

'Praise God, from whom all blessings flow.'

"There was a request that I would sing to them the 'Missionary Call.' Afterwards I pointed to the dear pictures [of Mr. and Mrs. Cunningham] hanging over the harmonium, and said to them there was no sight would delight that dear lady and gentleman much more than the present; and told them of our Sunday evenings at home. They were much interested, and said they were glad they had some one who liked to sing with them in Africa, and who had such a nice instrument. It did us all good; my husband was cheered, and to me it was like a refreshing pool in the midst of a 'dry and thirsty land.' My spirit had been sad and weary; I had sighed for the refreshment of those times when I had gone to the House of God in my own favoured country. I had thought many times of those lines in Tupper's 'Proverbial Philosophy,'

'Take courage, prisoner of time, for there be
many comforts. Not few nor light are the, burdens
of life; then load it not with heaviness of spirit.'

"But there is a better word still, in a far better book, 'Cast thy burden upon the Lord, and He shall sustain thee.' And so, amidst trials and discouragements, we have our bright sunshiny places; yes, many little streams are given us on our journey, though we are sometimes cast down by reason of the hardness of the way. Yet can we sing again, 'My mouth shall praise Thee with joyful lips.'"

"More than a month elapsed between the dates of the last and the next quotation. Her silence is accounted for by the recurrence of illness, a hindrance which already, in the four months since their arrival, had made such serious inroads into the work of the mission. The story continues as follows, to the end of the year

"**August** 20th —I am again permitted to write to you, after a most severe sickness. What a wonderful thing, in the midst of all, not to have been prevented sending something every mail. "With a weak hand I wrote a few lines last month, telling you I had inflammation in the lungs; after that was gone I was much worse for three whole weeks, touched nothing but water, tea, a little raspberry vinegar, and in very **sinking moments**, once or twice, I think they gave me weak brandy and water.

AT DEATHS DOOR

"A whole week they had looked for my end; several times I seemed almost gone; I feel I was prayed back to life, for once I was quite conscious, arid felt the journey of life ending, and that I should be with my Saviour, the body of clay sleeping the sleep of death, with those who so lately have been taken from amongst us, till the resurrection morn. My poor afflicted husband had sent a special messenger to Abeokuta on horseback, to request their prayers, and on the day he arrived, they appointed an hour in the evening for special pleading on my behalf; and that self-same hour, after an intensely suffering day, I became easier and better; God listened to their cry, and while they were speaking He graciously answered. **Here I am, weaker indeed, but getting on day by day, through God's infinite mercy, and oh, I trust, for some good purpose to my own soul, and the souls of others.**

"Everyone says this is a great encouragement for the future, that I am become more 'Africanized,' My dear husband, Mr. Kefer, and our good Olubi shared in the night nursings. My husband had not recovered from his illness, and had fever every evening for weeks, and after a few hours' watching, was obliged to throw himself on the sofa from exhaustion. Mr. Kefer soon had an attack of fever, and I was deprived of his help. Poor sleepy Olubi with his master did all they could, and my needs were abundantly supplied. Oh, that I could praise the Lord for His goodness!

"God has raised me up again, and though I was sorry at one time to be called back to the things of time and sense, yet with returning health and strength, I can but rejoice at being spared a little longer, I trust for the *glory of God, to my thankful husband, to the little bright black faces which attend our school, and to many a tearful eye which has greeted me since I have been up. The weather is cool, which is helpful to me, and I go out often in a hammock.*

"I was amused to hear that you remarked, when I said in my letter I laughed at something, that it was the first time you had heard of my laughing in Africa: I assure you I do laugh very often, it would be against my nature not to laugh. I am now in the best of spirits, cheerful and happy, and often laugh at my snail-like pace, and what would you say to see me, instead of jumping up two steps at a time, and frisking about, crawling about our little farm, and feeling it a long journey."

*"**August 26th**. —I have had a treat today, my sixteen school children to dinner. They were so good while I was ill that I wished to give them a treat when well again. We gave them a large bowl of palaver sauce[18], with a. huge quantity of beaten yams; afterwards pictures, then an examination as to what they had learned in school, a little talk, which was followed by a good game at ball, then each had a present from my toy-*

---

[18] Expatriate English slang for red pepper soup

box, such as a knife, or a box for cowries. They were delighted indeed, and after a little more eating of agidi, and an orange, I sent them off by six o'clock, and then we had visits from their parents to thank us. It was a real pleasure to me to see them getting on so nicely, four of them now begin to read the Yoruba Testament; all have learned Watts's little catechism, which has been translated, and the commandments; two are also learning the English primer; they extremely like to learn English sentences, and names of things. I am always saluted by them with 'Good-morning, ma'am.' When walking out with my four boys, they tell me Yoruba names of things, and then ask for the English in return, and they remember the English name much better than I do the Yoruba. A mistake now and then occurs; one boy had come to school for a short time, and had picked up a few words, but was called away to the farm, and of course forgot them. The other day he paid me a visit, and poor fellow! had evidently been trying to think of his former salutation, but only the word 'Yes!' could be remembered. I was sitting writing in the piazza, when suddenly I heard with the strongest emphasis, 'Yes!' and I looked up at a countenance full of satisfaction at his salutation. It was too ridiculous for my four boys who were sitting on a mat over a picture book; they all laughed heartily, but took the poor fellow, and very kindly taught him his forgotten English. It was quite a scene.

"My four boys go on most comfortably together, and I am quite encouraged about them. Akielle, the youngest of them, fell asleep once during the Sunday evening singing, and was carried to his mat. The next morning he came to me, saying, 'Iya, I did not say my prayers last night, shall I now?' I am teaching them to sew and to knit, for I want occupation for them, as the school only lasts from nine to twelve. From five to six we generally walk, play ball, and all sorts of things, and 'Iya must play with them as well as work;' their great delight is truly doubled when my husband will run and let them catch him. So with one thing and another, you can believe, I have not much idle time. We have very pleasant Sunday evenings over the Noah's ark or Mrs. Buxton's beautiful Scripture pictures. After that, the whole household come in for singing. The children are now very good at church. On Sunday, in speaking on the vanity and helplessness of idols, Mr. Hinderer quoted the Psalm, 'They have mouths and speak not: the boys burst out laughing, and said it was 'true, very true' this was not very decorous truly, but it showed they were attentive. The other day, one was with us in a compound, where a man told us 'God was good, for He gave them orishas,' the child instantly replied, 'No, God did not, the devil gave us orishas'

"Our palm leaf shed has stood the rainy season very well, and has been nicely filled, we recognize a few regular attendants, and all like Sunday school.

PERSECUTION

Anna's letter ...

"One young woman has been a constant attendant, and a frequent visitor. She bought a Yoruba primer, and was very diligent in learning to read. Her husband, who is one of the great men with a multitude of wives, gave her into her father's hands, who is a thorough idolater, for coming to church and 'taking book.' They asked for the book, but she refused to give it them, so then she was put in chains for three days. On the following Sunday she came to church. We did not see her for more than a week, when one evening in the dark she came to us to say she had been punished again, but not so much. She said they told her to read the book she had, so she began the alphabet, which was all she knew, and being unintelligible to them they were angry. They have not prevented her coming to us now, but they are very anxious she should give back such a fearful thing as that book which 'will do harm to her and her family.'

"Mr. Kefer has been twice disturbed in public preaching; ordered away from under the tree; 'We will not have you white men, you are the world's spoilers.'"

'Sep. 11th — A very bright Sunday. I awoke singing,

'Oh, may my heart in tune be found,
Like David's harp of solemn sound.'

"I am thankful I did value my Sunday privileges. I cannot help on Sunday longing once more for my corner in St. Peter's. I long to hear our beautiful prayers in an English church. I am generally rather low on Sunday in heart; I can get hold of so little Sunday feeling. The scenes and sounds around us are so different from home; drums, guns, farms, markets, all the same as any other day, and though I can heartily mingle my 'Amen,' in our simple shed, yet all seems strange; but what a comfort our God is not confined to time or place I only long for my soul to be filled more and more with the quickening and enlivening influences of His blessed Spirit; to rise above things temporal, and to lay hold on things eternal, that as earthly comforts and privileges fail, I may be so hidden in the Rock, and live so near to the Fountain that I sigh not so much for the streams, and that I may rejoice in the Lord in the midst of all. But one is apt to get flat, sad cold, and heartless sometimes, and to go down,

down. Oh, my dearest friends, we need your prayers lest we faint and be weary and feel the hardness of the way, instead of rejoicing to be counted worthy, looking into the future. In my late illness, one Monday night, a cloud hung over me and hid all that was bright; all at once it came into my mind that it was the day of the monthly Missionary Meeting [at Lowestoft], when many were not only praying for the heathen but for those of their own country who were dwelling in the midst of them, that they might be comforted and refreshed in hours of sickness and sorrow. I was quite cheered, and revived a little; the thought of your constant remembrance of us was and is always a comfort

"Abudu came to us on Monday; a nice bright little fellow. Ifa gave notice at his birth that he was to be a 'book boy,' so his father gave him a Mohammedan name."

"Oct. lst. — 'Mr. and Mrs. Townsend came to pay us a visit; we were very glad to have them with us in our little dwelling which I was almost inclined to think must be made of something elastic, for we packed in very comfortably, and were truly glad of a little white society. The people were astonished, and frightened too, to see five white people together; and when we all went out it was amusing and fatiguing enough. We are still much surrounded by visitors, who wonder at all they see; they think me much more industrious than I think myself; they laugh to see me write, and wonder that I can read so many books; and the wonderful things I can do with a needle and scissors make them open their mouths and say, 'Ah, ah, ah!'

SUPERSTITIONS

"Our school does not increase at present, people are afraid to send their children; they think 'book' will make them cowards, but those we have are going on very nicely. One Sunday, at school, I endeavoured to explain some of the texts which they had learned, at least to talk about them. They spoke a long time to each other about the eyes of the Lord being over the righteous, but His face being turned away from those who were wicked; they looked, very sorrowful, but soon one said, 'It is only the devil God does not look at.' On the text, Jesus did no sin, neither was guile found in His mouth,' one said I was 'good, very good, more good than anybody; the devil was very wicked,' he himself was 'a good boy, and Robert, and Akielle; Idowu was naughty sometimes,' but he evidently was happy in the thought that they were all extremely good. It is very interesting to have them talk out in this way, and it makes me very anxious to get on with the language, that I may hear them always, and be able to answer them. You would smile to see us trying to understand one another. They are so fond of singing; after their evening prayers they now begin to sing 'There is a happy land' very prettily. Last night, after it was finished, one of them clapped his hands and said, 'That is sweet.' I sometimes feel sad at the thought how little I do, how little there is I can do; and then I look at these little creatures, and hope they are being trained for future good, so I take comfort. My little black boys are my greatest occupation, so that they and their doings, or mine with them, are interspersed through everything, for I am mother, play fellow, teacher."

PLEA FOR HEALTH & LONGEVITY

"Nov 19th. —*This has been an eventful week. On Monday, the 14th, we commenced building the wall of our compound; the foundation of our house also is laid, and the corners built up a little way. The first floor will be about six or seven feet high, which will be used for stores, and we shall mount up, said have three good rooms, and smaller rooms made in the piazza. I can hardly fancy I am to have such comfort, yet it is with a loose hand one holds it.* **The uncertainty of everything, especially here, makes one only long for the 'house not made with hands, eternal, in the**

heavens.' Yet, if it pleases God to spare us a few years, it will be very desirable, and we may accept it gratefully, an earthly dwelling, secure from the rain and wind, and room to turn round in.

"We have a class on Saturday for candidates for baptism, some of our own servants not being baptized. A woman of this town has joined it; she has attended regularly every Sunday for four or five months, giving up all Sunday labour. She seems to have long desired to know the right way to serve God, feeling that orishas were of no use; she joined the Mohammedans, but that did not meet the want of her heart either. Now we do hope and pray that in hearing of Jesus the Saviour, 'the Way, the Truth, and the Life,' she may find Him her 'all in all"'

"*Nov. 21st.*— This will greet my beloved friends in a new year; this year will have passed away, with its multitude of events, but its unnumbered mercies cannot cease to be remembered. The uncertain future is before us; shall we fear to tread it? No! Mercies past only encourage one to hope, and to commit the keeping of our souls and bodies unto our faithful Creator. Oh, for grace to live nearer and nearer to Him, and to be found more and more meet for the kingdom above! I have found it is not our circumstances or position in life which will tend to this.

*'We need not bid for cloistered cell
Our neighbour and our work farewell.'*

"Not the more passive life in Africa, or the more active and busy movements of Lowestoft, will help us in communion with our God, or lead us nearer to heaven; the Holy Spirit must be our guide, our helper, our defender, with watching and prayer in ourselves."

GROWTH

"**Dec.**—It is a heart-cheering sight to behold, Sunday after Sunday, such a goodly gathering as we have, and they are so quiet and attentive. I think I told you we had a young schoolmaster, but we have given him up, in order to have a man who can go about in the town, and talk, and be of use to the people. This was more necessary to us in this immense town; and, as they could not afford us both from Abeokuta, we were glad to be able to choose between the two. We have made a sacrifice, and given up our faithful Olubi for the school. It is a sacrifice, for he was the only one in the house we could look to for everything, but he is a good creature, and very ready to 'give a helping hand when school is over, and I believe he will make an excellent schoolmaster, he is so fond of children, and has so much heart in everything.

> "The dear children are very ready to receive instruction, and it was quite a grief to them when, they had a few days' holiday; they were not a little delighted to have some lessons with me. It is so interesting to watch their opening minds. I asked one of my little boys if he liked to 'sit down' with me? 'O yes, indeed I do,' was his answer. 'Why?' 'Because I learn so many nice things here, and you, Iya, love me, and are so kind to me.' I asked, 'Do you love God?' 'O yes, because He is so great and good.' 'Do you love Jesus?' 'Yes, yes.' 'Why?' I asked, but that seemed too much to explain, it seemed too deep, and he ended with saying, 'I want to hear more of Jesus, and know more.'"

The first quotation from the memorials of the next year begins with another sad record of illness, but soon Mrs. Hinderer was able to resume her work, encouraged by tokens that God's blessing rested on her labours.

> "*Jan. 20th, 1854.* —I have again been laid very low, in consequence, in some measure I doubt not, of the late anxious nursing of Mr. Kefer. When a fellow-labourer is brought down to the gates of death, all one's endeavours, anxieties, and sympathies are called forth, and one feels the effects afterwards, the body and the nerves suffer; but we are also passing through the trying season, the harmattan. I have had lingering fever; I feel very weak, and unable to do anything; the

bed and the sofa are very much my resources, and I cannot get round as I usually do; however, we hope on, and are as cheerful as is possible with a weary body of clay. **My dear husband is always cheerful and cheering, never despairing, never doubting, never distrusting; even in the dark cloudy day he passes on with all his burdens.** I must confess I have had a low time, and have been walking on the dark and shady side of life. I have felt, 'What am I?' and could not bear to be looked at by the people who are all day watching us. I felt they must think me a very lazy white woman, but yet I think my pale thin face and tottering limbs must have been an excuse for me; however, the happiest way of thinking was that this was my time of education and preparation for future work, and so I endeavoured to lie passive, only seeking to be made entirely resigned to do or to suffer my Father's will. **This is a grace one especially needs in a missionary's calling. You come with a desire to do something; you see your work before you, see thousands of children, hundreds of people, and you are utterly helpless in mind and body; it is hard work, and only One can give strength to bear it.** Oh, that it may all work in me the good He designs who sends it, the spirit of patience, meekness, gentleness, forbearance, and love. God has been gracious, and He has promised never to leave nor forsake us. I do feel and believe this; but I long *for more of the spirit of repose, confidence, and assurance, in the suffering day, and in the time of weakness.*

"Truly, the African climate is fearful, and it seems to me that it will require the sacrifice of the gold that perisheth, and of life to a considerable extent, before it can be helped by her own sons. God calls for this; will men hear or not? They will not repent the sacrifice in the better world. Oh, that there may be a true church here, boldly to lift up a standard against error, in the name of the Lord of Hosts."

FIRST FRUITS

*"**Feb. 21st.**—Now I must tell you some of our encouragements, not perhaps conversions, but something approaching thereto. Many people in this town are not exactly slaves, but are in pawn. Their parents have wanted money, perhaps, and have given their children as security, so that after a time the one in pawn has to work so many days for his master without any reward, and the remaining days, according to the master's generosity, for himself, to earn enough for his entire food and clothing. A poor fellow in this position came to church whenever his master's working day did not fall upon a Sunday, and became so interested in all he*

heard, that he said he could not work on Sunday, he should beg his master to give him that day always, and he would give him one of his own week days. Now that is something like self-denial, is it not! "One of our church builders also is full of enquiry, and says his heart cannot sit down, he cannot follow his past fashion, neither can he take white man's fashion altogether.

CONVERSIONS

"Our sawyer is a heathen from Abeokuta, whom we begged to come and saw for us. His friends sent for him the other day to go and make the usual 'country fashion' with them. He sent them word. 'No; since he had been here he had seen and heard things so different. They begged, they threatened, he said he could not help what they did, but he could not join with them in their heathen worship. He attends church regularly, and Sunday school too, and is eager to learn to read.

"There are some other hopeful signs. A country priest who has troubled us, and tried to prejudice others against us, came the other day, saying, 'I get no peace, I want to give my heart to God.'

"A famous priestess came to convert us, but returned to think for herself, and has had some serious talks with

Olubi. So we are greatly encouraged in our work, and if thus permitted to do something for Christ's sake, what is a little suffering or an earlier grave? White and black will the sooner rejoice together, and the time be hastened when all shall know the Lord, from the least to the greatest.

"There is plenty to do, and I long to do it; I am certain there is more pain in sitting still than in the hardest work, but I find I must go 'softly,' or be laid by altogether. Africa is not England, I am not strong, but not ill either, and as time rolls on, I hope to be stronger: and in the compulsory retirement from continual active life, I trust there is some ingathering for one's own self, and for the good of others, in my future course.

"The house is making great progress. After my return from Abeokuta, we go into it. We do both look forward to it with real pleasure, and have bright visions, with God's help, of going to work in good earnest in divers ways. **Up to this time we feel to have done nothing, or hardly commenced, not at least in a way satisfactory to ourselves, but with feeble means God will do His own blessed work, and we hope and desire, from the depths of our hearts, to be more entirely used for His honour and glory, and for the good of Ibadan."**

REST IN ABEOKUTA

Reference is made in the above extract to an expected absence from home. Mrs. Hinderer had been for some time so much out of health, that under the advice of Dr. Irving, who had spent a fortnight with them in March, she was persuaded to go to Abeokuta to recruit. Mr. Hinderer accompanied her, but after a few days returned to Ibadan, to hasten the completion of the building of their house.

The following letter is dated —

"Abeokuta, April. —*It was by no means easy to get away from home, and I felt it much, the dear boys were so sorrowful. They came a little way on the road with us after many promises, before leaving the house, that I would not go to England, when I got as far as Abeokuta; and when we halted under a tree to take a final leave for a time, I got off my home, and if you could just have seen it, you would have said, African children have hearts, and very tender loving ones too. One of my boys, about ten or eleven years old, could bear it no longer; he laid his head on my side and sobbed, and as he could get the words out, said, 'Go, dear Iya, and make haste back,' and then turned his face and steps towards home.*

The Gospel in Ibadan

"You will not think me egotistical, but this I do think, if I am come to Africa for nothing else, I have found the way to a few children's hearts, and if spared, and I have health and strength, I think I shall not, with God's blessing, find it very difficult to do something with them. An inundation of seven, whom I expect to come to me when I return, seems rather formidable, but I do not fear it if I am well. If you can get at their affections, you can get obedience, and I think that is generally secured before hand. I have had many visits from them, and they are watching as eagerly as anybody for the completion of the house, that they may come and 'Sit down' in it. My boys that I have now, would never tell me an untruth, or touch a cowry or anything they should not. This is truly wonderful for heathen boys, brought up all their lives, hitherto, in the midst of every kind of deceit. Dear fellows, I feel sure the love and blessing of God is over them, and their young hearts are opening, I humbly trust, to receive Him as their only God and Saviour, and I hope I am very thankful to have found favour amongst them. I must add, though I may fill a larger place in their affections, having more to do with them, yet 'Baba,' my husband, shares in it considerably.

"There has been a fine gathering of black heads for the morning service, attentive listeners to the story of what was accomplished for them, and for all, on this day, (Good Friday.) The text was 'It is finished' I thought of the sermon I had heard from these words in my own tongue and country, and I felt a weary thirsty spirit for past privileges. No one knows what a loss it is. I felt with Keble, in his poetry for yesterday, it was a real striving

'To keep the lingering flame in my own heart alive.'"

"May 9. —*I long to be at home again, and grudge every hour from my beloved Ibadan*; only the assurance and advice of everybody, that I ought to have some sort of change, could have moved me. Tomorrow we hope to be on our way to Ibadan, and we go with joy and gladness of heart. I cannot be thankful enough to be able to return with renewed health and strength, and I hope never to have occasion for any move again till we leave for dear England once more. There is a great cry for Iya to go home again, and I certainly feel there is no place in all Africa like that home. But we are going, somewhat with the feelings of St. Paul, when he said, 'Not knowing the things that shall befall me there;' but the 'Fear not' of Him who cannot change, goes before us, said under its shield we can indeed go on our way fearlessly."

After her return, she made the following remarks on her visit to Abeokuta

"*The kindness and hospitality of Mr. and Mrs. Townsend are never to be forgotten; I enjoyed being under their roof and with them, and was much interested in all that is going on around them. Mrs. Townsend cared for me as a sister, and as a proof of its benefit, under God's blessing, I will quote a remark of my little maid Susanna. At first she would say, 'Please, ma'am, too much bone live here,' but when we were about returning, (for she sighed for Ibadan as well as myself,) 'Please, ma'am, bone all gone away, I think we may go home now.' It certainly would not have been very pleasant to lose all my bones, but there was some satisfaction in having them covered, and I fully agreed with Susanna on its being time to get back.'*

Journey from Lagos

Chapter IV

Progress in The Work

"All unseen, the Master walketh by the toiling
 servant's side;
Comfortable words He speaketh,
While His hands uphold and guide.
"Grief, nor pain, nor any sorrow,
Rends thy heart to Him unknown;
He today and He tomorrow
Grace sufficient gives His own."

ON MRS. HINDERER'S RETURN from Abeokuta, she was welcomed by her husband and her native children to the new mission-house, which had been completed during her absence. The building of this house, with its upper story and outside staircase (a marvellous production in the eyes of the people), and likewise the erection of a substantial church, had hitherto occupied much of the time of the missionaries, who, besides making the plans and directing and superintending the labourers, were often obliged to render further assistance by working with their own hands.

Anna's letter . . .

"*Ibadan, May 14th*. —Yesterday I reached my loved Ibadan home, amidst a hearty greeting from the dear boys. Laniyono, who was the most sorrowful when I left, gave a shriek of delight, and sprang into my arms, with his legs round my waist, hanging there to his heart's content, shouting and making the oddest remarks you ever heard; that I was never to go away again, seemed to be a certainty to his mind. But a tinge of bitterness is generally mixed with every cup, so I found here. Two of my boys had been taken away by their parents in my absence: Adelotan is not allowed to appear anywhere, but Abudu came at once to see me. I put my hand on his shoulder, and he burst into a flood of tears. -' O Iya, it is not me, it is not me, it is my father who has done it.' Poor child! I could only soothe and calm him, and bid him be patient. I believe he will soon get leave from his father to come back.

NEW LODGINGS

"Our new house, after all the toil in building it promises to possess all the comfort we could expect or desire in this country; it is water-tight, has a good-sized sitting and bed-room, white-washed walls, and a good iron roof; comfortable piazzas, and all very airy, and as cool as anything can be in Africa, which was my principal desire. It is wonderful what my dear husband has achieved in my absence, and now he rejoices to have his wife in it, and so does she to be there. We pray that a rich blessing may be given us with it, and that though we have the comfort of a dwelling, we may never forget that this is not Our home, but a tent pitched for the day."

"**May 17th.** — Bale, the head chief, paid us a special visit today. He came in great state, with drums and various strange instruments of music, with his host of attendants, singing men and singing women. He marvelled greatly at our house, and could not imagine how it was made. He was quite alarmed to think of mounting the steps; but with my husband pulling, and others pushing, we got him up. I stood at the top to receive him, in his mass of silks and velvets; he very graciously took my hand, and we walked into the room, at the sight of which he gave a great shout and wondered; he then took a fancy to the sofa, and sat there. We admitted upstairs his wives, his eldest son, and a few of his great people, and then were obliged to move away the steps, or the house, strong as it is, must have broken down with the mass of people. We gave him, and those in the room with him, a little refreshment, English bread, biscuits, and a few raisins. They looked at the bedroom, and all the things in both rooms. Bale was extremely amused to see himself in the looking glass. I took the women by themselves; the washing-stand attracted their attention, so I washed my hands to show them the use of it. My soap was wonderful; and that I wiped my hands after I had washed them, was a thing unheard of. But they took it into their heads to follow my example, and all hands must touch the soap, and go into the water and there was a fine splashing, and a pretty towel, for the indigo dye comes off their clothes so very much, that I believe the towel will be blue and white for ever. At last we got into a state of composure again, and all being quiet, Mr. Hinderer made a little speech, telling Bale how glad we were to see him, why we built the house, and what brought us to this country."

"**May 22nd.** —*A woman of about fifty years of age came to me. I noticed her in church, two or three Sundays before I went away, and again she was there yesterday. She brought with her a fowl, and corn to feed it with, and yams; she put them before me as a present, and said, 'Iya, all my life I have served the devil; he has been my god; but he never gave me peace in my heart. My husband was stolen away by war, the devil did not help me; my children all died, the devil could not help me; but since you white people have come, I have heard* the words of the Great God, which we never heard before, and they are sweet to me. I want to hear more, and to walk in the right road, for it has been a wrong road all my life.' She has thrown her husband's images into the water. After our last words, 'God bless you, and give you peace in your heart!' she uttered a most fervent and hearty 'Amen.' As it is the constant practice to take fowls, cowries, and other offerings to their gods, I thought it necessary to tell her we did not desire she should bring a 'full hand' to us: she said she knew it, but begged we would accept her little present, to make her happy. I had a little chintz bag hanging up, with not a handful of cowries in it; she would not have had cowries as a payment on any account, but the bag she could not refuse; such a possession she never thought to have, and she went off with it greatly delighted.

"Now, dear friends, farewell; remember us in our work, our weakness and infirmities, bodily and mental, and may all your love, sympathy, and prayers be returned in tenfold measure in blessings on yourselves."

"**June 22nd**. — We are both in very good health, and both as busy as bees. A day is never long enough for me; a great deal falls to my share, and I can fancy no one more happy than myself in being equal to it in bodily power.

"My dear little boys give me great comfort and satisfaction. I must tell you one story about them. On Sunday week we had studied and talked over the picture of Dorcas. Yesterday evening they came to me for their prayers in my bedroom, and particularly noticed the beautiful figure I have of dear Mrs. Fry, which stands on my dressing-table, and which always seems to say, 'Be ye followers of them who through faith and patience inherit the promises.' They asked me who it was, I told them; and, as far as I could, of her love to all people, especially the afflicted ones, the prisoner, the slave, &c. They listened attentively till big tears stood in the eyes of one. I then asked if they had ever heard of any one being so kind. One said she was like Dorcas, full of good deeds; another that she was like their own Iya, who could leave her own country arid friends and come to them, and love little black boys and girls and people so much. 'No,' I said, 'there was one whose example Mrs. Fry followed, who did far more than either Dorcas or Iya.' A little fellow, the youngest of all, exclaimed, 'It is Jesus, Iya means, who went about always doing good, and then gave His life for all.' **Do you know, I thought it was worth while to come to Africa, only to hear this from little lips which, such a short time ago, were taught senseless words over wood, and stone, and charms.**"

A SLAVE BOY REDEEMED

"*July 11th*. — Early this morning the wife of one of our native agents and our young schoolmaster went into the town, to accompany a friend on the road to Ijaye. On their way back they saw a little boy, not three years old, looking cold, starved, and filthy; they went towards the poor little thing, who said, 'Era mi,' - ' Buy me, buy me; I want to go home with you.' On enquiring they found that he was the child of a slave; the mother was sold many months ago, far away; the master of the house where the child was is gone to war, and so what was everybody's charge became nobody's. One man, who did just feed him for a time, got tired of him, and said he had enough to do to feed himself, for he also was a slave; so the poor child was cast out into the street. No one would dare to take him, lest they should be charged with stealing a slave, and for three moons, as the people say, he had been there, night and day; a few days more, and he must have died. All the food he got would be a bit of agidi, or corn, which would be thrown to him by passers by, as you would to a fowl. Olubi talked with the people, but they only said they could not help it, and wondered any one should care about a little slave boy.

"Mr. Hinderer immediately returned with Olubi. Meantime a woman in the yard had washed the child, and shaved his head; be had also been abundantly oiled, and rubbed over with canewood. Mr. Hinderer talked with the people, and at last they said, 'Take him if you like; if he live, he live; if he die, well; no one make palaver with you;' so my husband hired a woman to carry him on her back, and bring him to me; and here he is, a pretty-looking little child, but with a countenance so full of SORROW, and he is a poor miserable skeleton. After a little more washing, I put on him a frock, and wrapped him in a warm cloth, which he seemed thoroughly to enjoy. I took him on my lap, and he seemed quite at home there. We gave him a little food, which he ate most greedily. We must be very careful about his food for some little time, or he would kill himself with eating. He soon fell fast asleep in my arms. As I was watching his sweet sleep, 'Take this child and nurse it for me, and I will give thee thy wages,' seemed to ring in my ears, and we do receive him as a precious little charge. May I be enabled to bring him up for God. He may be a bright and shining light. I wish his poor mother could know he was well taken care of."

"**July 20th**. — *The little boy improves in health, but is not very good-tempered. The poor dear child has all the effects of being starved and unkindly treated, and at present all he can think of is eating. The other day I played with him a little, and he condescended to look at me. On my saying, 'I think you like me a little better to-day,' the reply was, 'What will you give me to eat?'*

This dear child has hardly a mind to appreciate kindness, having only known cruelty and oppression."

July 23rd was a day peculiarly interesting to both missionaries and converts, who for the first time assembled for worship in the church. Months had still to pass before the building could be completed, but they were glad to make use of the bare mud walls, with their grass roof, as the old palm-leaf church had been destroyed by the heavy tornadoes.

She writes on this subject....

"Now we have the outward walls, and we pray God, to build up a spiritual house within. Grant that the sons and daughters of Ibadan may become polished corners of the temple! Hear Thou from heaven Thy dwelling-place, and send out Thy grace and Thy blessing!

"It is curious to watch people listening for the first time to the new tidings, a little gentle remark, then an expression of doubt, then such a hearty 'Amen.'"

Anna's letter...

"August 13th. —My husband was going to visit Laniyono, who had been taken away by his father a week ago, at his father's house to-day, but, hearing his

voice as in prayer, he waited, and heard him pour forth his petitions most earnestly, 'I want to love Thee, I want to be Thy child.' When his voice ceased, he went in, and there he found the dear child alone with his little heathen brothers and sisters; and, as he came away, they burst forth in singing an English hymn, which he had evidently taught them in the week. I think we may trust that a work of grace is commenced in that dear boy's heart, and hope his being at home for a short time may not be for harm, but for good. I went in, a few days since, and they were all gathered round their meal; he was standing up, and, with eyes shut and hands folded, repeated the grace we had taught him, and all the children said 'Amen.'"

"**August 20th.** —Another bright Sunday! How I love to feel bright and happy on Sundays, they have been such blessed days to me, and I am so thankful to find their brightness returning. There is so much more peace and quietness round about us now; our neighbours seem to feel it is a holy day with us, and those who do not yet join in keeping it with us are ashamed to be seen by us doing their own work. No one thinks of coming to offer anything for sale in our yard."

"On the 5th of October a real treat was given us in the arrival of a beautiful box of things from Lady Buxton. It was such a feast that the children were wild with delight, whilst I myself was not much less so. The children were greatly pleased with the playthings, and not less so with Iya's new dress. They do so curiously enjoy any new thing for me, and fail not to admire it abundantly. Even when the letters arrive, they give a loud shout, and go singing about, 'Iya gets book from her father and mother, sisters and brothers, and friends, far far away. Oh, it is good 'followed by more shouts; and then they creep up for the empty envelopes, which is their share of the feast.

"The month of November is marked by the arrival of our good and valued Bishop (Vidal). On the 9th he arrived in Ibadan, accompanied by Archdeacon Graf, Mr. Townsend, and Dr. Irving; so that, including our three selves, we were seven white people in Ibadan, quite an event! On Sunday the Bishop confirmed nine of our people, and delivered, through an interpreter, a most striking address.

"On Monday evening he addressed the confirmed, and our native helpers. It was so solemn, so tender, so impressive: Phil. ii. 1-18, is indelibly stamped on our minds. The visit of our beloved and honoured Bishop, his kind interest and tender sympathy in us and our work, have been as a refreshing draught in a dry and thirsty land. We rejoice and give thanks that such a head has been granted us; his brilliant example must

have some effect upon us all. Every grace mentioned in
Gal. v. 22, seems to dwell in him."

VISIT TO IJEBULAND

In December, Mr. Hinderer, accompanied by Dr. Irving, paid a visit to the country of Ijebu, which bad hitherto been inaccessible to Europeans. He had been encouraged to undertake the journey by an invitation, sent to him some months before, from the king of that country. It was given in the form of a symbolical letter, composed of ten cowries strung together, and a seed of the osan[19] fruit. The word "ewa,"—ten, is also a verb, and means "come ye," and the cowries, being strung in pairs, gave force to the request that the white man of Ibadan and the king of Ijebu should meet face to face. The word "osan" is not only the name of a fruit, but also means "well," and conveyed an enquiry after Mr. Hinderer's welfare.

Of this time Mrs. Hinderer writes: *"My husband left on Friday. I felt parting with him, but was glad he should go on such an errand, and trust they may have much blessing in their journey.* ***It will be a wonderful blow to slavery and all sorts of cruelties, if the banner of the Cross be erected,***

---

[19] Yoruba – 'orange fruit'

and light and salvation be proclaimed and accepted there. So here I am all alone. I think it says much for a town in Africa, of one hundred thousand inhabitants, that one white woman can be left alone, in perfect safety, and with no fear.

"These Yoruba people have some very nice arrangements about their form of government. I found out that there was an 'Iyalode' or mother of the town, to whom all the women's palavers (disputes) are brought before they are taken to the king. She is, in fact, a sort of queen, a person of much influence, and looked up to with much respect I sent my messenger to her, to tell her I should like to visit her. She sent word she should be delighted; so on Monday the 18th, I went with the children, and we found a most respectable, motherly looking person, surrounded by her attendants and people, in great order, and some measure of state. I told them why I came to this country, and entreated them to come and hear the Word of God for themselves, and send their children to us to be taught. We two Iyas made strong friendship, by my giving, and her receiving, a fine velvet head-tie, and a silk bag; and the lady settled that we were to be the two mothers of the town, she the Iyalode still, and I the 'Iyalode funfun,' (the white Iyalode). I then spoke to myriads of children; and after sundry shouts, a variety of blessings, and divers shakes of my hand which seemed to be a great honour and privilege, I at last got away. Three days after my visit, the Iyalode sent to salute me, begging me to accept from her a goat, and a calabash of yams, to make a feast for my children and people."

This had been in many ways an eventful year, and her journal, at the close of it, expresses the feelings with which she regarded the past, and looked forward to the future.

"*Sunday, December 31.* — *The last day of this year. I have felt bowed before my God in humility, in shame and confusion of face, and heart, and mind; the burden of my cry is 'God be merciful to me a sinner.' 'Hide Thy face from my sins, blot out all my iniquities.' Though I have felt sorrowful and sad, under the sense of the intolerable burden of sin, there has been great comfort in being brought thus to His footstool, in heart-felt sighing and tears; and a sweet peace has come over my mind. I trust and believe that the Lord God, the compassionate Friend of sinners, will hear and bless me.'*

The dawn of the New Year brought with it thoughts in harmony with those with which the old year had ended, only with an additional strain of hopefulness and filial confidence.

"Jan. 18th 1855. — Welcome New Year! I hail thy approach as a special opportunity for a fresh start in the journey of life. Oh, may it be a new and blessed era. Oh, I do seek this day help and blessing for our work, our great and holy calling. O God, Thou knowest the multitude of my thoughts within me, and the many desires of my heart, and I would cast myself on Thee who dost care for me, even me; and on this new scene of time I desire to enter with hope and faith, committing myself body, soul and spirit, to Thy gracious care and keeping, with all whom Thou knowest to be near and dear to me."

"Jan. 3rd, Wednesday. — I went with all our people far on the Ijebu road, to meet my husband, but alas, he did not come. We were a nice large party; Odehinde joined us, which was very kind, and showed real love to his minister by losing a whole day's labour for the pleasure of meeting him. We were all much disappointed."

"Jan. 4th. —At 4 A.M., a man arrived with letters to say my husband expected to be back on Thursday or Friday, but this afternoon, about half-past two, to our great joy, he arrived with Dr. Irving, tired enough, but delighted to be home.

"I do enjoy having D. safe at home again, after such a journey of mercies, and such a successful one. We thank Thee, O Lord of heaven and earth! Dr. Irving left us on the following Monday." Mr. Hinderer returned from this journey apparently in good health, and there seemed to be no reason to fear that any ill effects would follow, although he had travelled under the rays of a burning sun; but in a few days he was laid low with fever. She writes

DISCOURAGEMENT FROM SICKNESS

"*Jan. 19.* — Now, alas, I have my tale of sorrow to tell. I told you my beloved husband had gone on a journey, he returned on Thursday afternoon, the 4th instant, worn and tired, but he soon got quite refreshed. On the following Monday he was so cheerful, talking of the pleasure of being at home, and making plans for the future for visiting every part of this immense town. In the afternoon he was rather feverish, and went to lie down, but from that bed he has never been up since, except for an hour or so from restlessness, or because he thought himself better."

THREAT OF DEATH

This was the beginning of a severe illness which for several days imperiled his life, and filled his devoted wife with anxious and disturbing thoughts, the more trying because she was overstrained by incessant watching and nursing. **What if she were to be left alone in that far-off land? Or what if he, with life restored, but with his constitution impaired, were to be constrained to resign his work in Africa, the very, object for which life was precious to them both?** The few words, which he was from time to time able to utter, showed plainly that he was under the impression that his days in the battle-field' were over.

The helplessness of her situation added to Mrs. Hinderer's distress. The fever had been subdued by the usual remedies, but on the 18th new symptoms of an alarming character appeared, and she dispatched a messenger to her friends at Abeokuta. To her great comfort and relief Mr. Crowther arrived on the 21st; his skill and care proved to be of the utmost service. Through the mercy of God, Mr. Hinderer was brought back from the very borders of death, and in a few weeks he was sufficiently recovered to resume in some measure his much-loved work.

On Sunday, February 11th, he preached for the first time since his illness. **On that day joy and sorrow were**

especially mingled together, for while their hearts were overflowing with gratitude for the mercies they had received, the mail brought the painful intelligence that God had called from his labours another, and, he the most influential, of the little band who had sailed together from England two years before.

"How shall I put down," she writes, "the sad, sad tidings of the death of our dear Bishop? He had been amongst us, cheering and comforting us on our way, had entered into our joys and sorrows, and had entirely won our hearts. His ministrations will not soon be forgotten and all his kind words and interest in everything. It was a most valuable season. He said he quite loved my boys, and the last morning he took them into his room and prayed with them. No one since I left you, my dearest friend, has ever given me such a kind word of comfort, encouragement, and exhortation; but now come the heavy tidings that we may see his face no more on earth, and we feel it deeply. Our Africans' explanation is,' 'The shepherd came to look after his sheep, and his life has fallen a sacrifice to it.' Poor Africa! What sorrows and trials do pass over it, wave upon wave; its climate is sad. **Of the fourteen who sailed together in one ship two years ago, only four are left to labour here. May we be spared awhile!** *We ought to desire to live, and to be enabled to toil and labour in this dark land. But for this, I should*

long more and more to pass away to the heavenly land. I often feel weary of loving what passeth away;'—weary of sin and sorrow.

The narrative proceeds in her own words...

"**March 16th**. — *Dear Laniyono has a very bad father, but his mother is an interesting young woman, and has attended church for some time. Last Saturday her husband took out one of his idols, and ordered all his household to bow down before it and worship, but his wife refused, at which the man was much enraged, and said he would never allow her to go to church any more. Poor Laniyono had a tearful Saturday, and in the Sunday-school, finding his mother was not there, he could hardly take his turn in the reading lesson, for sorrow; but to his great joy when service commenced, in she came, the father having gone out for the whole day. How she will be able to go on we cannot tell, but hardly, we fear, without persecution.*

"*Mr. Hinderer hopes on Whit-Sunday to admit a few of our candidates for baptism to that Holy Sacrament; and I trust they will not be members of Christ's flock in name only, but living members of the same. The private persecutions are very severe, but our little band have hitherto been enabled to stand strong in. the Lord, and in the power of His might.' Three of my boys have been* taken away by their parents, through the orders of these gods of wood and stone, or rather, of the country priests. It has been a bitter trial to me, but my husband tries to comfort me by the assurance that good will come out of the present evil."

On Sunday, March 18th, the following affecting entry is made in her journal. It is almost too sacred to be published, and yet it is difficult to withhold it when it may render essential service to other souls undergoing the like experience....

"I have tried to draw near to my God this day, and had one comfortable half hour, between breakfast and school, in prayer and tears. I have been too cold, too hard, too far from my God. I have deserved that He should hide His face from me. I have not drawn nigh unto Him; the heart-achings from outward things have drawn me away from the only place of comfort; the sins and sorrowing have been a sort of excuse, but I do desire to struggle, to wrestle.

"*March. 29th.* —I long to be living nearer to heaven, though I must stay on earth awhile. If the wings droop, and one bends towards earth in this heathen land, it is so hard to soar again."

She was encouraged by the progress the children were making at this time, they were quick and ready in drawing lessons from the objects around them.

She wrote...

"March. 20th. —We stood by a beautiful brook, where short palm-trees were growing luxuriantly; the children were much struck in comparing these with a dry and withered one further off. I just mentioned their having learned a Psalm with me, which they might remember while looking at the two trees; they at once thought of the first, and we had such an eager earnest talk. They went on comparing things around us with scripture illustrations...

*"April 26th. Good Friday. —I trust we have, in a measure, enjoyed this solemn week, and truly have we desired to lead our minds to meditation and contemplation on our gracious Saviour's cross and passion. **It is hard in a heathen land, away from such privileges as we had at home, to have the mind in full tune for such a season. Yet why should not we? If we can only fix our eye on the cross, on a bleeding Saviour, and not only so but on a risen One also, and if we can each feel, He is my Saviour, He has washed away my sins, He is mine and I am His, we are as near to Him in the wilds of Africa as in dear privileged England.**"*

MORE DEATHS AMONG THE MISSIONARIES

The uncertainty of life was again brought specially before them early in May, when the news reached them that their kind friend, Dr. Irving, was numbered with the dead. She wrote: -

Anna's letter...

"May 4th. — *I look at our little church, and the fence which is erecting around it to enclose a space for burials, and think, though no white person sleeps there yet, how soon there may be, how soon I may lie there. May we only be ready; and if so, through the mercy and righteousness of a Saviour, when the work appointed for us to do is done, and the summons is given, I do feel I could gladly exchange 'the tumults of earth, for the pleasures of heaven.' The weakness, frailty, and suffering of the poor body, the imperfect state in which one now is, the constant feeling, when I would do good evil is present with me,' all make me long for the time when we shall serve our God and Saviour without a veil between, without any impediment. At the same time, if it pleases God to spare us, I hope I should not only be content to live, but rejoice in it, if I may live to His honour and glory."*

Before the month closed, the first grave was opened in that little churchyard, and they laid their faithful friend and fellow-labourer, Mr. Kefer, in his last-resting-place till the morning of the resurrection. He was struck down by yellow fever, while itinerating in the outlying towns and villages. He had set forth in his usual health, May 22nd. On the following Monday, his horse was led into the town without a rider, While Mr. Kefer was borne to the mission-house in a hammock. When he saw Mr. and Mrs. Hinderer, he was just able to give them a smile of recognition. In the evening they gathered round his bed for prayer, but apparently it was unheard by the departing spirit, which was going to a happier scene, in which prayer would be turned into praise.

Mrs. Hinderer's anticipation, that the new churchyard might soon be the resting place of one of the missionaries, was thus early realised, though her own life was prolonged for many years of glad and faithful service.

Contemplating this event, which was so serious a loss to the mission, she tried to catch such rays of encouragement as might possibly diminish the gloom. "Now that we have the white man's grave in Ibadan, may we not hope for a harvest,' as one of our friends remarked, 'now that the Lord has watered Ibadan with the life of His servant?'" From this point, till the close of the year, the story may be continued in her own language.

ARRIVAL OF A SLAVE BOY

"June 23rd.—I have been gladdened this day by receiving into our house a dear bright intelligent little fellow, a slave; he is delighted with everything, asking, 'What is this? And what is that?' He is very affectionate too—once he sprang into my arms and put his arms round my neck, saying, 'you won't let me be sold away, will you? For I want to stop with you,' and then looking me full in the face, and laughing, he said, 'You can't kiss me, because I am black, and you are white,' I gave him immediately two or three kisses, which amused him immensely."

"Sunday, June 24th—My dear husband had the joy of admitting, by baptism, into the visible church, five converts, the Ibadan first-fruits. Our church was roofless, through the heavy gale, but in the neat and orderly place where service has been since conducted, knelt two women, two young men, and an old man, to receive the seal and sign that they were to be henceforth Christ's faithful soldiers and servants. Instead of their usual blue cloths, they wore each a white one; and their countenances showed great

seriousness, and a thorough understanding of the service in which they were engaged. The congregation was very good, many heathen were present, and all seemed struck with the whole service. I think I never felt such a solemn silence as there was on this occasion—many a tear glistened in a bright black eye. It was very touching and beautiful, and most encouraging. We could but think many might come forth, from among these same lookers on, to enlist under the same banner. Our Sunday congregations are increasing, and the good tidings are not without effect."

*"**July 21st**. — A gatekeeper has sent us two fowls, two large baskets of yams, a basket of fruit for the children, and some kolas especially for me. This is extremely kind, for the Matthews[20] at the receipt of custom get nothing from us; we and our goods are allowed to go free through every gate without paying tribute, so that this present is quite a token of love. I think among the rich Africans I never saw a more affectionate heart; he wept bitterly when we sent to inform him of Mr. Kefer's death, and came himself to express his sympathy.*

---

[20] Slang for tax collector

KINDNESS FROM A HEATHEN

"*My husband wanted bamboos, which are very scarce in this town, to repair the roof of the church. He went to quite a stranger, hearing he had some, and was treated with all civility and kindness, and when he came to settling the price of them, he was content with a mere trifle; so unusual with these people who generally want white men to pay three times as much as others; and when we sent him a little present in return for his kindness, he was so delighted, that he says the whole bamboo field is ours, and while bamboos grow, white man shall never want any. These may seem little things to friends at home, and hardly worth putting on paper, but they are great things to us, for we hail with joy and thankfulness any sign of kind feeling and willingness to help us, knowing that when they get confidence in us, and a friendly feeling towards us, they will listen to the good word we are come to bring to them.*"

FIRST WEDDING

"*August 13th. — We have had our first Christian wedding, and very nice and simple it was. We superintended the, dinner; and the speeches (for Africans can make fine speeches) were surprising to me, so marked by their Christian tone. The bride and* bridegroom were quite touched by them and their eyes filled with tears.

"Our Sunday school numbers between forty and fifty adults, all in earnest to learn, and it is surprising what progress they make in reading. They buy the translations of the Scriptures as soon as they come out and treasure them up as gold; but by the rest of the people, till their own eyes are opened, those are looked down upon as contemptible, and are called book-followers, forsakers of their forefathers, and despisers of their gods, who have given them strength, power, and everything. It must be remembered that here where things are only commencing, where a book had never been seen, no one man, woman, or child, could know a letter till we came to teach them. To leave books anywhere would be useless, and worse than useless; we have to be careful not even to throw down a little piece of paper, for it would surely be taken and used as a charm."

When Mrs. Hinderer was left alone, her husband having gone to Lagos on business she wrote: —

"*Oct. 1st*. — I am so thankful for the peace and quietness which is given me. I lie down as quietly at night as if I had every earthly guard. Now this not natural to me, but is given me by a loving God."

"**Oct. 5th.** —*My husband arrived today, alone and unannounced. Such a delight I had given him up till tomorrow, but soon I heard a terrific shout from the children and people, 'Baba de,' and there he was! He comes well and happy, after a pleasant visit. He is so full of delight at being at home again. But he brings the mail also, that tells of the death of our beloved friend Mrs. Cunningham. While we mourn for ourselves, it is yet to think of that pure and beautiful spirit a the realms above, with her God and Saviour, where all is peace, and joy, and love. I love to think of her, what she was here below, and what she must be now. I feel continually what a privilege it has been to me to have had such an example and such a friend; to have lived under her roof, and to have shared her counsel, advice, and affectionate love and interest. May every thought of her make me remember the account I must give of the privileges and blessings I have enjoyed, and stimulate me to follow her example in industry, perseverance, gentleness, meekness, and every Christian grace which shone so very brightly in her. I feel, in every step of my African career, how much I owe to her and to Mr. Cunningham, which can never be told!*"

Sunday Nov. 9th — *Eight of the dear children living with me partook of the blessed ordinance of baptism with six others. It was with peculiar interest I presented them, one by one, to their loved minister, to receive 'the* outward and visible sign;' I hope and believe they may be made partakers of 'the inward and spiritual grace.' They were Onisaga, Akielle, Laniyono, Arubo, Elukolo, Abudu, Ogunyomi, and Mary Ann Macaulay, a child from Sierra Leone. I dressed them all in new white clothes, with an earnest desire in my heart that they might be possessors of the robe made white in the blood of the Lamb. O God, keep these little lambs of Thy fold, shield them from all evil, and accept them for Thine own, through the love of Thy Son, our Saviour!

PERSECUTION

Anna's letter...

"Many of our neighbours had had a meeting, and made a solemn promise that, for a certain season, they would not allow one of their people to come near God's house. They seemed to succeed at first, but the spies carried the report of that Sunday, 'It is no use we keep our people away, the white man can still do his own work and way, whatever we do:

This day he has given fourteen the new name.' That expression, 'the new name,' was very striking to me. How one does desire our gracious God may give them, and those now baptised, that new name which He has promised."

RECUPERATION FROM ILLNESS IN LAGOS

"She wrote as follows from Lagos, whither they had gone, much broken down in health, to seek rest and refreshment.

Nov. 17th. — I am now writing in the room where, nearly three years ago, I had my first African fever. It is wonderful to sit here, and think on the way in which we have been led; many and, great have been the sorrows, trials and afflictions; but how great, how rich the love and mercy of our God and Saviour: everything must be swallowed up in the remembrance that truly goodness and mercy have followed me all the days of my life."

"**Nov. 26th** — The mail arrived with a most delightful packet of letters. Though fortunate and favoured every mail, I never had such a goodly heap, forty-one letters, or notes I and such boxes and parcels of things for ourselves, the children, and people. How very kind are friends, known and unknown, in dear England. It is very pleasant and refreshing to us to be so kindly remembered and cared for by many, rich and poor, enabling us to give so much pleasure, not only to the little ones, but to chiefs and others, to whom it is necessary to make presents..."

ARRIVAL OF NEW MISSIONARIES

"But by this mail came another rich present for Africa, two new missionaries, Mr. Buhler and Mr. loch. They appear so fresh, and full of spirit and energy, quite refreshing to us to see, who have been melting away, as it were, in the past three years."

*"**Ibadan, Dec. l5th**. — We reached our dear home again, with our friend Mr. Hoch, brought safely through the bush by the good hand of God upon us. We arrived amidst warm greetings and welcomes from many, surprising others greatly by the sight of another white man, when they had been doing their best to get rid of us by their persecution of our young converts. The fire and fury of persecution has raged to a very great extent; our hearts have ached, and still ache, for the sufferings of the little flock. Satan fights because his kingdom is endangered. The country priests fight under their master', banner, because their cruel lies and deceit are being exposed. The second Psalm just describes our state : — ' The heathen rage; the people imagine a vain thing; kings set themselves; the rulers take counsel together against the Lord.' Their power of endurance is wonderful. There is, no doubt, something of this in the natural character of the Africans; but that there is something much deeper, is quite evident; even their persecutors ask, 'What is it?' and they think we have*

some charm in our eye, and they are therefore trying to keep some of them quite out of our sight.

VICTORY OVER PERSECUTIONS

"The story of one young woman is most touching and interesting. She stands with the courage of a dependant child on the love, mercy, and help of a great and gracious God. Her marriage was hastened by her parents, who thought it would prevent her coming to church. Her husband treated her even more cruelly than her parents, which had been hard enough. When told by him, 'You shall never enter white man's house again,' she said. 'Very well; as you wish it, it shall be.' Neither shall you go to this church.' To this she replied' I cannot and will not submit; it is God's house; I will go.' **She was then cruelly beaten with a stick and cutlasses, and stoned, till her body was swelled all over; a rope was tied round her neck, and she was dragged, as an ox to the slaughter, to her father's house.** Mr. Hinderer went to beg them to cease their cruelties. He found her lying prostrate before the idols, which had been brought out for her to worship: she was held there by furious people, who were shouting, 'Now she bows down! Now she bows down!' She exclaimed, 'No, I do not it is you who have put me here; I can never bow down to gods of wood and stone,

Progress in The Work

which cannot hear me. Only in Jesus Christ, the Son of God, the only Saviour of poor sinners, can I trust.' She was then dragged up; they took a rope to put round her throat, saying, 'Well, we will take you away, and kill you!' She replied, 'Kill me if you will, the sooner I shall be with my Saviour in heaven; but I will not, I cannot, serve these foolish things.' They did not kill her; but for months she endured every kind of ill treatment, and at last ran away to Abeokuta. The history of her journey is little short of a miracle, and reminded me of the angel opening the door for Peter.

"One of her companions in suffering had run away before; she told me she felt she could stand it no longer; she was weak in body and mind, and she feared they would lead her back to heathenism, so she would go away the first opportunity. She is the seventh child who has run from her father's house; the former six went on account of the tyranny and cruelty of the father; but now they rally round him, and help him with cowries to make charms, and to bribe the chiefs to be angry with us and say, 'What a bad girl this is to go away, and what a bad thing this church matter is.'

"Another young woman has been set free; her intended husband refused to have her, and made her parents pay back what he had given for her, which they gladly did

139

for fear lest she should run away. So she comes to church, and lives at home as usual.

"A young girl of sixteen years has been nearly killed by her father for coming to church; beaten with a cutlass till she could not feed herself, or turn on her mat. She has endured very much, but I fear she is giving way now; she does not come to church, *On a week-day she visited me; I reminded her of the words of our Saviour, which she had learned with me, 'Whosoever shall confess Me before men, him shall the Son of man also confess before the angels of God; but he that denieth Me before men, shall be denied before the angels of God.' She wept, poor child, but alas! I saw her last Sunday go to fetch water from the brook, which, with every other kind of work, she had stoutly refused hitherto, even when they would not let her leave the house. She has told them for nearly twelve months, 'This is God's day!' Will you not pray for her, and for these young beginners in the ways of the Lord, that they may be kept, helped, and strengthened?*

"Another has equally and patiently, suffered the whip, the rope, and the chain, has been dragged about from one town to another, to make her forget about coming to church and serving God; but she was too much in earnest to forget by being carried to a far country. After some weeks of absence, she was brought back; her father

promised her great things, clothes, beads, honour, and added, 'Now you- will never go there!' pointing to the church. 'Father,' she replied, 'I am just the same as before, I will be a good daughter to you, I 'will earn cowries for you, only let me go to God's house, to hear His word and follow it, for this I cannot give up.' The father said, 'What strength do these white people give I what charm have they! Nothing will make these people give up!' and he nearly yielded. 'It is of no use,' he said, 'I am tired.'

"But his neighbours came about him, and gave him no rest till he promised to prevent his daughter coming to us, The mother came and said that if we would persuade her to worship idols as well, she might come to church. The girl has since often been sent to Ijaye to buy things; she was to go on Saturday, and. come back on Monday; but then they found she could go to God's house there, so that was given up; and one Sunday she was called out of church, but did not go. On the following Sunday, hearing her mother getting the chain ready to tie her, she ran to us, and what a fearful noise we heard! The whole family came into our yard, and flourished about their swords and knives, which we knew they would not use: we left them until they were tired, and then they went away. The girl was then advised to go home and sit down quietly for that day, which she did; and, though the house is close to us, we *heard no more noise. She visited me secretly a few evening since, and told me her heart was in the same place, and that she would follow the way God had sent us to teach, unto death. They have told her they will carry her to those who sell slaves, and who send them far away; her answer was, 'Well, where you send me, I will go: God, the great God, my God, is in all the world.'* You will readily believe how keenly we partake with them in their sufferings; though we weep, yet do we rejoice that they are so wonderfully supported; and we thank God that He has permitted His children to make such a good confession of their faith before so many.

TESTIMONIES OF CHANGED HEARTS

Anna's letter . . .

"The father of one of these young women has this morning set her free to go to God's house, and to walk in the way she sees right; for he says, 'It is true what that white man says, it is no use to fight against God.' Another man is greatly troubled at what he has done, and is quite in an agony to see his child once more. The mother of a third now begs me to help her to find her child; her heart yearns after her whom she so fearfully persecuted, under evil direction. In other houses the cry

is, about those who escaped, 'Oh, if it had not been for you, this would not have happened.' So our God has graciously made His arm to be felt among us, and many hear Him say, 'Why persecutest thou Me? it is hard for thee to kick against the pricks.' The Lord will not forsake His own work; when it pleaseth Him, He can put all His enemies to silence. Even these poor deluded heathen tell us, 'Have patience, white man; your words and ways are new, we are dark and have no sense, tell your word day after day, it will go into the ear, and bye and bye many will follow it."'

PRAYERS OF HEALING FROM THE LIPS OF INFANTS

The first quotation to be made from the journals and letters of 1856 relates to some of those children who so affectionately loved their *Iya*, and who had so securely possessed themselves of a place in her heart.

"Feb. 4th — My little African boys and girls are going on well so far, and are sheltered from much evil, but need the rod of correction now and then. The three younger boys must eat a fruit which I told them not to eat, as it was not ripe. They thought it was ripe, or that it would not do them any harm. The consequence was, after a little while, they were crying with smarting and

immensely swelled lips. One of the elder boys laughed at them, and told them they would die. They were now quite frightened, and did not know what to do. So one of them, Akieile, said, 'What naughty boys we have been! We have been like Adam and Eve, eating the forbidden fruit, let us go and pray to God, and ask Him not to let us die this time, and we will not do so any more,' and so they went with all childlike simplicity and prayed, and then came to me to forgive them for not obeying my word. The next morning to their great joy their lips were better. It was a simple affair, but I was glad to feel these little ones knew the meaning of prayer, and I did indeed desire they might always remember the Throne of grace and mercy, in all their future paths, with the same simplicity and confidence.

FEARS AND SUPERSTITIONS

"May — It is fearful to see the poor heathens' intense love of life, they will do anything, spend anything and everything, to be assured by priests and orishas that they shall live long; and their principal salutation, by way of desiring a special blessing, is 'Olurun bunolemi'—' God grant you long life' and no wonder, for what is their hope beyond the grave? It is so very dark to them; they never like to talk about it. But from what one can gather, it seems to them something so

completely unknown, they have no idea what is to follow death. They have I think a belief in the transmigration of spirits, by the fact that there is one kind of animal which the bush-hunter never kills, because he thinks it is one into which the spirits of hunters will go after death. Others are supposed to inhabit palm-trees. This is I think confirmed by the practice of consulting the orisha at the birth of a child, with a view to ascertaining which of his ancestors now inhabits that child, and when it is decided, the 'country fashion' of that ancestor must be followed by the child. Then there is the custom of the spirits appearing, called egungun, the bone people; the ancestors are supposed to be called from the other world, to come and speak with their relatives. They are not to be seen in the grove, but their voices are to be heard; and to gain this, yams, fowls, sheep, goats, and cowries must be brought, which of course become the property of the country priests, whose hands are full through these delusions. There is an egungun grove not far from us, and the yells and groans and miserable sounds are terrible. I have felt, it sometimes as most awful in the solemn stillness of the night, while watching my poor husband or others in illness.

"There are bad spirits too, who are supposed to cause most of the evils of life, and those who have reason to fear them wear rattling clinking irons round their ankles, which are heard at every movement of the foot, and the noise is supposed to frighten the spirits away. When a pair of these jingling feet walks in, during our Sunday services, it gives one a thrill of horror, it is so demon-like. These poor people year after year, day after day, are seeking for relief from the greatest burden of the heart, but are so slow to believe the word of Jesus, 'I will give unto you eternal life;' so deaf to the exhortation, 'Come unto Me that ye may have life; without money and without price.' Oh that the Spirit of God would descend and enlighten these dark souls, and breathe upon these dead bones! Then would this wilderness rejoice and blossom as the rose."

LABOUR FOR GOD

"I think no preacher or teacher of the gospel can feel so entirely his own weakness and helplessness, the entire dependence he must rest on the Spirit and blessing of God, as the missionary amongst the heathen. It is not the planter or waterer, but God alone, who must do His own work; but as He chooseth to use means, He commits the outward work to earthen vessels, in

His inscrutable wisdom. *May we in the day of toil, in the ploughing and sowing, labour cheerfully and with a rejoicing hopeful spirit, leaning on the strong arm; and if the reaping and ingathering day into the church militant be given us here below, may we give the honour and glory where alone it is due, as we surely shall if the fruit of the seed sown now is not seen till we have become inhabitants of the better land.*

MISCHIEF FROM A LITTLE BOY

"We are now in the midst of the rainy season, and very cooling and refreshing it is. A few days since, I went with the children to the rice farm. A shower came on, but we had set our minds upon it, therefore I would not mind pushing through the 'wet grass; but there was a brook to cross, and, 'What will Iya do now?' was the cry. There was a large stone on which the people wash clothes; this stone was placed in the middle of the brook, and by it I could step nicely across. There was a little boy there, a stranger to us, watching the whole affair, who seemed to think it very extraordinary I could not walk through the water like other people. Now their little black skins are as full of roguery and mischief as any little boy at home, so in our absence he prepared an adventure for our return. There lay the stone, but underneath, the little urchin had placed a smaller and

uneven one, so when I stepped on it, over it goes, and plump go my feet into the water, and then he comes forward with his salutation of sympathy,' Pele, pele, pele o,'—' Softly, take care, don't hurt yourself.' We should not call this very civil, but I could not help thoroughly enjoying the bit of fun for the little rogue."

TIME FOR FUN

Fun, and quickness of perception, with a tinge of poetry were remarkable and attractive features in the character of the little untutored children of Ibadan. An amusing example may be quoted, in an incident which once occurred to Mr. Hinderer. A little girl came to the Kudeti brook to seek water, but in vain, for the brook was dry. While she was there, Mr. Hinderer rode by in his cool white clothing. Seeing the white man, she at once in a most humorous manner charged him with being the cause of her disappointment, and improvised the song

"*Oibo de Kudeti*
O we roro
Ko je ki n'romi we
'E kilo fun ko ma we iru re mo."

Which has been translated thus..

Progress in The Work

*"The white man of Kudeti's hill,
Has used the black child very ill;
He washed his clothes so white, you see,
That not a drop is left for me.
Oh! Tell him when he comes next day,
To wash his clothes some other way."*

MIRACLE OF A MOTHER & DAUGHTER SOLD INTO SLAVERY AND RESTORED IN THE MIDST OF TRIBAL WARS

Mrs. Hinderer notes in her journal for May 6, "Ogunyomi finds her mother." The story of both mother and child was written in German[21] for children, and from it the following account is gathered.

"In 1854, a war broke out between Ibadan arid Efon. Until that time Ogunyomi was a happy child at home, living in peace with her father, mother, and two brothers in the town of Efon. When the war began, all the able-bodied men were compelled to join the army, and amongst them was Ogunyomi's father. He was never heard of again, and most probably had fallen in battle. His town was destroyed, the men and youths were killed; and the women and children, after

---

[21] They Hinderers were of both English and German ancestry

wandering about in despair and misery, were taken prisoners, and sold for slaves. A few, stronger than the rest, contrived to escape into the bush, and amongst them were Ogunyomi and her mother. Fear drove them farther and farther. Their only food was roots and leaves. When they had threaded their way for two or three days through the dark and pathless thicket, they began to hope that they were safe from their enemies. But they were afraid to speak above a whisper, lest they should be heard and overtaken. Exhausted with hunger and fatigue, they at last lay down to rest, under the shelter of a great tree. At once two men sprang suddenly upon them, one seized the mother, and the other the child. Their tears and entreaties were useless, they were torn from each other, and hurried off in different directions. The little girl, who was only seven years old, was taken to Ibadan, and put up for sale in the market. A Christian man, who himself had once been a slave, touched by her sorrowful face, took her in his arms, and tried to comfort her. Hearing that she was soon to be taken down to the coast and stowed away in a slave ship, he longed to purchase her and set her free; but it was beyond his power. He therefore went to the mission-house, told her sad story to Mr. and Mrs. Hinderer, and entreated them to redeem her. They gladly gave him money for her ransom, and in a few minutes the kind-hearted man brought the little girl to her new home. The poor child had never before seen a white face, and she screamed with terror when she found herself in the presence of the missionaries. The other children in the compound gathered round her, and told her how happy they were and that all who lived in the mission-house were safe from slavery. She soon learned herself to love her "white mother," and was constantly found at her side. When strangers came to the house, she clung closely to her, fearing lest they should carry her away.

But her great delight was to sit on the floor near to Mrs. Hinderer, and puzzle over the alphabet, or the still greater mysteries of needle and thread. Singing was a pleasure to her, and she quickly learned simple prayers and easy texts. She was a child of a happy disposition, and often her hearty laugh rang through the compound. But a change came over her. Her laugh was heard no more, and her countenance was sad and troubled. Mrs. Hinderer asked, "What is the matter, Ogunyomi? Is any one unkind to you. ?" "Oh, no," she said quickly. "Then what makes you sad?" She burst into tears, and sobbed out, *"Iya mi, Iya mi!"* — " My mother, my mother!" Mrs. Hinderer tried to comfort her, and promised to have a diligent search made for her mother. But, in a large town of more than a hundred thousand people, this was no easy task, especially as slaves usually received a new name; besides which, it was not known whether the poor woman was in Ibadan, or had been carried away to some other place. Meanwhile she said to Ogunyomi, "You have learned to pray to God, He loves to receive the prayers of little children. Pray to Him, if it be His will, to restore your mother to you."

From that time forward, to all her prayers she added the simple petition, " O God, give me back my mother." Ogunyomi gradually became happier, but there was still an expression of sorrow upon her face, stamped there by her longing after her lost mother.

When she had lived about six months in the mission-house, she went one morning, as usual, with the other little girls, to draw water from the neighbouring brook. The children were laughing and playing together when a woman passed by and, being attracted by the unusual sight of their white clothes, she stood still for a moment, and watched them as they played. One voice appeared to be familiar to her. She raised the basket from her head, placed it on the ground, and listened attentively. Yes, it was her child's voice trembling in every limb, she cried out "Ogunyomi!" Ogunyomi turned round, stared for a long time at the woman, and then, with the cry "My mother, my mother!" threw herself into her arms. The other children ran to the house, exclaiming, "Ogunyomi has found her mother." It was difficult to believe the joyful news. The poor woman was at first afraid of the white people; but when she heard from Ogunyomi how kind and good they were, and that they had rescued her from slavery, she was at a loss for words wherewith to express her joy and gratitude. She threw herself on the ground and sobbed aloud. When her mind was somewhat more composed, she listened with interest to the story of her child, and then explained that she herself bad been sold for a slave in Ibadan, but that happily she had been bought by a kind master. She was obliged to hurry away, but she was comforted by the thought of Ogunyomi's happiness, and ,rejoiced in the prospect of being able to see her, whenever she might have permission from her master.

Ogunyomi's heart that night overflowed with gratitude to God, who had so graciously heard and answered her prayers.

For many weeks all went on well. The mother often came to see her child. Then her visits ceased, without any explanation. Mr. and Mrs. Hinderer were troubled for the child, and, after much enquiry, they discovered that the mother was seriously ill, and that all hope of her recovery was gone. For Ogunyomi's sake they paid the poor woman's ransom, and removed her to the missions house. For ten months she was nursed and cared for by these new friends, and then, to the joy of all, especially of her own child, she recovered. When her health was sufficiently re-established, she was employed as cook for the children, and found much happiness in the altered circumstances of her life.

VISIT TO OYO KINGDOM

At the end of May, Mr. and Mrs. Hinderer visited the King of Oyo. The following letter, telling of their visit, begins with an amusing description of the journey: —

"June. —Our visit to Oyo, the king's city, is happily accomplished, and now I sit down to tell you about it.

On May 28th we started, I travelling partly on horseback and partly in my hammock It was very, very hot, and no~ having been out for same time, I soon felt very tired, and was thankful for willing carriers, two of our own people, and two from our young friend's house, the Balogun Olumloyo. I was much amused on th6 road by the conversation of those two men; they were so extremely polite to one another, that I had the benefit of quite a grammatical exercise. A fallen tree lies in the road, the foremost one mentions this fact, the other thanks him. Then follows, 'Have you passed over the tree?' 'I have passed over the tree.' Then they salute one another for the load they carry; I joined them in this, which pleased them. At last I forgot them, and was thinking, thinking, thinking, oh, of so many things! When they called me back from my thoughts by saying,

'Iya, do you sleep? For you have not saluted us so long.' I apologised for my forgetfulness, and promised to do better. They said, 'It helps us to carry you, and makes us think you are a light load, when you salute and talk to us.' The road was very bad, and bye and bye the foot of one slips into an unseen hole; off goes the end of the hammock from his head, but he catches it in his strong hands. I gave a shriek, expecting to go out head first, when he coolly asks, 'Iya, why did you lift your voice?' I told him fear caught me; he said, fear must not catch me any more, for he would not let me fall. At last we reached Ijaye, after full seven hours' journey, and glad indeed we were to be under the shelter of a mission-house, with Mr. Mann. We intended to start for Oyo next day, but Mr. Mann's invitation to stay and rest a day was too tempting, so on the third day we left for Oyo. The road lay through grass fields, but it was such a nice sandy road that I enjoyed riding nearly a]] the way, and it was rather a cloudy day too, which is such a luxury in this country. In six hours we reached the king's city, and Mr. Hinderer was received by the people as an old friend.

"Our Daniel Olubi had been there several weeks Mr. Hinderer had placed him there to commence teaching till the appointed person came up. He was very glad to see us, and so were all the people of the compound. A nice little place the king had given Mr. Hinderer, for *any one to reside in till a proper house was built. This had all been repaired and made comfortable, by the king's orders, so that we had quite a home to go to; a great deal larger than the native house here, in which we lived more than a year. We had hardly changed our clothes, and begun to refresh ourselves, before the king's messenger came to say we must go to the palace; and before he had done speaking, came another and another, saying the king was in haste to see us. A good deal of this was court etiquette. So we made haste, and were received in great state, but the king's face was quite uncovered; and he received Mr. Hinderer with great joy, saying he was his friend, his beloved friend, and had not forgotten that his name was Dabidi (David).*

AUDIENCE WITH THE ALAFIN[22] OF OYO

"He praised him for bringing his wife, and thou asked if he might salute me; then he asked me of my welfare, how I had left Ibadan, and if I had heard lately from my own country of my father and mother, brothers and sisters (for in Africa every one who comes from your town is your brother or sister), and was the good Queen of England well? I answered that 'all was peace,' — 'Alafia ombe mbe;' he was pleased, and said his heart

---

[22] Traditional title of the King of Oyo

rejoiced to see us, and then with true gentlemanly thought and politeness, he said he would not keep us longer, as we musk be tired from our journey: we must go and eat and rest, and tomorrow see him.

"On Sunday we had nice services in the piazza, though I was obliged to be on my stretcher in a corner, having fever, but I rejoiced to see quite a goodly gathering of regular attendants, whom our Olubi had drawn together.

Before leaving Oyo, **Mr. Hinderer had a conversation with the king, and described to him the purpose, then turning to his people, said, "The white man is my beloved friend, he shall teach God's word, and preach it in my town; what do you say?"** They answered, "It is good, we receive white man with all our hearts." The king treated his missionary friends with the greatest kindness, during the few days I which they spent at Oyo, and was sorry to part with them. **They departed full of thankfulness to God for giving them favour in a heathen town, and praying that the blessing of the Gospel of peace might be granted to the people.**

A little girl in Oyo took a great fancy to Mrs. Hinderer, and begged to be allowed to go home with her. Her name was Konigbagbe. When the time came for starting, the mother asked if it was true that her child was going to "sit down with the white woman?" Mrs.

Hinderer said she would very much like to take charge of her. The woman was pleased, and said, "Only you must ask the king first, as we live in one of his houses, and none of us may leave the town without his permission." The King gladly gave his consent, and said, "I think she is very wise, and I only wish that I were a little girl that I might go too." From that time Konigbagbe lived in the mission compound at Ibadan, and when she was old enough she became Mrs. Hinderer's servant.

Anna's letter . . .

"We reached Ijaye, and started the next morning early for Ibadan, and found all well, and a joyful welcome. On Sunday we were surprised and rejoiced to see a large attendance at the church, of men and women. The agreement the persecutors made to prevent any one coming, is now broken, and the road is once more free again. The Lord, the God of hosts, hath done great things for us, and for the honour of His name, whereof we are glad."

ANOTHER TRAGIC DEATH

But sorrow soon succeeded this joyful return to Ibadan, for in the following month Mrs. Hinderer wrote:

"But now hath the bright picture become dimmed. We were just rejoicing and girding up our loins with fresh zeal and vigour for our work, when my dear husband is laid very low with yellow fever, just what poor Mr. Kefer died of. He has not been well the last six months, not three weeks without fever. For ten or twelve days he is well, and goes out preaching, and then is sick again. After all this, I did not think he would have a severe illness, but it has come, and he is now as weak as a baby.

"It has pleased God once more to spare his life, seeing how he is, and the danger of another attack we all feel it is a real duty that he should go at once to England for health's sake, so that I am nursing him, and packing, and preparing to leave poor Ibadan by the mail which will leave the next month, July; so a month after you this, you may expect to see us, if it please I give us a safe and prosperous voyage. I am you will feel for us in the real sorrow and trial it is to have to go so suddenly. It is such a sorrow and such a wrench, which even the joy of beloved friends again cannot mitigate. I write more; it is well I shall have hard work.

JOINING OF OLUBI & SUSANNA

"June 19ᵗʰ — It has come out today that Olubi & and Susanne, have fallen in love with each other and wish to be married before we leave. So here is another iron in the fire, but one that gives us real satisfaction. I must now prepare for the brides outfit."

Susanna was the child of a Christian convert in Abeokuta, who had committed her to Mr. Hinderers care. On Mrs. Hinderer's arrival, Susanna was taken into the mission-house, where she as a servant until the time of her marriage

OLUBI'S CONVERSION

The history of Olubi is remarkable. As a boy he was strongly opposed to Christianity. He was dedicated at his birth to the idol Abatala, and his mother was a devoted priestess of her god Igun. When the Gospel was preached in Abeokuta, his native place, he was full of indignation. From day to day Mr. Muller gathered hearers together in the principal streets, and the boy's anger increased. "This white man preaches," he said, "that we must give up our idols. If I were a. war chief, like my uncle Ogubonna, I would kill him; and if ever be comes into my street, I will do so myself." The missionary came again, and without knowing anything about the boy, stood under a tree close to his house, and preached the words of eternal life. But where was Olubi? In some act of worship, rendered to his idol, he had injured himself; and now he was lying on his mat, suffering and helpless. He heard a great noise of people assembling, and saw the white man comes but he could not move, and was unable to carry out his threat. This went on for many days Olubi would gladly have been far away from the home, but that was impossible, and he could not avoid hearing what the missionary preached, "After all," he began to think, "it is not anything so very bad that he is saying." And when he recovered, he said, "I will go and see how these white people -worship." Accordingly, he went to the mission school, and enjoyed what he heard so much that he told his mother he must go again. She threatened him and beat him, but the boy went to the school and began to learn the Lord's Prayer. Soon after this, the yearly festival came round, when, according to custom, great preparations were made for religious observances. Olubi went with his mother to the idol's house, and they spent seventeen days together in sacrifices and worship. Before they returned to their home, he said to his mother, "I am sure that I shall not be with you next new year at Obatala's house, for I shall follow white man's fashion." This revived his mother's displeasure, and she refused him food and cowries for many days; but his father-in-law treated him with kindness, and even went so far as to accompany him to the church. The boy soon began to be a regular attendant at the school, God's word touched his heart, and he joined the class of candidates for baptism. His, mother opposed him to the utmost of her power, but he was enabled to stand firm, and in due time he was baptized by the name of Daniel. It was now his most earnest desire that his mother might be brought to a knowledge of Christ; and happily his prayers for her were graciously answered. She was attracted to the church in Abeokuta; God's word came with power to her heart, she cast away the beads and charms of her heathen superstition, she forsook her idol Igun, and worshipped God alone. Both she and her husband were subsequently baptized, and became regular partakers of the Holy Communion. **Olubi served Mr. Hinderer with fidelity and affection, and after several years he was judged to be the most fitting person to take charge of the first mission school in Ibadan.**

Church and Mission House in Ibadan

CHAPTER V

Visit to England & Return to Ibadan

"Leading little children,
And blessing manhood's years,
Showing to the sinful
How God's forgiveness cheers;
Scattering sweet roses
Along another's path,
Smiling by the wayside,
Content with what she hath."

THERE WAS MUCH TO be done before Mr. and Mrs. Hinderer could leave Ibadan, and the interval was a time of sadness alike to them and to their people. Mrs. Hinderer wrote in her journal "I must pass over all those trying preparations; they were very sorrowful. O my children, I shall never forget your weeping, and how you held me to keep me back, so that grown up people wept at the sight. We reached Lagos in July, to be ready for the mail, and had a miserable time there; but on the 1st of

August we went on board the steamer, homeward bound, though I think I then felt that I was rather leaving home. I was ill from the day we left Lagos till the very day we reached Plymouth. When the captain kindly helped me up the steps on landing, he said, 'Thank God, Mrs. Hinderer, that I land you in England! I never expected this, but always had the misery of thinking that we should bury you in the deep sea.' On a Saturday evening we arrived in London, and lodged near the Church Missionary House. We much enjoyed our peaceful Sabbath, though feeling the cold."

Two short extracts from her letters indicate the varied feelings called forth by her return to her native land: -

Anna's letter . . .

"Through God's great mercy here we arrived last evening. It is hard to believe that I am not asleep and dreaming, but my heart is tenderly awake to the changes which have taken place among us in these last four years. The only resting-place under it all is the sweet thought —

'The saints above how sweet their joys,

How bright their glories be'

"Can you understand my relief to have my dear husband under medical care and skill, after all we have

gone through? He has had much suffering, and certainly was never really well the last year and a half; but I do trust in a short time he will be in a very different state. I am thankful to feel very fairly well; a little tired sometimes; and I find I am not the strong person I was before I went to poor Africa'

When Mr. Hinderer's health was sufficiently restored, they removed to Lowestoft, where unhappily, Mrs. Hinderer was almost immediately prostrated by a severe and painful illness. In her hours of suffering, she was cheered and refreshed by the love end sympathy of many old friends, rich and poor; but she felt acutely the absence of the friend, whom she had loved and honoured, as a mother, and who had done so much to shed a glow of brightness over her earlier days. To that revered name she referred in her journal, after her recovery from this Illness. "The churchyard I used to love to go to, and by dearest Mrs. Cunningham's grave I could weep and pray."

HER LATE FATHER

She also missed the loving welcome that she would have received from her father, of whom she wrote thus in her journal: -

"Just before starting for England, I heard of my dear father's rather sudden but peaceful and happy death. I cannot mourn for him, for I believe him to be one ~whom his Saviour loved, but, one deeply tried and afflicted in this world; he now rests with Jesus."

Circumstances had taken her away from her father's care at a very early period of her life, but she always loved him with tender affection, and entered into the heavy trials of his life with feelings of sorrow and sympathy.

Early in the next year they were again in London, and, while enjoying the society of friends, they availed themselves of many opportunities of usefulness. Mr. Hinderer spoke at missionary meetings, and Mrs. Hinderer told the interesting story of their life in Africa, at working parties, anal other private gatherings.

HELP FROM BRETHREN HITHERTO UNKNOWN

It was in April of this year that they became personally known to those to whom has been committed the sacred trust of preparing these memorials for publication. When Mrs. Hinderer was on the eve of sailing for Africa, in December, 1852, a selection of passages from holy scripture was sent to liar by a member of the family, who had been deeply interested by the narrative, in the Church Mission Intelligencer, of Mr. Hinderer's early exploring expeditions, and of his first visit to Ibadan. This token of sympathy was offered under the influence of an observation made by another missionary, that many who are engaged in that important service, might be cheered and comforted in their loneliness, by a short letter, or a few verses of the Bible, even written by those who are personally strangers to them, if sent as an expression of interest in their work.

ACTS OF KINDNESS APPRECIATED

In due time the following welcome acknowledgment was received by the otherwise unknown correspondent.

"Ibadan July 1853. —Your very kind little note, and the pink sheets containing so many sweet and encouraging passages of Scripture, which you were kind enough to write out for me, have often and often been before me, and have been doubly refreshing as coming from one whom I have never seen or known. It was so very, very kind of you to write to me, and to take the trouble of copying so much for me, a stranger; they have, I assure you, been a comfort and pleasure to me."

This, led to an occasional interchange of letters, and to a box of clothing being sent to Ibadan by the members of the Halesowen missionary working party, for the African

Lest We Forget

children, together with a scarf, intended as a present for one of the chiefs.

After the lapse of four years, in April 1857, the friendship which had been commenced by a letter was ripened by personal intercourse. A visit of three weeks at Halesowen Rectory established an abiding affection and lively interest on both sides. Mr. and Mrs. Hinderer at once took a place in every heart, which subsequent correspondence and visits, in after years, only made more and more secure.

AMONG FRIENDS AND FAMILY IN EUROPE

From Halesowen they went into Yorkshire, and then returned to London. A letter, written a few weeks later, accounted for their next movements: —

Anna's letter...

"I was all this time often in much suffering, but wonderfully helped through in times of necessity, for meetings and working-parties, and I had a most kind and helpful physician in Dr. Johnson. He recommended mineral baths, so this hastened our intended visit to Germany; and on June the 5th we started, and had a most delightful and refreshing tour."

Visit to England and Return to Ibadan

Travelling by the Rhine and railway to Basle, they proceeded to some of the principal places of interest in the Bornese Oberland, thoroughly enjoying the beauties of the Alpine scenery and spent the rest of their time in Wurtemberg, partly at Berg, for the benefit of the waters, but chiefly with Mr. Hinderers relations and friends in its neighbourhood. This was a season of much happiness and refreshment of spirit. Among many cheering proofs of sympathy with them "for their work's sake," Mrs. Hinderer relates the following...

> "The sincere and earnest piety of these simple Christians is very beautiful. One poor woman said to me, 'For five years and sixteen days I have not failed to pray for you and your husband every day.' Just five years ago D— was in this country, and told them about Africa, and that we were going soon together; and from that time the good woman had borne us on her heart before God. Oh, what a comfort it is to know their prayers are heard by our Father in heaven! Oh, how blessed it is to labour for Him, and, for the little we give up, so abundantly does He reward!"

SAD NEWS FROM AFRICA

They were again in England in September, and soon began to make preparations for their return to Africa. Mrs. Hinderer wrote: -

"We rejoice to go to our work, and to our dear people in Ibadan; their earnest desire for us is very pleasing. We had cheering accounts on the whole, last mail. The few disciples are drawing others to hear the blessed words of the Gospel; but another thing touches our hearts. Our good friend Olumloyo is killed in battle; we have shed tears for him. Alas! Alas! He heard the Gospel, and acknowledged its sweetness and its truth, but could not follow it. Yet we may hope, perhaps; 'with God all things are possible, and perhaps at the eleventh hour He permitted him to call upon Him.

"Almost the last interview with his little boy Akielle was that at the annual feast, when the child was enabled to be a witness of the truth."

The story of that festival, so far as it concerned Akielle, is simply told by Olubi[23], in a letter from Ibadan:

---

[23] Later, the Rev Daniel Olubi

"You will be glad to hear Akielle begins to show light to his parent... A few days ago his father sent for him; the boy went, and found all his family engaged making yearly sacrifice; sheep were slain, and the blood sprinkled about, a number of the people rubbing their foreheads in the dust, and the orishas of the family all brought out. The little boy thought to himself he had better go back, but the father, seeing him, called him near and said, 'Now, Akielle! I want you to worship with us; here is Erinle' (pointing to one of the idols), 'here is the god who gave you to me.' The child, quite in African character, replied by asking some witty question, 'If Erinle gave me to you, father, how many children has he left for himself' The father was puzzled, and said, 'Perhaps none.' 'Well, then, said the boy, 'I don't think he would have been so foolish as to give me to you, if he had none left to himself.' Then the father said, 'Well, you must worship with us.' The boy answered, 'No, father, I cannot.' 'Why can't you?' 'Why, father, because the Word of God says, "Thou shalt have none other gods but me."' As they remained quiet, the child went on and repeated the second Commandment. He was then asked several questions, which he answered readily and respectfully, when the father ended by saying, 'Well, Akielle, there is one thing you shall do.' The little fellow now thought, 'My father is going to flog me, or make me worship these things;'

but the end of the sentence was, 'You shall go back to the mission-house, where you have been taught.' So he came back with great pleasure."

RETURN TO AFRICA

On Saturday, October 24th, 1857, Mr. and Mrs. **Hinderer** again set sail for Africa, on board the **"Candace,"** and landed at Sierra Leone on the seventeenth day of their voyage. While there, Mrs. Hinderer wrote: -

"I long to be in Yoruba again, yet I am glad to have stayed here. I am very well, but my poor husband had a sharp attack of fever for one night and day; not the acclimatizing fever, we do not expect to have that here, but soon enough when we get further. Oh, may we be preserved to labour on; we more and more rejoice in our work there, and feel its blessing and privilege as well as the duty; only, dear friends, pray for us; we need it more and more."

From Sierra Leone they went up into **the** neighbouring mountains, halting at many of the 'villages by the way; and making an interesting visit to Mrs. **Clemens** and her school at Charlotte. Mrs. Hinderer's own words will best describe their short sojourn at Regent, the scene of Mr. Johnson's labours, in the early days of the mission.

Visit to England and Return to Ibadan

Anna's letter . . .

"We passed through Regent, the place itself is a picture. I cannot describe it; it is equal to some parts of Switzerland, and that is saying much. There was no missionary there then, but we went to the empty mission-house, and there we found an old man, with his woolly hair quite white. It seems he lived there all alone, to take care of the empty house. I asked him if he remembered Mr. Johnson, and I touched a chord in the old man's heart. 'Ah, me know Massa Johnson, me know him; I been live with him all the time he live here.' I wish I could give you the whole account, but we talked together for an hour and a half; and the old man took us into the garden, and showed us a very large orange-tree. He gave me plenty of fruit, and said, 'Eat these oranges, and take the seeds, and plant them in the Yoruba country, and call it Massa Johnson's orange-tree. Mesas Johnson plant this tree, I stand by him, and you now, a stranger, eat the fruit;' and the dear old man never tired of talking of Massa Johnson, and we talked of heaven, the home of the blessed and faithful missionary. He added, 'Ah, I done old now; poor old Josiah here a little while, but soon Massa Jesus, my Jesus, will say, 'sow, **old Josiah**, come up here,' and then I see my Saviour, I see my dear Massa Johnson—though he been bury in the sea—and we no die no more;' and when we parted, 'Goodbye, Missis, me no *know you, but I glad I been see you; God go with you, and bring us all to heaven at last.' This was a delightful visit; I am only sorry I cannot do justice to it with my pen."*

HOME IN IBADAN ONCE MORE

Early in January, 1858, Mr. and Mrs. Hinderer began the last stage of their journey, proceeding from Lagos to Ibadan, a distance of about eighty miles, by the most frequented route, which is a rugged path through bush, and forest, and occasional tracts of coarse grass, six or eight feet high, interspersed with trees. The bush is a dense thicket of shrubs, and saplings, and tangled climbing plants, adorned with a profusion of beautiful flowers, and many a gaudy butterfly adds life and brilliancy to the scene. The stately cotton-tree, the graceful palm, and other gigantic forest trees, tower above this mass of luxuriant vegetation, and by their deep shade afford a welcome protection to the traveller from the glare and heat of a tropical sun. The track is, in most parts, only just wide enough for a horseman, or for foot-passengers in single file; and now and then inconvenient obstructions are encountered in the form of trees which have fallen across the path, or of a new growth of the bush asserting its ordinary rights. The loveliness of the country, diversified as it is by hill and

Visit to England and Return to Ibadan

dale, is most striking, wherever a point of view can be obtained. The fertile soil will reward the labours of the cultivator whenever peace may settle itself in the land, and the people have again replenished it. Such towns and villages of the Ijebus as have escaped the hands of the destroyer, are off the usual track, sheltered in the depths of the jungle or forest.

The next letter was written from Ibadan: -

Anna's letter ...

> *"Jan. 27, 1858. — We are too busy settling in this dear place to write much by this mail. Thank God, we are in excellent health, after having suffered a good deal in Sierra Leone and Lagos. We stayed at Lagos till we could send up and have people from the interior to fetch us and our loads, and then was it not a treat to see Ibadan faces once more? We had a delightful journey through the bush, the people so pleased to be taking us back again, and when we halted for the night, with our tent pitched, and three or four fires about, maid all resting after our day's journey, it was so nice to talk for an hour or more, and hear all about Ibadan doings in our absence; and on the fourth day, when we were within sight of the town, we were all at once startled by such a shout as that bush has hardly heard before. Our children and people had come out to meet us, and just caught sight of us. Oh, it was such a happy meeting I*

> Besides our own people there were many of our heathen neighbours and friends, whose welcome was most hearty, the horsemen galloped and danced backwards and forwards, and guns were fired, so that altogether we were nearly deafened. I was in a hammock, and my carriers had hard work to get on, and my husband was nearly pulled off his horse. As we went on, the numbers increased, till we were brought to our own door, on Saturday, January 9.
>
> "It was delightful to be in our old house again, everything was made so neat and clean, and a nice meal prepared for us. But all this joy had its sorrow; we missed our friend, Olumloyo, and the people also talked of him, saying how pleased he would have been to have met us, and how far he accompanied us on the road when we went away, and could not bear to part with us, and then tears glistened in many an eye, for he was much respected; but tears could not last long that day. For three weeks or more we had visitors constantly, and such kind presents. We have still quite a farmyard from them. I wish you could see our beautiful ducks, with their green and gold feathers sparkling in the sun, quantities of chickens, goats, and three sheep. Besides these we had corn and yams given us.

A CONVERTED SLAVE TRADER

"The chiefs and people seem as though they could not give us welcome enough, and say they were afraid we should not come again, as we had so many troubles from the persecution; but now they love us more than ever. Far better than all, many people are coming regularly to church, and are anxious to be 'taught the Word of God. Some have been attending a few meetings and are now bringing their idols to us, saying, 'These things cannot save us, we want to follow Jesus,' and then desire that their names may be put down as candidates for baptism. We have now a huge basketful of idols, and last evening a man who had been a large dealer in slaves, brought the irons with which he used to chain the poor creatures, saying, 'that having been made free by the blood of Jesus, he never should want such cruel things again.'

Anna's letter . . .

"We very soon went to pay our respects to the four chiefs of the town; they had sent some of their servants on the road to help us. They were so pleased to see us. Some time ago these same chiefs were afraid to touch our hands, lest we should convey poison to them: or that our eyes should, meet, lest they die. Their cruel

country priests and Mohammedan Alufas[24] had told them that these things would surely happen if we were allowed to go near to them. But now, in the face of their deceivers, they took our hands, and expressed their joy in every way, and the head chief would make me sit on his own mat, quite close to him. But I am sorry to tell you that chief is now very ill, and, wonderful to say, Mr. Hinderer was allowed to go and see him. We hope he will be spared, as he is rather better than he was. We sent him a mattress and pillow, and though the chief has a very fine one, Mr. Hinderer saw he needed something more comfortable. The poor man was so pleased, and tried to thank him, though he can hardly speak.

"The dear children were all well, and so happy to have us back; they have been kindly taken care of in our absence, and we thank God for our helpful Catechist and his wife, and our good Olubi. Susanna and Olubi were in full force, very happy, and they have a most charming little boy; his name is Daniel, he is the best-tempered child possible, full of fun, and very amusing. Ogunyomi and her mother are extremely happy, and little Arubo, little still. Some of them, we have every reason to believe, are truly converted by the Spirit of God."

---

[24] Moslem priests

"Feb. 15. —My writing time gets less and less, and this terribly hot weather does not help one to push for, it. We are thoroughly parched, and must now send far for water. The hot seasons are indeed increasing in intensity, but what a mercy that we are preserved in health, though we look, like everything else, bleached and colourless. My own special flock of twenty-seven children occupy much of my bodily and mental strength, my former ones requiring further instruction, the others a breaking in, and training; but it is an encouraging work, and when my strength is gone some one will be ready to stand in my room. Our Sundays are now quite cheering, such a nice attendance of so many earnest listeners."

In this and many other extracts from Mrs. Hinderer's journals, she appears as taking a lively interest in children, and especially those who were under her care in the mission compound. They introduced as illustrating that love for children which was a distinguishing feature of her character. Through all her life in Africa it appears to have been her special vocation to minister to the happiness of the young, to civilize them by kind and winning treatment, and gently to lead them to Christ, and it was one of her greatest joys to perceive that the good seed so lovingly sown had taken root in some of their hearts.

In May, Mrs. Hinderer was seriously ill, but next month she was able to write, "I begin to sit up now in my comfortable chair, and I am getting on gradually. I must try to take life more quietly, though it is hard in such a place for work. I am glad to be able to leave the future, to lean on the strong Arm, He will do all things well, and it is His will for us to do or to suffer."

EXPANSION OF THE WORK & TIMES OF WAR

Anna's letter . . .

"July 26th. —I sit down to write again, thank God, in good health. We have been on the eve of civil war, may God preserve us from it, it is only since the Word of God entered this town, it has been free from it. My children can tell me dreadful tales of these wars, which before used to happen two or three times a year, when the women and children would run into the farms, or hide in their houses for two or three days. Well may so many of the people say, 'Ah white man, you are our friend, you have brought peace into this town.' How cheering it is to see many (yet few) wishing to hear and read the Word of God, which tells of the peace which passeth all understanding, and which tells of, and leads to, the land where wars, and sorrows, and sins shall be known no more. Our chiefs were never more friendly to

us than at the present moment; they say 'we are seeing which is truth.' Ground is cheerfully given, and they are desirous to have other stations. The two men my husband chose in Sierra Leone are very satisfactory, and are much liked. They are now having the ground cleared in two places in this town, about four miles apart from each other. We stand in about the middle. In the dry season the building is to begin, and then Johnson will live in one, and Allen in the other, so that in less than a year, we trust there will be three bells on a Sunday, calling to the house of God. Several persons from both these quarters come to our church now."

SICKNESS TO DEATHS DOOR AND BACK

The following letter gives more particulars of her illness, and tells of Mr. Hinderers journey up the country:

"August — *"In May I began to be ill, and a most serious illness I had. I had not been so prudent, perhaps, as I ought to have been. They used often to tell me I was doing too much. For six weeks I could not leave my bedroom. One whole week I knew no one or anything. Many times they gathered round my bed for last moments, but it graciously pleased God to listen to their cry, and to restore me. I do not know what my illness was, but it seems principally caused by my great* and constant sufferings at sea; and on coming back, with so much to urge me on, I did a little too much. But I am now quite strong, the cold season came on just when I began to mend, and it has tended greatly to my restoration. We never had it so long or so cold before, but though so good for me, I am sorry to say it does not agree with the natives, and I have still many sick people to attend to.

"I am just now alone; my dear husband is on his long and important journey eastward. Having been permitted to labour here for seven month with uninterrupted health, to get things to rights and set other things going, and my health being so thoroughly re-established, he felt quite happy in starting the 2nd of this month. He has been gone nearly three weeks; I do not expect him before four or five more. I am getting weary to hear from him, it is long now; but as he gets further and further away, it is impossible.

"One cannot help getting a wee bit anxious, in this land of sickness and death, but he is in good keeping, and it is such a favour to be permitted to commit each other to the gracious care of such a Father, such a friend. Truly I do not grudge him to his Master's work, and this is one part of it, for which he is peculiarly fitted. Yet I must constantly feel the absence of one so ready to take every burden, and lessen every care for me. *He carries a happy loving heart and cheerful face; and so thoroughly understands these people, and has such tact in dealing with them.*

"Olubi went with him to the first resting-place, and came back next day; he dearly loves his master, and was sorry not to follow him, but he also likes taking care of me in his absence. He and his wife and little boy are very flourishing; the child is quite my pet and plaything, when I have time to play; he is a funny quick little fellow, and though only fourteen months old, has long run alone, and imitates all I say and do.

"My thirty children are very prosperous, very good, very naughty, and very noisy, just as it happens; then there are lots of people to be cared for and watched over: the sick also fall to my share, and I have had many the last six weeks. I have gone about this town to a greater extent than ever on my good little pony's back; I must do it, our converts cannot go to heathen doctors, where they must make sacrifice, or perhaps be quietly poisoned."

DISCOVERY OF AN ABANDONED BABY

Anna's letter ...

"What do you think Olubi found, when he returned on the 3rd, in this town, in the bush, near a running

Lest We Forget

brook? A little baby not a week old; it had been thrown away-by some cruel mother. It was shrieking; no one dared to touch it in this heathen land, but Olubi picked it up, and brought it home, as nice a child as you can see. We know nothing about it, perhaps it was a twin child; the gods do not like twins, so one is often got rid of, and perhaps the poor mother had not the heart to kill her child, and so thought, if the pigs or vultures ate it, the gods would be appeased, and take its spirit to a good place. I always make a point of helping a woman who has twins, if she brings them up carefully, which some do in spite of the idols; but this poor little boy only lived with us three weeks. We did all we could, but it seems he had taken a violent cold, and he must die. I was so sorry D. was not at home to baptize him; we should have named him 'Moses,' but I was glad the poor little thing should be cared for, and die, and be buried, instead of the pigs and vultures feasting upon him, though I did wish he might live. We buried him under a shady tree in the bush. We have had a great loss here in the death of our native catechist, he was a faithful labourer, and we miss him much. How wonderful are the ways of Providence!"

Visit to England and Return to Ibadan

REPORT ON THE WORKS PROGRESS

Anna's letter...

"We have twenty-nine communicants, thirty-nine candidates for baptism, and twelve beside who asked to be taken as candidates for baptism last Saturday. Then we have some baptized who have not come to the Communion yet, and we have several inquirers. Thus the Lord's work is going on, and ought we not to be the more encouraged as it is truly hard ground to work upon?"

"*September. 23rd.*—My husband came home from his journey in excellent health, and much cheered and refreshed by his interesting tour. It is wonderful to see him; he has not had a day's illness since we came to Ibadan (in January), I quite feel it is in answer to prayer. We enjoy seeing our little church grow. One of the converts, who lives more than three miles from this station, has been so earnest that he has brought many from his quarter to hear the Word of God; and, thank God, many have not heard in vain. Being so far off, they bring their dinners, and stay here all day; but in the evening those that live anywhere near, before they disperse for the night, meet at his house, and have prayer together. They pray for their minister and teachers, for themselves and for the heathen. Touchingly simple and childlike must their petitions be when we think that such a little while ago they were all enveloped in heathen darkness.

"A blessing will come, and does come, from such a state of things as this. Though there are so few to do the work of the Lord, in this immense place, He is graciously doing it Himself in the hearts of His dear children gathered here, and will do much by them, the little seed, the small piece of leaven. The jewels in preparing, and bye and bye they shall adorn their Redeemer's crown, in His kingdom above"

"Oct. 18th. —We had the men of our congregation to a little treat one day this month. We showed them our magic lantern, which delighted and surprised them much; then we gave them sweet tea and biscuits, with a little yam, after which they made nice little speeches, comparing their former state with their present, and spoke of the happiness of believing and trusting in God, and Christ-their Saviour, and they thanked me so nicely for the pleasure and information we had given them Then they talked of their former days of heathenism and how they used to gather round their war captain and after a grand feast prepared for them, they would promise to fight for him, 'But: said one, 'now you, our dear minister, our friend, our father, and you, our mother, call us so kindly, and show us such *wonderful things, and tell us about them. It is God who has given such sense to people to make such things, that we may get instruction from them, and then you have given us such nice refreshment, and we are very pleased; but you do not want us to fight and catch slaves for you, so we will now end by asking our minister to put up a prayer for us to the great God, that we may be His children and His faithful servants.' All knelt immediately, and with a full heart my dear husband 'put up a prayer' for them and for ourselves, and there was such a beautiful and hearty 'Amin' at the end from every heart and lip. Our dear children are progressing in many things, but we have our hopes and fears, our joys and sorrows, there is much of true labour, but a. blessed one, a work which brings its reward even in this life."*

NATIVE LABOURERS

In a letter dated Oct. 20, Mrs. Hinderer spoke of the comfort they found in the native teachers: -

Anna's letter . . .

"God be praised, we are enabled to go on in our work, and with some cheer and joy. We are thankful for our present native helpers. You know a little what Olubi is; and Johnson and Allen, whom we brought from Sierra

Leone, are turning out as well. They are truly attached to us, and are so thankful for advice and instruction. They have also learned to read Yoruba, and address the people now very well."

And again on Nov. 19th, she wrote of them: -

"They are real helpers, satisfied in their calling, liking the place, and attached to us. Johnson is a sterling man, so straightforward, and rare quality in an African, I am sorry to say; a man well acquainted with his Bible, loving and reverencing it: and he quotes it so readily and appropriately. He is quite his master's right hand, for work among the people, and in trying to get up another station. He is now watching and caring so nicely for the new candidates, and they much respect him. Several of them have chosen him as the witness at their baptism. Allen is a younger man and very well disposed, and our regard for him increases. He addresses an assembly of people remarkably well, whether in the church or the street, and is becoming much more active. You ask about our singing; it is hearty, but not beautiful the Africans have not sweet voices, but their enjoyment in it makes up for a good deal."

"My dear husband was cheered by his interesting service yesterday (Advent Sunday), nine women and

five men gathered round him for baptism, and a most interesting sight it was, trusting as we did they were truly converted persons. They looked so earnest, and had been well instructed; their answers, during the time of preparation, were often quite touching, and in the service, instead of 'That is my desire,' two or three burst forth with 'I will, I will, I will,' folding the hands in their earnest way, and again to 'Dost thou believe?' 'Yes, yes, sir, that only I believe and trust in.' All the fourteen were idolaters not long ago. We now have the idols which some of them used to worship; but some worshipped the god of water, others the god of war, and another the god of thunder."

"Nov. 24th. — *"God give us grace to labour on for Him, and for the poor heathen around! He has mercifully owned and blessed our labours in this town. We are happy and thankful in our Master's service, and only entreat you most earnestly to pray for us, that we may be kept faithful unto the end, and that our heavenly Father may do His own work, notwithstanding the infirmities and sinfulness and helplessness of poor frail man!"*

"Christmas Day. — *"We have had a pleasant day altogether, though in the broiling heat it is next to impossible to believe in its being Christmas time. Every one of our people came today to church, and. all came* *up to salute us first, and were delighted to receive each a Christmas present of a nice new print bag, to put their books in. My children had a fresh supply of clothes, which made them look so comfortable. We had a nice little service, and, in about an hour after it, all dispersed, and my children sat down to a plentiful supply of food, with all sorts of things in their palaver sauce, which I gave them the pleasure of choosing for themselves yesterday. We then sat down to our own meal, and the children went out to salute some of their friends and relatives, while D. and I had a quiet afternoon, quite to ourselves, and we had such a long talk together as is not often our portion. Since tea we have had a pleasant time with the children, and a nice bright short little service, and plenty of Christmas hymns, and then they went to bed."*

SEARCH FOR MORE LABOURERS

"Dec. 28th. —On Friday my dear husband starts for Sierra Leone. Those places he visited eastward wish for teachers, so he proposed to go to Sierra Leone to select Yoruba men from the congregations there, who will make good scripture readers."

Visit to England and Return to Ibadan

JOY MIXED WITH TRAGEDY

Anna's letter...

"Death has entered our dwelling this month, and taken away my youngest little African girl, a little, little sorrowful creature whom we found here on coming back. Her name was Sophy Ajele, she was taken by our catechist in our absence because her own mother wanted to sell her; her case had to be taken before the chiefs, and they decided, as the father was willing, that she should be brought up by us. Poor little thing, her early days seem indeed to have been sad ones; for three days at a time her mother would give her no food. Then the parents went away to Ijaye, and I never saw them till the end of last month, when the mother came very quietly, as we afterwards found, to steal the child away; but she found her full of measles. Then she pretended to be so grieved for the dear child, and cursed me for 'letting' her get sick; we had at last to drive her out of the yard, but alas I not before she had given the child something very bad, which produced a complaint for which no means we could use did any good. In a few days the mother came again, and we were obliged to have her driven out of the compound; it was quite afflicting to see the dear child clinging to me, and crying: 'Oh, do not let my mother take me away, she will only sell me; you are my mother!' and then take my hand and say, 'I can go to sleep if you sit by me.' The two Sundays she was ill I could not leave her, and thankful was I for health to be with her almost night and day. She was a very silent child, but very obedient, and so attentive to any instruction; I never had to punish her but once, and I shall not forget her sorrow.

"She was very patient in her illness; during the early part she was so happy, lying or sitting on her mat by my chair, with all the pictures to herself; but when she became too weak for that, she chose out her favourite picture, of Christ blessing little children, and putting it by her side she gave me the others, saying, 'Iya, let this always stop here, and when I am better I can look at it.' A few days more, and my little Sophy had gone, I humbly believe, where she would see her dear loving Saviour face to face, that same Jesus who so loved little children when on earth. I suppose she must have been about eight years old. She was so small and so grave, that any one might have thought her sullen; but sorrow had evidently given her that expression. Nothing she liked so much as stories from the Bible, and hearing about the love of Jesus.

"She would never miss morning and evening prayers, and even when full of measles would come in. She said very little in her illness; but once, when I said to her, 'Sophy dear, you are very ill, perhaps it is God's will you should not get well again, would you like to die?' She replied, 'I should like to go to Jesus, but I do not want to die.' Poor dear child, she shrank from that last enemy, but it was made very easy to her; she sweetly fell asleep, so gently, so beautifully, like a, little babe on its mother's arms. The other children were much affected at the loss of their little companion. That same evening we all followed her to the silent grave, where we laid her just as the shades of night were coming over us. The speedy burial, which we must have in this country, is a very painful thing. The busy wheel rolls on again, but we miss our little Sophy. My remaining children are well now; I have had five ill, and poor little Ogunyomi has been at death's door, but mercifully raised again. I find these African people and children are very delicate, they have very little constitution.

"Our house is very comfortable now, a light grass roof over the iron makes it cooler; all is boarded, no more mats, and we have been painting the whole outside, the boards white and the shutters green, and it really looks so bright and pretty, that people come from far to see what we have done, they seem to wonder what will happen next. I must tell you, because you kindly pity us more than we deserve, — about bread, we have such nice flour this time, and we make delicious bread; this makes up if we should now and then have the barrel low or spoiled. I feel so ashamed to have mentioned that such is the case sometimes, when I think of our dear Red River friends, and their real sufferings."

ANOTHER YEAR OF FAITHFUL SERVICE

The new year, 1859, found Mrs. Hinderer alone in Ibadan, if such an expression is admissible in speaking of one whose active life found few solitary hours, excepting those necessary for repose. Mr. Hinderer was still in Sierra Leone.

Her story continues:

Anna's letter . . .

"*January, 1859. — We had a very happy new year's day in Ibadan. We had always intended to carry out the suggestion which came originally from America, that at twelve o'clock in the day, in all parts of the world, that hymn should be sung: — 'Jesu shall reign where'er the sun.'*

"*As my dear husband was obliged to leave before the new year, our people begged that I should have it, and at half-past eleven the room and piazzas were full. I read a few selected passages of scripture, and we had prayer, then entire silence for several minutes, and when the clock struck, we all burst out in that beautiful hymn. We had two or three prayers afterwards, and* separated with full hearts. I felt there was much blessing in this little gathering, and the remarks, prayers, and tearful eyes showed that I was not alone in this belief. We have much for which to bless and praise our God at this time in Ibadan; oh, may He continue it! It was a deeply touching day to me, I felt I was not to see my dear husband again, and I could not bear the sight of his clothes. But in a day or two I was better, and set about a thorough house-cleaning, and papering the parlour, which I have now accomplished, and have made ready to start on the 20th to Abeokuta for a little visit, and to Lagos, following my good husband's parting advice. Only Konigbagbe and Durojula will be my companions on the journey, with two persons to carry my box, bed, &c. It is rather an adventure, but more pleasant and amusing than not in prospect. Dear Lord, bless my going out and coming in, keep us all under the shadow of Thy wing."

In an account of this expedition written a few weeks later, Mrs. Hinderer related the following story: -

"One of the little girls who accompanied her: — "When my husband was in Sierra Leone, one lovely moonlight night, we had the usual Monday prayer-meeting on the grass in front of our house; and, when all had dispersed, the children and I still lingered on, and they talked, not thinking I listened, about the prayers. One said this person's prayer was too long, and another said whom she liked to hear pray on a Monday night, when one of my girls, sitting very quietly, replied, 'Well, prayer is always sweet to me) I like prayer from every one, and nobody's is too long;' and then they talked of the difference of our prayers from those offered to idols."

After giving some details of the journey to Abeokuta, Mrs. Hinderer continued: -

"At night we took shelter under a shed. About twelve o'clock I woke, and found my little girl at prayer; I supposed she thought it morning, and time to get up, for one good heathen practice is kept up now that they are Christians—in the morning, on waking, every person salutes his or her idol before anything else; and now, though you may wake any of our people in the morning, they do not speak to or salute you until they have bowed in prayer to thank God for His mercy, and to ask His blessing for the day. So, when we were on the road the next day, I asked my little damsel if she had thought it was morning. 'O no, ma'am; but I think I hardly ever woke in the night before, so I thought it would be so nice to pray now.' This was said in the simplicity of her heart, and I was pleased to have this truthful testimony that prayer was to her. Truly do I desire it may be her joy, comfort, and resort to the end of her life here, when prayer shall be changed for never-ending praise."

Writing from Lagos, she spoke of the pleasure she had experienced in these two visits: -

Anna's letter ...

> "A little society is so refreshing to the spirit. A little communion, and interchange of thought and words with Europeans, can hardly be appreciated except by those who live far away in a heathen land. I spent more than a week at Abeokuta very pleasantly, and then I came down to this place."

FRESH ILLNESS

She was attacked by illness at Lagos, and received much kindness at the hands of her friends Mr. and Mrs. Maser; but she longed to return to Ibadan, as will be seen by the following extract, dated Feb. 27th: —

> "The mail has arrived, which brought my dear husband and to-morrow we are homeward bound. That is a joy! There is no place like Ibadan in all Africa, to our taste, and I am quite home-sick !"

DELIVERED FROM DROWNING

In crossing the strait which flows between the continent and Lagos, their canoe went to pieces, and, though they escaped with their lives, their stores were sadly injured, and many things lost. Wet clothes by day, and a damp mattress at night, were productive of serious injury to one in so delicate a state of health, while, independently of these things, she was scarcely equal to a four days journey to Abeokuta.

> "But," as she expressed her grateful feelings, March 16th, "with good nursing, medicine, kind friends, and our merciful Father's love, I was restored, and reached Ibadan, through the great kindness of our Christian people, who, on hearing of my sickness, came to carry me in a hammock every step of the way."

> "March 28th — How pleasant it is to write from this place again; we are so thankful to be settled once more in our home and our work, having had a most delightful and refreshing few days' visit from our dear Bishop [Bowen]. He has left us this morning, and has left a blessing behind him. I wish I could give you a vivid description of him; lie is a most delightful man, and well fitted for his work in Africa. Oh, may our God preserve him to us, and to His Church on earth! The Bishop has good health, he has gone through some sharp

attacks of fever, and is able, to endure much in the way of travelling, and is very free from excitement. He has been in every quarter of the globe, preserved from fears and anxieties; and you can see constantly, with all his vigour and energy, the man who is 'stayed' upon his God. He has been greatly afflicted by the loss of his sweet wife, so mercifully given, so wonderfully adapted to himself and to his important calling, and then so quickly taken from him. It is a grievous affliction, but the peaceable fruits of righteousness are not withheld, and he is comforted by the God of all comfort and consolation. He has been so kind to us, interested in the work, visiting the chiefs, and doing good in every way; ready to listen to our lamentations and rejoicings, so capable of advising or reproving, quick of speech and decided, but with such true Christian courteousness. I think that is the feature in his character which strikes you particularly, and a sweet spiritual tone pervading all. You feel the better for a reproof from him it is a kindness, the 'precious oil' which does not break the head. We had some delightful little seasons of prayer by ourselves, with our children, and our people. On Sunday he confirmed twenty-two persons, and gave a most beautiful address, so earnest, faithful, and suitable. The church was nicely filled, and you might have heard a pin fall, all seemed solemnized. In the evening he had all the native agents; he gave an exhortation, and his prayer was the pouring out of the full heart of one 'who holds communion with the skies.' It has been a ray of sunshine which will not quickly fade."

"Good Friday, 1859. — I must write a few lines at the close of this most solemn day. It is very interesting to feel it has been kept by a little band who have long been struggling, in heathen darkness, to find a mediator between poor sinful man and the holy God. The glorious Gospel has come to them, and they have been enabled to lay hold on the one only and true Mediator, to believe in Jesus, who left His Father's glory and came down to suffer and die for poor sinful man of every tribe, nation, and people. My dear husband had service this morning; every person who comes to church was there. Then he had a prayer-meeting in the afternoon, in which there was much: life and heart. Two of the converts, and one of the scripture-readers, prayed most earnestly and beautifully; they were evidently not strangers to prayer, they knew what it is to lift up their hearts to God their Saviour. This has been a great cause of thankfulness to my dear husband, for it is joy to the true missionary when his children walk in the truth, walk in the light, grow in grace.

DEATH OF THE ALAFIN OF OYO

"April 27th. — Our old friend the King of Oyo is dead; there were not so many persons put to death as is usual on such occasions, not more than four men. But forty-two of his wives poisoned themselves, for the honour of accompanying him to the other world. Oh, heathenism! What can it not do what cannot its superstitions lead to!"

PASSAGE OF BISHOP BOWEN

"July 26th. — What tidings does this mail bring to us! that our most beloved Bishop Bowen's course on earth is finished! He reached home well, and in a time of sickness and trouble worked incessantly, and sunk under an attack of the general epidemic. This beloved servant of God preached his last sermon on the 22nd May, a most solemn one, from Col iii. 1,2, and on the Saturday evening following, the 28th May, breathed his last. We are true mourners; we could not have service this afternoon. Our people were so heartily grieved they could not take a service, and dear D. was too utterly broken down; the people had assembled, so Olubi went and told them what we had heard. There was true sorrow, not the loud wailing of the Africans in general, but quiet weeping; and all

dispersed to their homes. Today, every man and woman who comes to church has been to salute and sympathise with us. Some have just got into the house, and instead of a word you hear a sob, and they have turned round and gone home. Others have tried to speak words of comfort, or sat down in silence. One young woman who is not baptized, but in preparation for it, came and laid her hand gently on my shoulder, saying, with tears, 'Iya, it is true the fathers pass away; they go, but God is still here, He will never go away.' O beloved, honoured friend, we will not grudge thee thy blessed rest, the arrival at thy congenial home with thy beloved Saviour and the sweet partner of thy short African pilgrimage; but oh, we mourn bitterly and deeply for ourselves and for Africa, for who can see thy like again!

Two such treasures as our most dearly loved Bishop Vidal, and this Bishop Bowen, cannot be seen in this afflicted land. Dear Lord, heal, bind up our broken hearts, and make us followers of Thee and of them.

INTERACTIONS WITH MOSLEMS

"I have been having a visit from some Fulani people; they are Mohammedans, and take care of the cows. No Yoruba may milk a cow, so there are always some Fulani slaves, belonging to the chiefs, to

take care of these creatures. They all live together, and are very independent, but staunch Mohammedans. They are excessively fond of music, and when I bring out my musical box, or play the harmonium, they are so happy, and would stay all day. But if I sing to them, they are more than happy, and will sit with tears in their eyes. They are intensely loving to me, and have much more sentiment than any other tribe of Africans that I know. They were saying today, after some hand grasping and coaxing, 'Ah! Iya, we are both alike, we are strangers in this country; we both speak a different language from this people, so we are one. I replied, That is just what I want, that we should be one; there is much in which we are alike, but something remains. I want that we should both love and serve the great God who made us and both, when we die, reach heaven.' To this there was a ready assent; but I said, 'We want help to reach there, and not all the gods of the poor heathen can carry them or us there.' 'O no, no,' was the reply; 'and we cannot bear to look upon these foolish idols which the people here trust in: we are not half-Mohammedans, like many here.' 'Ah; but,' I said, 'my good friends neither can Mohammed carry us there;' and I went on to tell them of Jesus; but that name was not sweet to their ear. Yet I got them to learn, by repeating after me, St. John iii. 16.

"Alas! They did not want to go to heaven by the hand of Jesus, and quickly began to talk of the weather, and other things. So you see it is with us as with you at home, a 'sowing beside all waters.' But how great is our privilege! It is said, 'Blessed are ye that sow beside all waters.'"

MEMORIES OF HER YEARS IN TRAINING

In the next letter, written to Mr. Cunningham, Mrs. Hinderer showed how fondly she cherished the remembrance of the happy time she bad spent in Lowestoft Vicarage, which had been such a help to her in preparing for missionary work.

"July 7ᵗʰ. — Our little church goes on steadily and we look on in hope, but not without some fear and trembling; yet we desire to labour on in faith and hope, and with thankfulness; we are in good health, fully occupied, and very happy. **I have felt so much lately what a blessing, what a gift is good spirits and a cheerful heart. If we had not this blessing, I think we might break down sometimes;** *and how constantly do I feel what a blessing, help and preparation your dear vicarage life was to me, with you and dear Mr Cunningham the head; and all one saw, and learned, and felt there; the regular occupied life, the*

kindness and love which reigned there! Sorrow and care came, but there one saw how it was to be borne, and a cheerful blessed spirit presided, loving and loved, all under the banner of Jesus: so much happiness existed, because He was the honoured and beloved Head.

"Well, I ought to be better than I am for all I learned there; but I always feel I owe everything of the earthly blessing to that dear home, my dear mother dying when I was so young, that I was tumbled up and down in the world a good deal. No! life is full of blessings, but it is light and shadow, cloud and sunshine, tears in the evening, joy in the morning. ***But in our home above it will be all joy, all peace, perpetual happiness, because there we shall be in the presence of Jesus, and there shall be no more sin, and we shall be delivered from this body of sin and death. O when we dwell on this, we long to be gone, to stretch our wings, and fly away; but it is blessed to labour and to wait.***

OVERCOMING CONSTANT ILLNESS

In August Mrs. Hinderer had another serious attack of illness. As soon as she was sufficiently recovered to be left alone; Mr. Hinderer set out on another missionary journey, from which he returned as she expressed it, "cheered and hopeful, bright and happy."

SLAVE BOY RESTORED TO HIS MOTHER

The following touching history of a little boy in the mission-house was written by Mrs. Hinderer, to interest children in her work of faith and love: -

Anna's letter...

"Oct. 25th—I must tell you a story of one of my little boys finding his mother, or, rather, of his mother finding him. Any one is free to enter our frontyard, and to look, and talk and be spoken to as much as they wish; but to the back yard we do not allow visitors, as it is necessary to keep that part more private. A few mornings ego, a woman came in to sell cooked yams; another woman followed her, wishing to buy a piece for herself, as soon as she should put the large calabash down from her head. The children all began singing, you must not come here, wait in the other yard, the yams will soon come to you.' So she was going away; but, on looking at one of the little boys, she thought by the marks on his face that she knew something of him. She called him by a certain name, but the little boy did not know it She asked him some questions, and at last she said, 'Don't you know me?' He said, 'No, I never

saw you before.' And then she said, bursting into tears, 'I am your mother.' She had lost all her four children by war, and this little boy was so small when he was taken away that he had quite forgotten his mother, and what his name was. There was great joy, as you may believe, in which we all shared; and soon the little boy began to recognise that it was his mother. You will like to know what his name was, though you will not understand it, and I must see his mother again before I can quite tell you the meaning. It was Atipui.

"And now, how came we by this little boy? A few years ago, a man of this town bought him, intending to make him his slave; but the man afterwards came to church, and became a Christian, and though he had several people whom he had bought, he did not like to hold them as slaves any longer. They come to church with him, and one of 'them is already baptized; they work for him, and live with him, but are quite free. This was very noble of the man; 'there are very few of the Africans who do such a thing. So he brought to me the little boy, to whom he gave the name of Ope, (Thanks) saying if I would take the little boy to live with me, and bring him up with my others, he should like it. I was very glad to do this, so here he has been these two years, and he has learned to read very nicely, and begins to write, and is a very happy little boy indeed. The mother is living in the town; the man who had her as a slave, had made her his *wife, and is very kind to her. She will be able to come and see her little boy whenever she likes. When she heard he would never be slave again, she did not know what to do with herself for joy. And now, who can tell, perhaps that poor woman, through finding her child, may also find a precious Saviour for her soul. Pray for her, that she and her dear boy may hear and believe the blessed Gospel of our Lord and Saviour, Jesus Christ, and that she may be amongst those who bless God for sending white people to this country to teach and preach good tidings."*

MORE BATTLES WITH SICKNESS

*"Oct. — **We are in the deep waters again, but 'they shall not overflow' is the sweet promise.** My dear husband is exceedingly ill with a terrible cough, which has lasted nearly three months; he has also violent fever, such an attack as he has not bad for some years, and he suffers agony from boils, a malady to which Europeans are subject in this country, but which he has entirely escaped until this year. It is a real trial to him to be as much laid aside, but he manages to get through a good deal of homework, and to take the services generally. He is has been much interested in having persons come to him together, and separately, for special instruction, before joining us at 'the Lord's*

table on Advent Sunday. He is now having his candidates for baptism, and hopes to baptize seventeen or nineteen on Christmas day. That he should have this work now is very comforting to him, as he is not able to speak five words in the streets."

VISITING THE CONVERTS

Anna's letter ...

"Last Tuesday it was a nice cloudy morning so after breakfast I went to see four of our Christians who were sick. I had to travel at least four miles about this town to see them but my little pony and I are capital friends, and when it is not so very hot, I am glad to be out. Visiting our people is not so easy as in Lowestoft, and how different is our power! I am always about in the house and compound, but if I walk outside a little way, my knees bend under me. So it seems with us all; my husband seldom can walk any distance, so our ponies are our legs and great comforts they are. They do not cost much, and are kept very cheaply.'

She described the simple, happy celebration of Christmas, 1859; by the Christian converts adding: -

"But the great interest of the day was the baptisms in the morning; the grey headed were there to receive the *sign, to seek the grace, to become faithful soldiers and servants of the Lord Jesus. I could only think of the words, 'Ye who sometime were strangers are made nigh.' There were also some young married women, and eighty youths from fifteen to nineteen years of age. Their preparation and examination has been extremely interesting to my husband; the boys seem to have grasped the root of the matter, and are so happy. It is remarkable in the African character but one hardly sees anything of sorrow for the past nor are we able to draw from them that they feel any. They are wonderfully light light-hearted people and when they receive the Gospel, they lay hold of it truly, and renounce heathenism most earnestly, and go on rejoicing. There is something very interesting in this, in the simple laying hold of the Gospel, yet we should sometimes like to see a little melting of the heart, under the wonderful love which God has shown. We often fear rather a tendency to self-righteousness. But oh, it was a goodly sight and heart-cheering, to see that little band of sixteen round the font, enrolling themselves as followers of Jesus, coming out from among the heathen darkness and sinfulness of this town; we did indeed pray that they might be faithful unto the end.*

BIRTH OF BABY BOY TO OLUBI

"On the same morning Olubi received a fine Christmas present, another little boy. Little Dan likes him very well, but clings to 'Missisi' more than ever; all the week I have washed, fed, and done everything for him; he is quite my child. The school is going on very well; Olubi teaches all the children from nine to twelve, and sometimes my husband or I go in to give a lesson. At twelve, the girls come to me, and Olubi has the boys alone till two; then he is free, but my work goes on with all, one way and the other, till eight o'clock in the evening. I often write till nine, and then go to my room tired, for there is no sleep after half-past five in the morning, and from that time till I go to bed, hardly any rest. I have the comfort of feeling my days are pretty well occupied, though often, it seems, with things of small importance, yet those things must be done, and so I desire to a quiet and comfortable mind about them.

Human Sacrifice in Yorubaland

CHAPTER VI

Trials In Wartime

"Hungry, their soul is faint,
Thou hear'st their cry;
Thirsty, their soul doth pant,
Lo! streams are nigh;
Cloth's by Thy bounteous hand,
Strong in Thy strength they stand,
O Thou most high!"

R.B.H

IN JANUARY 1860, THE strength of the mission was increased by the addition to its number of Mr. Jeffries, who had been sent out by the Church Missionary Society from England, and whom Mr. and Mrs. Hinderer gladly welcomed to the appointed scene of his labours. But Mr. Hinderer's health had been much impaired by serious illness, and therefore, after having nursed Mr. Jeffries through his first fever, they set out on a journey to Abeokuta, whither they had been invited by their friends, Mr. and Mrs. Townsend, for rest and change of scene. The time which they had thus selected was unfavourable to repose. The town of Abeokuta was almost immediately agitated by rumours of an invasion by the barbarous king of Dahomey, and soon they judged it prudent to hasten homeward, while yet the country might be safely traversed, On the eve of their journey, Mrs. Hinderer wrote the following description of her feelings in expectation of the near approach of war, so unlike the peaceful confidence with which she was afterward enabled to live for years in the midst of it.

"Abeokuta, Sunday Morning February 19th, 1860.
—We are just now set in the midst of many and great dangers. Dahomey is close upon us! It is said he is not far from the walls, and in the morning an attack is expected. This has been a most anxious trying day, yet the congregation in church was very large, and the Psalms in the morning, and the prayers, were truly comforting, and Mr. Townsend was able to get calmly through a comforting sermon on 'I know that my redeemer liveth' Almost the only peaceful place has been the church. All roads are being shut up, to prevent people from running away. The reports coming in all day are most distressing. I am sorry to say I am terribly upset by it, the anticipation of war unstrings all my nerves. My husband is rather anxious about me, because I have such sudden pains in my left side when the shouts and reports come; and he is determined to take me on the road to Ibadan, if possible, to-morrow. I

cannot tell you that I am calm and composed, when I am not; would that it were so! Yet amid the turmoil and disquietude and infirmity of this poor body, I am permitted an under-current of peace: I know 'This God is our God for ever and ever, He will be our Guide even unto death.'"

They accomplished the journey safely, but found Ibadan full of excitement in the prospect of war with the neighbouring town of Ijaye.

"February 28th. —We reached home, God be praised, safely, but it was a desolate journey, the road forsaken on account of wars everywhere. We did not know whether we should not be fired upon from the bush any minute, and my poor husband suffered much, but we have every cause to be thankful we came, and our people are glad to have us at home in these troublous times. The sea of life is by no means smoother here than it was in Abeokuta; the chiefs of this place and of Ijaye have quarrelled, and caught each other's people, and sold them. Most passionate messages were sent backwards and forwards. Calabashes were presented to one and another, with the request that the chief of Ijaye desires such and such, and Ibadan's chief's head in the calabash; then these people send back, 'We want Are's[25]

---

[25] The War Chief

head in this calabash first.' Now the roads to Ijaye have all been shut, and Ibadan kidnappers have been catching everybody, man, woman, or child, who ventured out in the Ijaye farms. Whether there is to be real war we cannot tell, there are various reports, but it is an anxious time. What a mercy it is when we have grace and faith to lean on the Strong Arm; how truly we can then feel, 'I will not fear what man can do unto me.'

"When you receive this, I hope many of our present anxieties will be over, but you will think of, and pray for us. I cannot tell you how soothed and comforted we often feel, in the remembrance of so many beloved ones praying truly and earnestly for us."

The faint hope entertained, that the questions which had arisen between these towns might be amicably settled, had vanished before the dispatch of the next letter, which told of the declaration of war, accompanied by deeds of cruelty.

"*March 16th.* — A general war is now proclaimed, and all whose business it is must go. Tremendous sacrifices have been made, and alas! On Saturday night, a human sacrifice; a man of about twenty-five or thirty. In the day he was paraded through the markets, that people might see what a fine fellow he was; for all the town is taxed to pay the expenses. Some of our people who saw him say that he looked as proud as possible of the honours that awaited him. From being a poor slave, on that day he is all but worshipped, and has the power of saying and doing all he likes, except escaping his death in the evening. But, poor fellow, he believes all kinds of glory await him in the other world, the world of mystery. The moment he is killed, all prostrate themselves in prayer (what prayer!), then follows feasting and rejoicing, and before the body spoils, certain generals must be off on the road to the war. The head of the poor victim is left to the fowls of the air, but the body receives great honour from the women; they rub and decorate it with everything precious, believing that this same man is to return to the world again as an infant, but that he will then, when he grows up, surely be a king. So hundreds of women pay honour to this dead body, each praying she may be the mother when he visits the world again. Yesterday the people were making other sacrifices at the graves of departed warriors, earnestly entreating their help from the other world.

"O the blindness, the darkness, the foolishness of heathenism! And in the midst of all this we are living; and when pressed down under the thought of these and a thousand other sorrows and horrors we can hardly help asking sometimes, are we of any use in such a *country? But then we are comforted by the thought that beginnings must be made; we are now, in a feeble way, hacking at the great unwieldy stone; it is a rough unsightly one, and we in our day shall hardly get beyond that part of the work; generations may pass before it is comely and pleasant to look upon, yet we shall all rejoice together in the end. I must finish my letter, for roads all about are shutting, and I may have no opportunity of sending down for the next mail. We have no personal danger to fear but discomfort enough; no communication with our friends, soon food will be dear, and of course all trade of every kind stopped. We partake, and must partake, of these calamities, and we feel heart-sick at the thought of all the bloodshed, all the sorrows, all the woes which will follow; but the Lord reigneth. He preserves us now, gives us favour in the eyes of these savages, and permits us still to work on for Him. He is and will be the wall of fire round about us. Our people are happy to have us remaining quietly amongst them, and we all feel peaceful, having no fear, and go on just as usual"*

In order to its being understood how town could rise up in arms against town, without interference on the part of any national authorities, a few words of explanation may be necessary.

Trials in Wartime

About the year 1817 or 1818, when the Yoruba country owned the supremacy of a king, and had a regularly constituted government, the Mohammedan Foulahs and houssas invaded the territory, taking possession of Ilorin, and making it their place of encampment. This was the first preparatory step towards the dismemberment of the nation; for the new form people were always on the watch for opportunities of weakening the country, by sowing seeds of discord between its towns.

At a somewhat later period, the tribes which constituted what might be, called the provinces of the Yoruba country (Egbas, Ijebus, and others), were drawn into actual conflict, one with another, not without encouragement from Ilorin. The causes were thirst for power and pre-eminence, mutual jealousies, and the prospect of gain in the slave-market at Lagos, to which the surprised and captured inhabitants of many a town and village were marched off for sale by the pitiless conquerors.

It may give some idea of the desolation which these slave wars produced, if it be mentioned that the town of Abeokuta was peopled by refugees from no less than one hundred and forty-five towns and villages, the sites of most of which have since been overrun by the bush, so that all traces of their existence have disappeared. The prevalence of these internecine wars had left to the king

221

of Yoruba little more than a royal name. The larger towns had assumed a position of independence; the smaller towns attached themselves to the larger, in hope of finding protection at their hands.

Even after the strong arm of Great Britain had destroyed the slave-market at Lagos in 1853, and had thus put an end to the exportation of slaves from the principal port in the Bight of Benin, the ancient unity of the Yoruba kingdom was not re-established, nor was goodwill towards each other restored amongst the towns. A spark might easily produce a conflagration, and there was always too much readiness to kindle the flame. There was therefore nothing strange in the fact that in 1860 Ibadan and Ijaye discovered grounds of dispute with one another; and war having once begun, it dragged on its slow and varying course, in characteristic African style, through many successive years. It was, in fact, war without many battles, and was rather a state of hostility, treachery, lying in wait for stragglers, and capturing prisoners for slaves. Occasionally there were severe engagements, involving the loss of many lives; but far more frequently, when reports had arrived telling of a "terrible battle," it was eventually ascertained that less than twenty men had fallen on either side. The war-chiefs of Ibadan, with their eager "war-boys," and as many other men as could be pressed into the service, were partly entrenched behind a fortified camp near

Ijaye, and partly spread over the country in all directions, they and their enemies alike watching for every opportunity of plundering property and kidnapping people. It was impossible even to conjecture when or how such a condition of things would be brought to an end.

It would be out of harmony with the purpose of these memorials to enter here into the details of this native war. But it seemed necessary to touch upon the subject so far, because the effects of the war were felt sooner or later in every department of the missionary work in Ibadan, and in every incident of the daily life of Mr. and Mrs. Hinderer. It was painful to be in the midst of such scenes as those described in the foregoing letter; it was far more painful to prove by experience, that the people generally were too much engrossed by thoughts of war to be disposed to receive the message of the gospel of peace; while the bearers of that message became, through the troubles which befell them, the objects of contempt to the more bigoted of the heathen around them. But the presence of the missionary was needed more than ever by those who as yet were but children in the faith, to inspire them with calmness and confidence, in the midst of the many disturbing influences which were at work, in those unsettled days. Mr. and Mrs. Hinderer resolved to remain at their post, ready to do or to suffer whatever might be their appointed lot; and from time to time cheering signs were vouchsafed to them that the blessing of God rested upon the work of His servants, carried on under circumstances of such peculiar difficulty. The Christians learned new lessons of faith and love in the school of affliction; while from among the heathen, one here, and another there, was gathered in and added to the little band of believers.

The year 1860, in which the war broke out, was marked to Mr. and Mrs. Hinderer, personally, rather by its perplexing rumours and alarms than by actual privations; but their position immediately became one of extreme isolation. All intercourse with their missionary brethren in the Yoruba country was rendered impossible; for the people of Abeokuta, and the rest of the Egbas, took the part of Ijaye in the war. Letters from England, also, which had usually been forwarded to Thadan from Lagos by way of Abeokuta, could now only reach them by new tracks and uncertain opportunities; while the possibility of receiving supplies of such things as had hitherto been reckoned amongst the necessaries of life was entirely at an end, within a few months after the commencement of the war. The Egba kidnappers watched every approach to Ibadan; and any goods sent up from Lagos were always in danger of falling into their hands.

In looking to the future, they could not but foresee that heavy trials were before them, if this state of things should continue; but they hoped that amongst the many conflicting rumours which reached their ears, those which told of peace being near at hand would prove true. In any case, they were content to commit themselves to His keeping, in whose name they had gone forth to dwell among the heathen, and who had again and again been to them "a very present help in time of trouble."

At first, the most pressing cause of anxiety to Mrs. Hinderer arose from her husband's constant sufferings, to which frequent reference is made in the following extracts from her letters; letters, it will be remembered, which were written to intimate friends, to whom in unburdening her cares and sorrows she found relief; at a time when the sympathy of loving hearts, and the aid of their prayers, were peculiarly precious.

"April 1860. — I never like writing on Sunday, but as we know of someone going on Monday morning, and in these times opportunities are so rare for sending letters, I gladly spend a little time in communicating with you. Our Sunday services are over, the children's picture lessons ended, and a hearty cheerful singing; and they are all fast asleep on their mats. War troubles are just the same, but we are thankful that food is as yet cheap, and likely to be so for some months, and perhaps then war will be over; but these foolish people like to go on for two or three years and then 'sit down' for two or

three more. However, we won't think of what they may do; to live a day at a time is the Christian's privilege. My children's appetites do not lessen because of war, and as soon as there were rumours of this time coming, I laid in a large store of yams, palm oil, and other things, and we have a good stock of cowries. You think of us, I am sure, in our varied and sometimes trying circumstances.. We rejoice in the love and care of our heavenly Father, which we daily and hourly feel in this heathen land, and we thank Him for the gift of so many dear friends at home, to sympathize with and pray for us. I always feel so nearly drawn to you all, on the blessed Sabbath-day, home ties are so strong on this day; there is so much here unlike our home Sabbaths, the language, the people, everything. But oh, it is a blessed day of rest from so many of the secular cares and labours which must attend a missionary life, a time when the mind can be, and is, drawn more towards spiritual things. I often feel a little tried by the thorough Martha life I am obliged to lead; with twenty children in the house, others out of it, and my husband, who is generally so active, now for many months disabled and suffering, my hands are more than full, and I am afraid my heart too, not in the pleasure of a Martha's life, but in the worry, and cares, and fatigues attending it. Yet I don't see for myself where it is to stop, until the end of the journey, for I am quite sure the more we do the more we find to do. I'm very thankful for the health and strength I enjoy; my husband says he looks at me with wonder sometimes. He took a service today, after many weeks' silence, and got through well; but his health is in a serious critical state; he has now confirmed asthma, which must greatly hinder him in his work."

*"**April 20th** — We are going to venture to send some of our people down to Abeokuta next week, as by that time the mail will have arrived, and we want the refreshment of letters from home more than ever in these times, so we must get some letters ready to send down by the same opportunity. It is well white people are yet in favour, for no soul except our very own people could walk that road now, it would be death, and it is very good of our people to venture to do it. There has been a long groaning for war, and now here it is begun; and where is the ending we know not. If it were not for the assurance that our Father in heaven knows all, and will do all things well, and the help He gives us, and little gleams of encouragement in the work, we should be utterly discouraged. Three women came this week to have their names put down as candidates for baptism. One we felt sure was not in earnest, so her name was not entered. The second was a nice sprightly looking woman without a particle of beauty, her woolly hair wanting to get grey, but in its transition state*

now, a dingy yellow; but when her countenance lighted up, and somewhat of the earnestness of her soul was shown in her ready and hearty replies to all D.'s questions, you could no more see her plainness. The name given at her birth means, 'Honour or riches shall never cease.' We talked of the honours and riches of the world, and of those she was now seeking in Christ her Saviour, the nothingness of the one, the truth of the other. At the sacrifices and worship at her birth, honour and riches were promised, but what has she seen of them? Sorrow, trouble, pain, and poverty instead; and what would they have done for her in the life to come? But what God promises in Christ Jesus shall never fail us: He will never deceive us. She was intensely interested in this little talk on her name. The third was a younger woman, very different in manner, timid and shy, but we found her heart was in the right place. She said to D., 'Father, I heard you in church last Sunday that you would baptize little babies next Sunday, so I could not stay longer; I have come to church nearly a year, and I want to be a Christian so please put my name down, that I may be among those whom you will baptize some future time.' My husband was surprised at the clearness of her knowledge of the way of salvation, and he gladly put down the names of Olaotanmo and Ifawe, rejoicing in the hope that their names were written in heaven. You will remember Ifa is

Trials in Wartime

the chief god of the Yoruba's. Many names are given in honour of him. Ifawe means 'Ifa washes.' This led us to speak to her of the only efficacious washing of our guilty souls in the precious blood of Jesus. D. will baptize eight little babies next Sunday. I am busy with some of my children, making little white gowns and caps for them. Olubi's child is to be called Jonathan Christmas, as he was born on Christmas day."

In the same letter she tells of two incidents which had brought unjust reproaches upon the Christian religion and its teachers. A woman who had been preparing for baptism died. Her illness was chiefly occasioned by the cruel persecution which she suffered from her relations. She was visited by several Christian women, and in simple language expressed to them her faith, telling them that she was like a little child who did not know and understand things fully, and adding, "But I do believe in. Jesus, the good Saviour, and I try to lay my soul on Him." After her death, her relations taunted the missionaries with their inability to bring her to life again, and said, "What is the use? People give up all the good ways of their fathers, they cast away their idols, and anger the gods, and then they die just the same as others!" Another woman, who was also a candidate for baptism, was prevailed upon, after enduring beating and starvation which reduced her to a skeleton, to return to idolatry, after which she became strong and well again. Mrs. Hinderer added,

> "These two cases, being so near together, have been, and are, a great triumph to the poor heathens. They exult in them, and look on us, and almost say, Where is now thy God? It has been some trial to our faith, but we know in Whom we have believed, we know that He will do what is right; we are to walk by faith, not by sight. This, the dark heathen cannot understand; the present, what he sees, what he holds, is all in all to him. And we take comfort in believing we shall see poor Maonni, babe as she was in the faith, yet, through the love of Jesus, in His kingdom above. So we go on day by day, 'faint' but I trust 'pursuing.'"

A characteristic illustration of African life is presented by the next letter. After relating some difficulties which Mrs. Hinderer met with in dealing with some of the young native Christians, she added,

> "These are troublesome people, you must either let them go on just as they please, or hold them with a strong hand; I think they like you better for the latter. At all events they respect you more. I must give you a little anecdote on the word 'respect.' One of our people beat his wife very badly, and she came to me to heal her bruises. When we remonstrated with the man on his

conduct, he answered, 'I tell you, you no understand the business at all. White people no understand husband and wife palaver at all. I tell you, in this country, if man no flog his wife now and then, she no 'spect him at all, no 'spect him one little bit.'"

In the same letter, dated May 17th, Mrs. Hinderer tells of the commencement, on Ascension day, of a week-day evening service, and speaks of her increasing anxiety and distress on account of her husband's severe illness.

"*May 29th.* — *Troubles increase.., but sufficient unto the day is the evil thereof, and the God of mercy and power reigneth. I sometimes wonder we are not more anxious; but we are mercifully kept in peace and quietness, though wars and rumours of war are around."*

"*June 20th.* — *We have finished a house about two miles off, in the town, where a native teacher has been for some time; and now Mr. Jeffries is settled there, under the same roof, and they will soon, I think, get up a little church, the outward walls and the spiritual building; and in another direction we are hoping to commence another station for a native teacher. It is a comfort, and an earnest for good, that our Master's work can go on in such times as these. Dear Mrs. Buxton's box has arrived, and Mr. Charles Buxton has* sent us a splendid box of tools. We *have* not got them all yet, for if we do get a few people to go down, they will not bring even half a load, because they may have to run from kidnappers."

"**August 7th** — *Our war position is much the same, yet a little worse, which is rather a relief, as it gives hope of a quicker end. We have a wonderful in-gathering in Ibadan, yams and corn, beyond all our expectations a few months ago; so that we have plenty of food, and not dear; but our people are troubled for want of cowries, and we have to open our store in faith; and hope that they will last till peace comes. European comforts, and what in a general way appear and are necessaries, we must do without, and be thankful for what yet remains in our hand. With tea, coffee, sugar, we think ourselves rich, and are glad to be able to share them with Mr. Jeffries. What we shall most regret is our flour, when that is gone. You can soon be weary of yams, if you have to take them as the staff of life. But by Christmas we hope war will be over."*

After referring to some of the many real causes for anxiety, with regard to the welfare of the mission, in this time of war, Mrs. Hinderer continued,

"**August 11th** — *It looks dark indeed, just now; but we know He liveth who will make all work after the counsel* of His most mighty will. It is a wonderful mercy that we are kept in such peace and quietness of mind in these troublous times. To be nervous and over-anxious in such a country must be a wonderful trial. How thankful we ought to be, and I trust we are, to be preserved from it. The work is also going on; only four of our church people are in the war, and they were obliged to go; and we have newcomers, and three of the greatest persecutors, two women and a man, have joined the class of candidates for baptism, and the man is to be baptised soon, with eleven or twelve others. Our children are all going on very steadily and amiably.

"My dear husband still suffers much, but he is thankful to be able to get on as well as he does; his presence is very necessary at this time. I continue in excellent health, and am very busy, and we are permitted to sing a joyful song of praise and thanksgiving unto our Father and our Redeemer, who has called us here, and makes us happy."

"October 13th. — I must write and yet have little inclination. Our future looks very dark. Today we hear that our only coast-road is going to be shut. This threat may blow over, as others have done; but it looks more real now. This mail brought me letters from a missionary sister on Mount Zion; we all seem companions in suffering and anxiety. However, our one

Ark of refuge is the same, in whatever quarter of the world our trials come. If only safe in Christ our Saviour, all will be well.

Yet of course the body shrinks from suffering, and any anticipation of it is too much for words. We are weary with war, —sounds of war, talks of war, anticipations of war; but we have been mercifully kept and comforted."

The misconduct of some members of their little flock gave a yet deeper tone of sadness to the letters of this date; but one of them concluded in terms which showed that, though "cast down," they were "not in despair."

"We have a cup of sorrow, but we are cheered and supported by our unseen Friend, and we are cheered sometimes by the sweet thought that He may have a blessing in store for us and His work; here, therefore, He suffers us to be so deeply tried just now. We see no end to the war troubles. Another feature has appeared; our farms in all directions are troubled with kidnappers. If this goes on, we may be troubled for food. I have been obliged in faithfulness to tell you some of our dark side, but we are thankful for some signs of a brighter one, and we do rejoice too in our way and our work, and are permitted to know what it is to be 'sorrowful, yet always rejoicing.' God be praised we do not work in a desponding mood."

Trials in Wartime

These were the last letters written in 1860. The report that the coast-road was to be "shut," proved to be too true; and months passed before the missionaries in Ibadan had any communication with the outer world. Trials of another kind now began. The store of cowries which had been laid in at the commencement of the war was rapidly diminishing, and there appeared to be no means of replenishing it. The traders, who at other times were glad to take dollars in exchange for cowries, could no longer make their way to Ibadan, with the attendant train of followers requisite in a country through which, for want of roads deserving of the name, goods could only be conveyed on men's heads; and where the value of the current coin, the cowry shell, is so small, that between £1 and £2 worth (i. e., a "bag" or 20,000 cowries, the rate of exchange varying extremely, according to the state of trade) is a "load," or as much as a man can carry. On his first visit to Ibadan, Mr. Hinderer himself had travelled with a trading-party consisting of no less than 4,000 people.

There were no Christmas festivities this year. "We could not afford it," wrote Mrs. Hinderer; "but the day was made bright to the children, and the Christians were full of sympathy, and assembled in goodly numbers in church, washed, and oiled, and dressed in their very best, their woolly hair freshly plaited (which sometimes is not done for months together), and looking as cheerful as possible; and they parted, having passed a blessed, happy day."

The close of the year found her in solitary charge of the large household, Mr. Hinderer having gone to the war camp, to ask the chiefs for the loan of some cowries to supply their nearly exhausted stores. "Sorrowful sighing" was mingled with the fervent desires which found expression in her journal at this season

"December 31st. — The last hours of this year of years are now fast drawing to a close, my children gone to sleep, my husband in the camp, and I have had a quiet day. Wonderful have been the mercies of this year of trial; sad have been the wars and fightings about us. Oh, we have a cup of sorrow to drink; but no more of this; only Thou, 0 God, have pity upon us! We have had no communication with anyone outside Ibadan for three months, and no mail for three months, a grievous loss, especially as there was no letter by the last from my dearest friend, the vicar. I am hungry to hear of my dear friends, but almost more anxious for them to hear of us; they will all be thinking of us in our war calamities in a heathen land. But I pray God to comfort them concerning us, and to keep them all in peace in the hollow of His hand, as He so mercifully does us, in the midst of all our troubles. Farewell, 1860! All the sins and sorrows, all the omissions and commissions, I take

to my merciful Saviour, and lay them at the foot of the Cross, and beseech Him to pardon and forgive, to wash all away in His precious cleansing blood; and oh, dear Saviour, give grace for the new period of time which will so soon commence. Give, oh, give me grace to live to Thee, to love and serve Thee in this dark land. Oh, have mercy upon us all in this house and compound, especially upon my dear children, in whom I so long to see a work of grace. Have mercy upon the little church gathered out here from among the heathen; give them life, breathe upon the dry bones; rouse us all from our coldness and deadness, and make us all burning and shining lights!"

The New Year dawned.

***"January 1st, 1861.** — We have had a nice day, and in some measure I enjoy beginning a new year; but I miss my ever-dear kind husband. How often we are separated at Christmas, New Year; even on our visit to England it was so; but we are one in heart, and meet in spirit, when absent in the body. Whenever he is away, it is in the path of duty. My heart's fervent desire is that our dear Lord and Master's work may flourish in Ibadan this year. Lord, make Thine own work prosper in our hands, and let us have the joy of seeing a fruitful vineyard here; but, above all, make our own souls to flourish, and keep us faithful, and vigorous, and earnest* in the work to which Thou hast called us, whether we see fruit or not. But oh! for the salvation of souls we do cry unto Thee; and oh! hear me for my dear children."

Her first letter in 1861, addressed to Mr. Cunningham, was written with much uncertainty whether she would be able to send it

"January 4th, 1861. — *D. having to go to the camp on December 31st, wrote an address for Olubi to deliver in his name on New Year's Day, which he did very well. We met together in the morning. Three persons prayed, and we sang hymns, and the address was given; in this way we started our new year, hoping you were engaged in much the same manner in one of your schoolrooms, and that we might be bearing one another on our hearts before our heavenly Father, at pretty much the same time; you gathering together in the dark and cold, we in the glaring sunshine of Africa; but each and all in our right places, where our wise and loving Father would have us to be. We feel so much at this time under the sweet influence of the Father's boundless love, and this, blended with the grace of Christ our Saviour, and the Holy Spirit's favour, will make, and does make all to be well.*

"We are quite shut up by war, but are always hoping we shall soon be in a better condition. Our God has been wonderfully gracious to us in preserving our health and spirits. My dear husband often suffers much with his cough, but he is not worse, and just now he is very much better. I have gone on with remarkable health, sometimes worn and weary with work and cares, as many a labourer is in dear old England; and of course all things are increased in wear and weight in a climate like this, but, God be praised, I have no illness. Our living is rather poor at this time; we cook yams in all sorts of ways, to make them palatable. I can eat palaver sauce and beans; D. cannot, but he likes Indian corn-flour made into porridge, which I do not, so we get on very fairly. There is plenty of this kind of food in the town, but our great trouble is the want of cowries, for, in the present state of things, there are no traders from whom we may buy them. Here we all are—ourselves, Mr. Jeffries, our school, our native teachers, in all seventy persons— and everyone has for more than two months eaten, and is now eating, from our store of cowries which we were enabled to lay in. That store is now nearly exhausted, though we have been as careful as possible, only allowing our two selves a pennyworth of meat in our soup, and glad to eat beans, with a little onion and pepper to flavour them, and pinching in the salt as if it were gold dust; but we have plenty of its kind to eat, and there is no poverty among the natives yet.'

> *"February. — Our work in general goes on steadily, but war is not conducive to its progress; the people are wild, restless, and unsettled."*

Mr. Hinderer's appeal for help had been received by the chiefs with many expressions of regard for his character and useful work, and of willingness to grant his request. But "Ifa must be consulted;" and a few days later the answer was given that Ifa forbade them "to lend the white man cowries;" and, though a present of cowries was shortly afterwards received from the head chief, such help could not be expected again. There was, throughout the war, considerable jealousy of European influence, which was supposed to be exercised in behalf of the Egbas, the enemies of Thadan. The existence of this suspicion which, as attaching to Mr. Hinderer, was utterly groundless, may account for the alleged unfriendliness of Ifa. Some of the consequences of the refusal of aid will be seen in the following letter: — "March 4th. — All my children who have parents or homes I have sent away today, making arrangements with them for the purpose; and we were comforted by the nice way in which the people took it.

> *"One woman offered to take one of my children, who has no other home, in order to help us; we have now tried all ways and means, but little is left in hand. We have tried to borrow, but none will lend; they say, and*

Trials in Wartime

very naturally, 'We cannot tell how long this war may last; it may be finished in a few weeks, or it may last some years.' Balogun, who promised to lend (a very easy thing for an African), now tells us we must have patience. He and all these poor heathen say, God will not and cannot suffer us to want, and truly in Him do we trust; and, now that we have tried all proper means, I do not believe He will put us to shame, but, for His great and blessed Name's sake, He will help us, till many shall say, 'They that wait upon the Lord shall want no manner of good thing.' But it is a long trial which our God sees meet to continue upon us. Some poor heathen look on and say, 'What is the use of their serving God? They die, and they get trouble;' and Ifa and Sango, &c., &c., often help us. The Mohammedans say, God loves us very well, but we do not worship Him the right way, and do not give honour to His prophet. But we know that Jehovah-Jireh liveth, and He will not forsake us. We do sometimes think of what might be, if these people were really to turn against us, but we are wonderfully delivered 'from fear of evil.' We had the comfort of getting our three months' mails in January, and a few days ago we received your letters written in December. Thus we have had all 1860 letters, so do not be discouraged about writing; we shall get them somehow or other, and think of the refreshment they must be to us."

In her journal of about the same date, she spoke of herself as being in a low state of health, the effect of poor living and anxiety; while Mr. Hinderer suffered yet more seriously. They had then been nearly six months without flour. Their food consisted principally of horse beans, the produce of their own little garden-plot, flavoured with palm-oil and pepper; and even of these the supply became so limited that they only allowed themselves a handful of beans daily. They could smile afterwards at the remembrance of having sometimes cried themselves to sleep with hunger, "like children;" but the suffering was terribly real at the time.

In the extremity of their need they thought of a new expedient, to sell such of their little possessions as would find purchasers in the Ibadan market. Everything that could be spared was quickly exchanged for food; again and again the house was searched, in hope that something more might be found. Amongst other things thus lighted on were some old tin match-boxes, biscuit-boxes, and the linings of deal chests, which had been put aside as useless, but were now regarded as a mine of wealth, being certain of meeting with ready customers; and the children spent hours in polishing them up for sale. When other stores were exhausted, they were obliged to part with household utensils, and even articles of clothing, all of which were sold for much less than their real value.

In after years, the details of the story of this time of privation and suffering were related with touching simplicity, the one feeling associated with the remembrance of them being that of thankfulness to Him who had sustained the faith of His servants, and brought them safely through those deep waters of affliction.

The native teachers and their families were dependent on Mr. Hinderer for food, when their salaries no longer reached them, and this increased their difficulties till the summer of 1861, when they were able to maintain themselves by cultivating farms.

The Christians would gladly have helped their minister, but most of them were poor, while the heathen generally knew little about the troubles of the "white man." Bale, the chief who looked upon them as his own "strangers," or guests, was suffering from paralysis, from which he never rallied, and the other chiefs were intent on war, and left them to take care of themselves as best they could. Nevertheless, Mr. and Mrs. Hinderer received, from time to time, many tokens of good-will, and substantial help, both from Christian and heathen neighbours; and such manifestations of their heavenly Father's love and care cheered their hearts and strengthened their faith. In her journal of Feb. 18th, Mrs. Hinderer noted with thankfulness the gift of two bags of cowries from one of the Christians, and the loan of two more from Olubi's aunt, who was a heathen; and similar gifts were acknowledged in letters written during the ensuing months.

DIVINE PROVISION

The following incidents, among many others, may serve as illustrations of the way in which unexpected help often came, in that time of need: -

One morning, when her husband was absent from home, Mrs. Hinderer assembled the children as usual for prayers, and the petition, "Give us this day our daily bread," came from a full heart, for there was nothing in the house which she could eat. The children, indeed, sat down to a hearty breakfast, but though she was faint with hunger, she could not touch their coarse food. While they were eating, she wandered to the gate of the compound to get a breath of air, and stood for some minutes watching the people going by, to the farm or the market. Amongst others who passed, was a woman carrying a bunch of Indian corn on her head, to whom she addressed, according to custom, the native salutation, and as she went on speaking the woman stood still, and stared with amused surprise, exclaiming at length, "How wonderful it is that you white people know how to talk our language." Mrs. Hinderer explained to her in a few words why she had come to Ibadan, and what she wanted to teach the people.

Having listened awhile, the woman asked, just as she was turning away, "Can you eat our corn?" and on learning that it would be acceptable, she gave Mrs. Hinderer a handful, which she hastened to roast and eat, gratefully acknowledging in this simple food, provided by a stranger's kindness, the speedy answer to her prayer for "daily bread."

When the stock of cowries was diminishing, Mrs. Hinderer ordered less and less milk for her household. The woman who supplied it, and who had always been most friendly to the missionaries, though she would not hear a word of the message which they brought, began to suspect that something was going wrong, and at length resolved to enquire how matters stood. She would not be satisfied without a distinct explanation and Mrs. Hinderer told her plainly, that she had no cowries to spare, and that, being unable to procure more, she could not buy the regular quantity of milk. The woman answered in a decided tone, "You must send as usual every day." Mrs. Hinderer told her that it was impossible to pay for it at present, but she only said, with still more determination than before," You must have your full quantity of milk every day as usual, and if you do not send for it, you will give me the trouble of sending it to you." For a whole year this charitable woman supplied them with her best milk, without payment, and when, at the end of that time, Mrs. Hinderer sent her a bag of cowries, as an acknowledgment of her kindness, though far from being an adequate payment for the milk, she at once returned it, and on being urged to accept it, answered with much feeling, "No, no! I did it because you were strangers in a strange land, and I will not take anything for it."

To return to the narrative. On the 6th of March Mr. Hinderer set forth on an expedition to Lagos, in hope of procuring cowries and a stock of European provisions. It was not until after much consideration, and earnest prayer, that he resolved to undertake so perilous a journey. But their need was urgent, their present precarious means of subsistence could not last much longer, and no other way of obtaining help appeared to be open to them.

The story of his journey cannot properly he omitted; as many of its circumstances are noticed in the letters which are to follow. His only companions were two of the boys; none of the adult Christians daring to accompany him, so great was the dread of kidnappers, while the war was in progress. The little party, however, did not meet with a single person in passing through the bush, which was the part of the journey most to be dreaded; and they reached their destination safely, on the third day after leaving Ibadan. At Lagos, Mr. Hinderer made arrangements with a trader, who undertook to supply him with cowries in Ibadan; and on the 23rd of

Trials in Wartime

March he sent off some flour and other provisions, in charge of a trading party, who intended, if possible, to make their way to Ibadan, and under whose protection he had hoped to travel. But on the eve of their departure, he was seized with a severe attack of illness, and thus was mercifully preserved from the calamities which befell the caravan. For they were attacked by the Ijebus; some of them were killed; and in the affray the goods were pillaged and wasted, and of all that Mr. Hinderer had sent, little more than one load reached its destination. On the 23rd of April, being sufficiently recovered to mount his horse, he commenced his homeward journey, the perils of which had greatly increased during his stay at Lagos, for the king of Ijebu, who had always been jealous of Europeans getting a footing in the interior, had now set a price upon his head, and had sent men to watch the road by which he would travel to Ibadan. Knowing all this, he nevertheless set forth on his perilous journey, and travelled in quiet confidence, trusting in the God who had so graciously protected him hitherto. The hearts of the boys were not so tranquil; they trembled, and not without cause. For some miles onwards, from the spot where the caravan had been attacked, the road was strewn with bones and skeletons, and Mr. Hinderer's horse was several times terrified by the sight of skulls lying on the narrow path through the forest. But again they saw no one on their long day's journey, though once they passed close by the smouldering fires of the Ijebus, who could only be supposed to have retreated to a hut at some distance, for shelter from a heavy shower of rain, which fell that morning, though rain at that season was most unusual. On the evening of that day they reached some outlying Ibadan farms, and the boys gave a shout of joy and thankfulness, acknowledging now that they had thought, "Truly our last day in the world will be this day." They were soon fast asleep in an empty hut, in which they found shelter for the night. Mr. Hinderer was kept awake by the rustling of a snake in the roof. Early the next morning they entered Ibadan. Truly the Lord had preserved His servant in his going out and in his coming in. When the king of Ijebu heard that he had reached his home in safety, he declared that it was God who had protected the white man, and none but God.

Of all the trials endured by Mrs. Hinderer during her eventful life, none probably surpassed her agony of suspense through the progress of those weeks, in which she had watched in vain, day by day, for the return of her husband. She had heard no tidings of him, beyond such as were conveyed by one little note from himself; telling of the commencement of his illness, while she had sufficient knowledge of the peril to which he was exposed, to justify her utmost fears as to the possible evils which might befall him. When at length she heard the sounds of the horse's feet, and the excited shouts of the people, announcing his arrival, her heart seemed to fail and faint, and consciousness almost forsook her; even the sorrowful exclamations which followed, "He so weak!" "He not able to get off his horse alone!" were heard by her as in a dream; and it was not until he had been tenderly lifted from his horse, and carried into the house by two men, that she awoke to a perception of the blessing which had been granted to her, in his safe return.

Her journal of that day, April 29th, contains these few but expressive words, "My beloved husband came home safely, having escaped many dangers, through God's great mercy. Oh, what thankfulness fills our home again! Her feelings during his absence, and on his arrival, were poured forth more fully in her letters.

"March, 13th. —On the 6th of this month, after having talked and thought long about it, my husband started for Lagos, to try what he could do to get some things up, and to make arrangements with some of the merchants to get cowries. Our two eldest boys only accompanied him, taking a few clothes, and a little food for the road; and he hung a rug across his horse for his bed by night, for three and a half days' journey, and went in faith and courage, trusting in the Good Shepherd of Israel. It is a greater trial to me than usual,

because I can hear nothing of him till he comes back; but I am mercifully kept in peace, and though I have many troubles and cares, especially just now, I feel so helped in my path of duty, and so delivered from fear or apprehension, that I can only adore the goodness and mercy of our faithful covenant-keeping God. In these times of trouble and difficulty, how wonderfully precious is the sense of dwelling under the shadow of the Almighty, hid in His tabernacle, held by His right hand, the very hairs of our head numbered, not even a sparrow falling to the ground without His notice!. Wonderful, wonderful compassion and love to the children of men. Yes, under His banner, we are able to dwell among the 'heathen.' My children, who go home to eat and sleep, come to school daily, and they go on very well. I shall be glad to get them back again; yet it may be of some good, settling their characters a little, showing what is, in them, and also bringing good desires into action; and they may be a little salt, a little leaven, in their own houses. God grant it! The rest are very good and amiable at this time, trying to help me to spare cowries, and of their own accord doing things which at another time they would not have thought of; and they seem to feel, in their own consciences, the reward of doing a good action. I am so thankful to have comfort and refreshment of spirit from them; it is too great a pain when they show a naughty rebellious spirit.

"Some of our converts are very kind in bringing us yams, and even a few cowries now and then, and we are glad to accept the value of two pence; but all this we hope one day well to reward. There are no riches in Africa; slaves and wives make a man great in this country, but the Christians are among the poor generally, for, as in our Saviour's time, 'to the poor the Gospel is preached,' and by them more frequently received. By great care, our little handful of cowries yet stays 'by us, which one thought must be finished long ago. I look upon them as blessed almost as the widow's barrel of meal and cruise of oil, and I do feel sure the daily bread will be given; yet we cannot but feel the trial which this present state of war and confusion brings to us.

"Our work outwardly is not progressing at this time, which is the heaviest part of our trial and discouragement. A blessing is promised to the sowing in tears, but even the sowing is checked by these troubles; but oh, a better time will come; may it be hastened!

"I hear today that there are kidnappers on the road by which my dear husband has to pass when he comes.

May the Lord preserve him, and the two boys with him. Oh, if it were not for the upholding hand, my heart would faint altogether."

"April 12th. *—My dear husband is not yet home, and I can hear nothing of him. On the 28th, a war-party went down, and I fully expected he would be in Ijebu to join that party. When, on their return, they were attacked and had a battle, I was almost thankful he was not there; but he had sent a little note to tell me he was ill, and could not mount his horse. He bid me not to be cast down; in a few days he hoped to be well again. This was written March 23rd, and from that day to this I have not heard a word, only all kinds of horrible reports from that road. But next week the Ibadans are going, it is said, and I write a few letters for the chance of getting them down by them, and am living upon the hope that somehow dear D. will be able to return with them, or that at least I shall hear something of him. Thus I have told you our tale, but I cannot tell you of my real anxiety. Not to know whether he is ill or well, or whether he has fallen into the hands of the Ijebus, or what really detains him, it is more easy to be imagined than for me to describe. I feel worn out with anxiety, apprehensions, and even hopes. The day I get through pretty well, cheered by hope that the end of that day will bring him; but I cannot tell you what it is when the evening closes in, and I have to exist for another day of* *vain hope. I would rather touch on the mercy which is granted from day to day, and from hour to hour, by a merciful Father. He has at times graciously enabled me to endure, as seeing Him who is invisible. One day especially, it had been such a day of hope and expectation, but the evening closed in without its realization; and the disappointment was so great that I went to my room and wept bitterly, mind and body being exhausted, when my eye lighted on the words, 'He shall deliver thee in six troubles, yea, in seven there shall no evil touch thee; in famine He shell redeem thee from death, and in war from the power of the sword.'*

"Oh, how unspeakably comforting were these promises! It was as if the blessed Saviour spoke to me in my ear, not only to my heart, and I had a night of sweet rest and peace, under the shadow of His loving wing. Since then my distress has never been so great; there has been more of entire rest in the sense of His mercy and love, and in the belief that He is a wall of fire round about His people, and that He will do all things well. Yet, as day after day goes on, knowing that nothing over which he had any control could keep my dearest husband from me, I do feel at times indescribably anxious."

Mrs. Hinderer afterwards spoke of the evening referred to in the preceding letter as having been a time of extreme distress; she was overwhelmed by alarm for her husband's safety, and by the sense of her own loneliness, and the weight of her cares. Her sobs were overheard by the children, and they entreated Olubi to go to her and comfort her, but in vain; for he had heard of the designs of the king of Ijebu against Mr. Hinderer, and he was afraid, lest instead of consoling her, he might unawares reveal to her a cause for anxiety beyond her utmost fears. Thus she was left to bear her sorrow alone. She took up her Bible, but with the bitter feeling that even there she would find no comfort. She turned to it again and again, but still with no heart to read it; and it was after this, while it lay open beside her, that her eyes caught the words which brought the message of peace to her troubled soul.

The next letter is in a very different strain. "May 3rd — I begin with the joyful news that my dear husband is safe at home once more in Ibadan. He arrived last Monday, to my great surprise, and very great thankfulness, but he is now in bed, in much suffering and fever. But how he has suffered in Lagos! He received the greatest kindness and careful nursing from our dear missionary friends there, Mr. and Mrs. Maser; he had the benefit also of a good doctor, and then good food. If he had had such an illness here, he must have sunk, and even now it is sad to see him, so broken-down and worn. The people's shouts of joy were speedily checked by their exclamations 'Master sick for true!' He has not only suffered bodily, but has had many anxieties of mind. The journey was one of real danger: the Ijebu king sent word to him in Lagos, and to the Consul, 'if the white man goes back to Ibadan, he will surely take off his head, as he cannot sell a white man.' My husband was of course greatly troubled, and tried to think of many ways to get back again, but at last he felt 'There is no road for me but the Ijebu road, and by that I must go; and after all, my time is in God's hand, and not in the Ijebu king's,' so he started with his two boys, as he went down, and reached here to our intense joy. Oh, I was weary and nearly sick with watching, as I could not tell whether he was living, or had fallen into the cruel hands of our enemies; yet I was greatly comforted by the God of all comfort and consolation. My poor husband was sadly unequal to such a journey; excitement and anxiety lent him strength to get through it, but another illness attacked him immediately, and for thirty days he has been fearfully ill. But he was so thankful to be at home, and I to have him, that we could feel nothing but thankfulness. He is, I trust, in some measure recovering now, but he is sadly broken down, and often thinks his days for work in this climate are numbered. Sometimes we feel we should like to go in search of some health, which is so sadly denied him here; but the door is so entirely shut upon us, that I feel thankful that he is happy in its being his Lord's will that he should remain at his post, and that he has no craving to get away, but hopes for some measure of strength to go on; and it is a comfort to us to feel we are of real use in keeping things together, though he is often so sadly afflicted. I cannot be thankful enough for my own health, and that we are both favoured with good spirits. My work is never done, and the days never long enough, and God's love and mercy are great. He seems so near to us in this time of trouble that we are never cast down for long, and He enables us to rejoice in Him. We never knew so much trouble as now, short of cowries, proper food, especially for D., poor health, separation from all people except in Ibadan, and from regular communication with you all; and yet I do not think we were ever more cheerful or hopeful, because of that blessed hand which is so kindly over us and near to us. He seems to be feeding and caring for us day by day, as clearly as He did Elijah by the ravens. When He giveth peace, who then can make trouble? We know and feel the troubles, crosses, losses, and privations, yet it is with us as the Psalmist says, 'They went through the flood on foot,' yet even 'there did we rejoice in Him.' I know that this great blessing, which can only come from Him, the Author and Giver of all good things will make you happy, and that you will give thanks, as well as pray, for us.

"The affection, attention, and kindness of our people and our native teachers, in this whole time of trouble,

while my husband was away, and now in his sickness, have been really cheering and comforting to us.

"We have not much missionary news to tell, in these sad times of war. All minds are set on its troubles and excitements, but we are thankful our church is but little shaken by it. Very few, not more than four, have been obliged to go into the war, but we have no new convert this year. My dear children have been very good lately, their conduct, habits and desires have much improved. I have laboured to make these children industrious, whether at work or play, for the natural idleness of Africans in general is trying. It often seemed a labour in vain, but I have been really repaid this year. They have known our trouble for want of cowries, and felt our every endeavour that they should not want, and this they did not behold with an African's usual indifference, but have done everything to help me. I have not bought one bit of wood this year, they have gone in the afternoons and fetched of their own accord, which at another time they would not have thought of doing; they wash the clothes for the whole school, and do many such things. It seems a small thing to write, but it has really pleased and comforted me.

"We have the prospect of a plentiful harvest, which begins to be reaped this month, and our burden is lighter respecting our people and teachers, as we made *them all plant for themselves, so they will get corn this month, and yams next, which will feed them for some time. I am thankful to have some flour for my dear husband that was saved from the great losses. He spent eighty pounds in Lagos, and all we have got for it is a little flour. One hundred and twenty dollars of it he gave to a merchant, who promised to give us cowries for it in Ibadan that same month, but he did not appear, and there has been no opportunity to come since. We hope we shall get the dollars, or their value, some day, but it is now we want them. However, patience is the lesson we have to learn at this time. I am afraid the war will yet last awhile, but we cannot tell; we can only live in. faith and hope. It is marvellous how we have been helped hitherto; if we attempt to look at the future, it is painfully dark and anxious. Yet having been so graciously kept and helped to this day, it seems a real sin to dare to fret for to-morrow, and we are enabled generally to cast our burden on our Father in heaven, who so tenderly careth for us."*

Some of the good fruits which ripened in the season of adversity are noted in a letter which appeared in the Church Missionary Intelligencer, for December, 1861.

"It was a time of trial to us all, but I am sure it has been for good. A love has been drawn out from all our people towards their minister, which they were hardly

Trials in Wartime

aware of before. Then it has called forth a spirit of prayer, which must and does bring good. There were many little gatherings together for prayer in the week, but in secret from me, lest I should suspect what they knew of my husband's danger; and now they have found such a full and ready answer to their earnest petitions, which has caused a joy and thankfulness which can be seen even in their faces, and much more in their expressions. There is a good deal of earnest prayer, I believe, called forth in Ibadan in this war-season, the natives regularly hold a daily meeting at seven o'clock, and there is a tone and spirit in it which there was not before. Then there are the Monday evening meetings, and our monthly prayer meetings, and also on a Wednesday afternoon our teachers all meet, with a few of the most earnest and true of the converts, and what gives us comfort and hope of their being heard is that the spirit is so different to what it was at first. At one time it used to be painful to hear certain individuals pray, it was so entirely for what they individually wished; but now it has come round so entirely to 'Do Thou, O Lord, what seemeth to Thee best: make all to work for good to this whole country, and for the coming of Thy kingdom.'''

Of the joy manifested on Mr. Hinderer's safe arrival, she wrote in the same letter: -

"It was a happy day, indeed. The news flew like lightning through the town, and our house was crammed by the converts and others, truly rejoicing. It reached the war-camp also, and the next day we had several messages from the chiefs and others of our friends. There was such an excitement, because all had heard of the king of Ijebus intention to kill him. I was the only one who did not know it." And again: —" One of the men, not yet baptized, though cowries are scarce in his hand, sent us a bag of cowries for joy that his minister had come home again.

"August 1st.—There is a chance again of communicating with dear friends in England. A few days ago we had. the joy of receiving our month's mail, letters written in April, including the beautiful specimen of dear E—'s work. I do enjoy and wonder at it, and if I wonder, what do not my little Africans? They look this way and that way, expressing a doubt that a little girl could do it, and then wondering how many years she was at it, and how it could be kept so clean is a marvel. They think it an utter impossibility that any of them should arrive at such a perfection of needlework. I hope it will make them try to work better than they do, but considering that they are the first children in Ibadan who ever handled a needle, I am fairly satisfied with their progress.

"I have more than enough to do in the common and uncommon business of African life, such work having lately increased for me., in having to look after the growing, as well as the using, of food. We are still in our cowry scarcity, and must be till the war is over; but we are wonderfully helped on by little presents of yams and corn, and by disposing of things. One of the war gentlemen has bought my large cloak, which was given me in England, and which I cannot wear except on the voyage home. I got 20,000 cowries for it (about LI), much less than it is worth, but the cowries are worth more to us now than six times the value at another time, so we laugh and say we have all been living on Iya's cloak. This week we are living on the proceeds of my onion beds: onions are much used here, and I determined by a little care to try and improve on my beds, and I have had fine ones. One of our church people sells them for us. It is wonderful how we get on all this time, and where we should be glad of five bags (about £5), are made content with five strings of cowries (5d). The Lord is, indeed, our Shepherd, and cares for His sheep, feeding us day by day, and giving us peace and quiet and comfort in Himself. On June 30th, we had a very interesting baptism of eighteen children; a few were infants, others our day-school children, and five of my own special charge. I think it was a season of good to us, they appeared solemnized, and expressed very nice and simple desires. The congregation was much impressed, and the eyes of some mothers standing round glistened with a tear-drop. It was an imposing sight in their white garments. Oh, for the heavenly baptism; we do indeed pray for it."

"We have nice weather now, but I take good care not to be too free in the enjoyment of it: the thermometer never below seventy-five in the night, and at eighty in the day. But oh, these people are shivering so, it is painful to see them. Fancy Susanna Olubi sending last night to beg me to lend her a blanket, for she was 'truly dying with cold.' She told me she really suffered from it, though in their rooms a thermometer could soon reach ninety degrees, for they shut up every chink and corner, yet was she sensitive to the present season, called by them cold. Poor things, to get themselves cowries they have lately sold their blankets; every African who can possibly afford it has a blanket, and I have come round to the belief that it is a necessity. As to my children, they would jump at a box of clothing such as is sent to the Red River. I try not to bring them up tenderly in that respect, but our house and the whole town is full of coughing and sneezing just now, as if every one had influenza, and I am obliged to give them fires. For the benefit of our house and clothes we have had fires upstairs, also a few times in an iron stove, and how the children have enjoyed it!"

At the end of the year, in writing to a friend in affliction, she said: -

"December 31st. —Pain, sorrow, suffering is in all the world, not only in this poor Africa no, into the brightest happiest home it enters, but a precious help is always at hand for those whose heart and desires are above, and who look for His glorious appearing, even in this weary sinful earth; at Whose coming, sorrow and sighing shall flee away, and sin, the cause of all. We sometimes seem to have our cup rather full of sorrow, but oh, great mercy-abounds. We are upheld and supported from day to day, and comforted sometimes by what our eyes see, and by what we yet hope for....

"We hope this week to get a few dollars, and our mails of July, August, September, October, and November; this will be a new year's treat to us indeed. In them we shall doubtless have the 'changeful song' of the old church-bells, but it will be sweet to have some communication with dearly-loved ones, and to be brought into union with the civilized and Christian part of the world.

"It is quite possible we may spend Christmas, 1862, in England, but if this war lasts twenty years, we cannot get away! Many people ask, why do we not go down, as we are so sick, etc.? But even if we our two selves could

escape on the road of danger, how can we leave our children, our native teachers and their families, in all this trouble?"

A letter written on New Year's Day, 1862, contained a review of the trials and mercies of the last few months.

"January 18th 1862. — Your kind hearts are, I well know, longing for tidings of us. We are weary for letters also, having had none since those written in June; we cannot help longing for home letters to perfect our New Year's Day, but we hope soon for the great treat of receiving the July, August, September and October mails, and some dollars to buy cowries with, for our daily needs. 1861 has passed away with its cares, sorrows, pains, and though last, not least, its many mercies; 1862 has commenced; we sometimes think it looks sad, dark and heavy, and we fear to tread it, but we know who is the same 'yesterday, today, and for ever,'—through war, sickness, all things, yes, through death itself.

This has been the subject of my husband's address at our early morning service. There is a prayer meeting every morning at six or earlier, but on this morning we have it at seven, to give time for our people who are far off in this large town, and all came so bright and happy, truly enjoying it. They were here long before seven, for kind greetings, good words, and blessings. My thoughts and musings are many on this day, but I must come to our matter-of-fact history, especially as I have only three thin sheets of paper besides this. War, so-called war, is still going on, with very little of real war, but roads shut up, and parties out kidnapping. We, of the mission in Ibadan, are the chief and almost the only sufferers; depending on the coast as we do, and with no road: European necessaries and comforts we have long been without, and cannot have again. My last pair of shoes are on my feet, and my clothes are so worn and so few, that if the war does not end soon, I shall have to come to a country cloth, and roll up like a native. These would be small troubles if we were in health, but my dear husband is a sad sufferer, and every bit of remedy or alleviation, in the, way of medicine, has been for some months entirely finished. I have had two most severe attacks of fever, one in August, and one in November. I only began to get out on Christmas Day, to the great pleasure of our people, who said it would be no Christmas at all if I were not with them. And I have been getting better ever since, creeping up hill, and falling by degrees into all my various duties; but recovering is slow work, when even a cup of tea can now only be taken sparingly, by way of a luxury, as very little is left. Goat meat and yams, though good enough at other times, are not very nourishing or congenial now, and the season is fearfully hot. We do sometimes feel weary and cast down, and then cheer and comfort are given; we are mercifully helped on from day to day.

> "Our Master's work is really going on; faults, infirmities falls, are in our little church, but there are some truly travelling heavenward. November was a month of trial; evil doings among some of the Christians were revealed to us, and they were only sorry because they were found out. Candidates for baptism were unsatisfactory, and we were ready to cry, 'We labour in vain, and spend our strength for nought,' when our merciful Father, instead of punishing us for our murmuring and want of faith, gave us a wonderful sign that He Himself was in our midst, to own, to bless, to save, in the death-bed of one of our converts, whose conduct had been consistent in the few years since he joined himself to those who profess to be on the Lord's side. He left behind him a beautiful testimony to the truth and reality of the religion of the Gospel, calling the converts together, exhorting them, and taking leave thus:
>
> "'For me it is no more hard; through my Saviour the fight is fought; through my Saviour the battle is won; and I now, through His love, go to be with Him; but for you, my brethren, it is hard; you have to go on in an evil world, in a land where the devil is very strong; but

hold on to Jesus, and all shall be well.' The last day he had strong convulsions, but, at intervals, happy looks and words, and when he could no more speak, on Olubi raising him, and asking if all was still well, with a happy smile he pointed his finger upwards, then folded his hands, as if in prayer, on his chest, and left his companions only to say, 'Blessed, indeed blessed, are those who die in the Lord.'

"It was a great comfort to us to have such a witness for the truth, and such a blessed entrance given to the mansions above; a soul safe from sin, Satan, and the evils and cruelties of a heathen land, of which none can have any idea but those who live in it. Thus a new song was put in our mouth, and in the refreshment of that we go on our way.

"There is a great talk that this war will come to an end before many months. We try to hope it, and if so, and we get a road and money and clothes for our children, (of which there are plenty waiting at Abeokuta) and everything to set all going comfortably, we may by the end of this year reach England, which refreshment we much need; but if the war lasts years, we cannot possibly leave, as far as we now see. But we look to Him, and lean upon Him, who is the Physician for body and soul, and who can keep us in sickness or health, in pain, and war, and troubles of various kinds, for His *own good purposes. We pray that we may not be weary or faint, but seek only His will in all things, to go or to stay, patiently and willingly."*

*"**March 3rd.**—On the 13th February came our precious six months' mail and I had fifty letters for my share, and how happy was I. We are most fortunate, in all this war and confusion, that up to this time we have received all our letters from home. There has been much small-pox among our school-children, but all are going on nicely, it is made nothing of in this country; it has been raging in. the town this year, and we know of only one death.*

"On January 15th, one of my little girls fell from some steps outside our house, broke the inner bone of the arm, and dislocated the wrist. We did our best to put it to rights immediately; and because we could not make splints, and did not like to wait, my husband cut up the strong board cover of a German book, and I bandaged it up. My lotion was vinegar and water, and all went on admirably. The third night she was in dreadful pain, but after that she had no more. Those first nights I was very anxious about her, not trusting my surgical doings; so I never left her, and would not let any one touch her but myself for three days. After that, she was very happy in my room, with her picture-book and doll; and when I released the bandages she could again move

her hand quite freely. I was greatly surprised at the perfect cure; all now to be seen is that the wrist is a little thicker than the other. So we have been helped over this trouble.

"I must tell you of a most useful gift. I have three pairs of new shoes! American shoes too, and from further in the interior. An American Baptist missionary sent me them from Oyo; they were his dear wife's, who died four years ago, after having been less than three months in Africa. Thus our daily wants are supplied, even in such a matter as shoes. Ah, how may we

'Praise God for all that is past,
And trust Him for all that's to come.'

"I am in good health, and my dear husband has longer intervals of rest from his trying cough than last year. If this war should end, and we could get a few comforts and necessaries about us, we shall almost forget weakness and want, and might yet be able to go on a year or two longer here. How happy this would make us, to carry on our work under the more favourable circumstances of peace; but we shall be rightly directed to go or stay, I truly believe; such goodness, such help, has mercifully been given us. The war has been a sad hindrance to us in many a way; preventing the completion of the second station in this town, where

Mr. Jeffries is residing, and also the making of a third station, where a native teacher lives. We have managed to build a little house for him and his family lately; he was only in a borrowed room in a large compound, and that was not so pleasant; but as we and he have all helped, we made it for very few cowries, and it will be well worth what it has cost, even if we have to make the proper place next year. We sadly want the opening of the roads which the end of this war will bring; my children are so out of clothes, such a shabby little party they are, and there are so many nice boxes waiting for us, clothes, books, and plates, &c.; when I think of it all, I am sure we shall not have time to go home. I am nicely well, if only my dear husband should get as well! But all will be rightly, wisely, kindly ordered for us. Oh, how sweet it is to feel that every step is ordered for us, if we only seek grace to walk in it."

There appeared to be good grounds for hope that peace would be concluded after the taking of Ijaye, which occurred in March, 1862, bringing such utter destruction upon the place, that, within a year, nothing but desolate and overgrown ruins remained to mark the spot where a flourishing town, containing upwards of sixty thousand inhabitants, had so lately stood. But, in the long contest, all the surrounding tribes had become involved in disputes with one another, some taking the part of Ibadan, and others that of Ijaye. The seat of war was eventually transferred to the Ijebu territory, which extended over the greater part of the country between Ibadan and the coast. The enemies of Ibadan well knew that to isolate 'would be to weaken it, and that to cut off its communication with Lagos, the market from which its supplies of ammunition were procured, might issue in its destruction. With this view, in fact, hostilities were still carried on with more or less of activity, and with varying success.

The effect of this new turn of affairs upon Mr. and Mrs. Hinderer was to increase the difficulties of their situation. To the number for whom it was necessary to provide was now added Mr. Roper, who had been sent out by the Church Missionary Society, and was captured in the taking of Ijaye. Mr. Jeffries, about the same time, returned to the mission-house to be nursed through a severe attack of fever. This fresh anxiety, and the increased weight of daily care, pressed heavily upon Mrs. Hinderer when she wrote again

> *"May 20th. —We are living just as we can, others helping us, out of their poverty. We get a yam here, and a yam there, and a little corn in the same manner. One of our converts yesterday lent us some cowries, which must, by pinching, last us three or four weeks, if possible; he had to borrow them from a heathen friend, before he could lend them to us. Dearest friends, you*

will think of us, and long to help us, but there is nothing left for your kind hearts to do for us, but to pray."

The next letter was more cheerful: -

*"**August l5th.** — I have a corner in the piazza, which I call my study. it is a funny little place, but very pleasant to me. Here I read and write, and receive any favoured visitors. Where there is wall, it is washed with a kind of red earth, but where it is of boards, they are very rough, and overlap one another. I took it into my head a little while ago to ornament it, for an amusement, and to enjoy it afterwards; so out of an old London Newspaper I have got some pretty English scenes, domestic groups, children, and animals, all of which are an immense delight to my little and big children, and form a never-ending subject of conversation when they are admitted there."*

This last extract was from a letter written in readiness for the earliest opportunity of sending down to the coast, which occurred towards the end of September. With it Mrs. Hinderer despatched another letter, telling that they were cheered again by a prospect of peace; telling also of the death of their young fellow-labourer, Mr. Jeffries. Worn out with sickness and privations, he slept in peace on the 22nd of September. "The next morning before five," wrote Mrs. Hinderer, "we committed all that remained of him to the grave, by lamp-light, in the blessed hope of everlasting life."

From that time Mr. Roper took charge of the Ogunpa station of the Ibadan mission, until his return to England in 1865. In the midst of so many and varied trials, it is pleasant to read of literary occupations beguiling the time, and turning it to account

> *"November 17th. — My husband is much interested in translating the 'Pilgrim's Progress.' We indulge in the hope of taking it home to print before long, and we think it will be particularly interesting and useful to our Africans. This work has been a great pleasure to him, and helps to reconcile him to the quiet life he has been obliged to lead of late. Through God's mercy, I do not think I have had even a day's ailing since last November. Pray for us, and give thanks also, for God's mercy endureth for ever."*

The hope of peace was much diminished in December, and the perplexities of daily life were on the increase. Happily faith could still discern and trust the mercy of God.

> *"December 9th — We and our people have sold everything which we can turn into money, and the thought and burden of all that is upon us is getting*

almost more than we can bear. A few days ago I did get cast down, but our gracious God was merciful to us, as He ever is; our troubles are many, but His support is mighty. My dear husband's state is most serious; some nights ago he had hours of fearful coughing, and every moment seemed as if it might be his last; and we have not the least, the simplest, remedy to relieve him. He was much exhausted for two or three days, and one of our people, who could ill afford it, brought us a bag of cowries (about one pound's worth), and told us to take it and use it freely to buy meat and more strengthening things than beans, &c., which we are generally content with. That bag of cowries, which was to have been for our comfort, and especially for my poor husband, we had to give up, to rescue the daughter of the scripture-reader of Awaye from being sold. [She had been captured by the Ibadan people.] I nearly cried, yet we were thankful we had it, and could thus rescue the poor girl; and so gracious, and merciful, and faithful has our God been, that we have, after all, been living better than for some time past. We sold a counterpane, and a few yards of damask which had been overlooked by us; so that we indulge every now and then in one hundred cowries' worth of meat (about one pennyworth), and such a morsel seems like a little feast to us in these days. I have been buying to-day ten baskets of corn, and hope to buy five more to-morrow, for our children

Trials in Wartime

especially; and I was sadly afraid I could not even buy one basket in store this season; and so, time after time, is our want of faith put to shame, and also our faith revived and strengthened. Those baskets of corn are such a delightful sight to me this evening that I can scarcely help running just to take a look at them, and be thankful. "I have made out an almanac, by the help of the Prayer-book; I shall gladly throw it away if the proper ones reach us by some good chance.

"This letter, if it reaches you, will have gone from here to Lagos such a roundabout way, twenty-five days' journey at least, instead of three; but these people are inveterate traders and walkers; where they can buy and sell, there is not a distance which will prevent their going."

The last days of 1862 were brightened by a visit from Captain J. P. L. Davis and the Rev. J. A. Lamb, from Lagos, and the Rev. G. F. Bühler, from Abeokuta. They had made their way to Ibadan with much difficulty, in the hope of being able to promote the restoration of peace, and at least to relieve the pressing necessities of the missionaries. But their negotiations were unsuccessful, and there was a long pause between the report of this generous though unavailing effort for their relief, and the next tidings of Mr. and Mrs. Hinderer which reached their anxious friends in England. When at length they wrote, it was only to tell of renewed disappointment. Who can wonder that they sometimes experienced the truth of the words of wisdom, "Hope deferred maketh the heart sick!"

During the next two years several attempts were made by the missionary brethren at Abeokuta and Lagos to send succour and relief to them, but with little or no success. Letters sometimes passed safely to or from the coast, but other supplies were almost always intercepted. On one occasion Mr. and Mrs. Hinderer were tantalized by a handful of tea being brought in to them from the bush, telling a tale of help which had travelled some distance, but had failed at last to reach them. The Governor of Lagos, Captain Glover, R.N., was unwearied in his efforts to relieve them, and three times was on the point of penetrating to Ibadan himself; but he was absolutely refused permission to pass through the Ijebu country.

The utter isolation in which Mr. and Mrs. Hinderer were thus left was a great aggravation of their trial through this prolonged affliction. But their hearts were stayed on God; His presence cheered their saddest days, and through His grace their faith failed not.

Few and scanty were the letters of 1863 and 1864. There was no heart to write, till the rare opportunity of sending off letters actually arrived, and then there was but time for few and hurried words; or, if a letter was written in anticipation of some happy chance, there might be long delay before it could be despatched, and then only by circuitous routes and uncertain means. Many letters, in fact, were lost during that period, while others did not reach their destination till long after they were due. One, for example, dated January 1864, was not received in England until the following October. Of direct missionary work there was little to relate. The war proved a hindrance to each new scheme devised for assembling and instructing the people. Preaching in the streets was impracticable. Of his experience in visiting from house to house Mr. Hinderer wrote:

> *"The first word may be the Gospel, but the second or third is sure to have to turn to this all-absorbing war." A new week-day service, in a distant part of the town, was tried, but shortly afterwards a press-gang system was brought into action, and the people feared to show themselves. The plan of visiting and assembling the people in farms outside the town was, for the same reason, equally fruitless. Little remained to be done except to carry on the regular Sunday and weekday services."*

Mr. Hinderer gladly turned the leisure time thus forced upon him to profit for his people, by continuing his translations, until another difficulty, resulting from the war, brought this good work to an end. Paper became so scarce that he almost grudged the use of a scrap for making notes for his sermons. His letters were written on paper cut out of old blank books, partly eaten by white ants, and even the fly-leaves of printed books were soon exhausted.

Meanwhile the schoolwork could not be carried on satisfactorily, the children being in some measure scattered abroad; and there was but a scanty supply of books and school-materials for the use of those who were able to attend. The slates were broken, and the little girls could learn no more sewing, for the contents of the workbox were at last reduced to two rusty needles, and half a bail of cotton, too precious to be used by any one except "Iya" herself

These details, trifling in themselves, may yet serve the purpose of filling up the picture of this life of privation, and almost of destitution. A few further particulars will be found in the following letters, which show also the unfailing patience and cheerful submission of spirit with which these varied and perplexing difficulties were met.

"March 16th, 1863. —We live a day at a time; we eat today, and trust for to-morrow. The prayer, 'Give us this day our daily bread,' is not unanswered. All are busy planting their farms, and, thank God! There is a good prospect of plenty of food; rains are beginning,

and corn already, five days after planting, shoots up, and in June we shall be eating it. We feel your prayers are answered every day on our behalf, in the care and love and presence and comfort given. We are not yet delivered, but kept and even comforted in our trial in a land of captivity."

"**September 29th.** —In August we had the joy of receiving precious packets of letters, and with them dollars and calico, and things to sell for cowries, and a little tea, and other comforts for ourselves. Food too is plentiful, and very cheap, and cowries are much more in circulation than last year, so We feel quite rich again, and I hope truly thankful. It is an utter impossibility for us to get away till this war is ended, and I see no chance of that now; but being so mercifully helped again, I hope we are enabled to bear our trials bettor, and are more cheerful and happy than we were inclined to be a year ago; and oh, it is such a comfort, we are sent here, put here. We met with some lines by Trench, on Sunday evening, which were quite refreshing; they begin thus: —

'Thou cam'st not to thy place by accident,

It is the very place God meant for thee, And shoiild'st thou here small scope for action see, Do not for this give room to discontent.'

"And so here we are. The Lord give us to feel the privilege of doing or suffering His holy will. Six years, next month, since we left England this last time. I wonder how many more it may be before we see it again."

*"**March 22nd, 1864.** —I have a new occupation now. About seven weeks ago a little babe of about six months was put out by a brook in some glass; whether because it is a slave, or its mother died, or an idol priest ordered it, we have no idea. No one in the whole town would dare to take it, and it remained there three nights and days, in the night shrieking bitterly (which effectually frightened the wild beasts away), in the day comforted by every mother who passed by giving it suck. As soon as we heard of it, we took it, and are bringing it up by hand. It has been quite ill from all the changes, and the night dew giving it cough, so that our poor little baby gives us much trouble and anxiety. As she will only take to myself and my eldest girl, she fills my hands extremely. She is very passionate, but when better, she can laugh with us, and seems clinging. We love her very much. We call her 'Eyila,' which means 'this has escaped,' or 'is saved.'*

"Oh, dearest friends, this sad war will not let us meet I did hope by this spring-time to be in your midst; but our Father knows where we are, and why; I am thankful

for the gift of a more reconciled spirit, submissive to all, feeling that His hand, His providence, is at work, though we may seem in the dark sometimes, and tried, and tossed, and discouraged.'

"**November 18th** — *About five weeks since I had such an attack of fever as I should have thought only a new-comer could have had, and such as I have not had for some years. I thought at one time I was to have a short journey home, the gates of which, through the love and mercy of Jesus, no one could shut. I wonder that I should have liked coming back to the storms and sorrows of life, but I did like the thought of working in better times in this country, and my dear husband seemed to want me, said a few people and children in Ibadan; and I should like to reach England once more first, and see dear friends and faces, and get refreshed in body and soul, and then to come back to work with fresh heart and zeal. We do get so cast down at times, we are so let and hindered in our work, our hearts faint, and our hands hang down. No materials for our schools, not even a Bible for each child, and we have such hard work and toil in only just holding things together; yet again we are comforted in the thought that we are not altogether useless, and we are enabled in the dark hour to stay ourselves upon our God, and receive innumerable helps and comforts from Him, our faithful covenant-keeping God. And we are very cheerful too,* though sorrowful sometimes. My little black boys and girls are doing well on the whole, and my blackest of black babies is very flourishing, and a real pleasure to us, always ready to come to Iya.' She can call me 'Iye.' now, though she makes no farther progress in talking, and none in walking, her feet are so tiny. She could not understand my being ill, and when I could not take her, she would sit on my bed and play, and if I say, 'Kiss Iya' she throws her pretty little arms round me, and kisses me, and laughs, as much amused."

Soon after the close of another year of trial, she wrote as follows

"January 14th, 1865. — *Because there is only time to write a scrap, and my heart longs to send you a letter, I am almost tempted to leave it for a better opportunity, but I do not like that either; so I send just what I can, and not what I would. Just now we hear of a person starting in an hour for Lagos, how or where we cannot tell, and I sit down for many such like scraps to let our dear and anxious friends hear of us, though we have no better news. We are both very poorly, so exhausted by the long stay, and we cannot get out till war is done; and it is such a sickly, dry season; we feel sometimes so weak in the morning, after a night of fever, that we say, 'Well, this day we must do nothing, but just try to keep ourselves alive,' but the day brings its work, and with it* *its cheer sometimes, as well as its care, and we rejoice in the evening coolness. We have had close and private examination and conversation with our dear people, at the close of 1864, and are much cheered and comforted, though we add none to our numbers. Our young men are truly hopeful, we see much of a real work of grace in their hearts."*

Those who look back along the course of these five years of native warfare, with all the consequences which ensued to the European missionaries, cannot but admire their faith and comparative cheerfulness, and adore the goodness of God who gave them all their strength by the continual presence and help of His upholding and sanctifying Spirit. Under the combined influences of a pestilential climate, extreme privation, and anxiety of mind, their health was constantly wasting and wearing out, and with it was declining the power of sustaining the work of Christ in Ibadan. But it is seen throughout, that God cares for His children as a gracious Father, and comforts them when they are cast down. To this alone is to be attributed that prevalent submission and trust which pervade this otherwise sad history of painful experience.

Rustic Bridge in the Ijebu Country

CHAPTER VII

Second Visit to England
Last Years in Ibadan

"Look not behind; seek to recall no more
The long dark shadow of past grief and fear,
Look not beyond, thou canst not see the shore
Now through the glooms yet may the port be near.
Let vain regrets and sad forebodings cease,
He will give strength and peace."

DELIVERANCE BY THE BRAVE

AN UNEXPECTED OPPORTUNITY OF deliverance out of Ibadan was presented to the missionaries in the month of April 1865. Their kind friend, the Governor of Lagos, had met his heart on devising some plan for their rescue, and he found trustworthy volunteer in Captain Maxwell, who undertook the charge of the expedition. Accordingly, in company with a few chosen men, and avoiding the ordinary route, this brave young officer cut a new pathway through the bush, and after a tedious journey arrived one night at the mission-house at Ibadan, with supplies of food, and a hammock, for the conveyance of Mrs. Hinderer. He urged the necessity of starting on the return journey the next morning at daybreak, before the enemy could discover the new track. There was little time for thought or preparation. Prompt decision and action were necessary. It was agreed that the mission could not be left to itself at a moment's notice, and that Mr. Hinderer must therefore remain at his post for the present; but it was no less clearly Mrs. Hinderer's duty to make use of the means of escape thus mercifully brought within her reach, and the trial of parting thus suddenly from her husband was softened by the hope that he would shortly be able to rejoin her.

It was now ten o'clock, and the travellers were to be on their way at five in the morning. Mrs. Hinderer spent the night in preparing for her journey to the coast and for the voyage to England, and in giving directions for the comfort of her household. The children were not told that their "Iya" was to be taken from them, lest their grief should add to her distress, and unfit her for the exertions which must be made in those few precious hours. But Konigbagbe learned how matters stood, and her anxiety on account of her beloved mistress was not pacified until she had obtained permission to accompany her to Lagos. In another hour she appeared, equipped for the journey, with her bundle on her head. The morning came, and the

Second Visit to England. Final Years in Ibadan

children awoke to learn the sorrow and loss which awaited them. Many bitter tears were shed, when Mrs. Hinderer entered her hammock, and the little band of travellers set forth. By forced marches they accomplished a six days' circuitous journey in a little more than three, notwithstanding the difficulties and perils to which they were exposed. The roughness of the path often made it necessary for Mrs. Hinderer to walk for a considerable distance; in some parts, as they advanced, they found the track already overgrown, and scarcely to be distinguished; and at times they passed within hearing of the voices of the enemy. On the third morning, having reason to fear that they were pursued, they left an untouched meal, and marched on for hours in hunger and unbroken silence. On the fourth day they entered Lagos, worn and weary, but with a deep sense of the mercies which they had received in the protecting care of God.

The poor girl Konigbagbe, unused to such travelling, had suffered dreadfully by the way, her feet were torn and swollen; but she had carefully concealed her sufferings from her mistress, and felt that she was being amply repaid by being permitted to minister to her to the last, and having seen her embark on board the next steamer for England, she returned to Ibadan.

SAFE ARRIVAL IN ENGLAND

Mrs. Hinderer arrived at Liverpool on the 13th of May. Two months later, Mr. Hinderer, having arranged matters in some measure to his satisfaction at Ibadan, was also enabled to return to England, leaving the mission under the care of Mr. and Mrs. Smith, missionaries from Badagry.

After staying some time in London, for communication with the Church Missionary Society, and for the transaction of business connected with the mission, they spent the autumn at Halesowen, and made visits in other places, increasing an interest in their work wherever they went. At this time Mr. Hinderer was much occupied in completing his translation of the Pilgrim's Progress, and preparing a book of hymns in the Yoruba language, many of them original, and the rest translated from the English. Under medical advice, required by Mr. Hinderer's state of health, they passed the winter in the south of England, and the first two months of 1866 found them at Dawlish, where they experienced much kindness, formed new friendships, and received a lasting memorial of the interest they had excited, by the gift of a harmonium for the church at Ibadan, and of clothing and other presents for the children. Early in the spring they quitted Dawlish, and having visited friends at Bedford, and in various parts of Norfolk, rested for a while at

Second Visit to England. Final Years in Ibadan

Lowestoft. The home in that town, which had endeared it to Mrs. Hinderer, had long since been broken up; and full as the place was of associations both sacred and happy; there was also a mournful consciousness that its strongest attractions had passed away. The news of Mr. Cunningham's death had reached her in Ibadan in 1863, but no reference to that event has been found in any of the letters available for this memoir, nor is any help supplied by her journal, in which she had ceased to make any entries soon after the commencement of the native war. But her latest letters to him had abounded in expressions of sympathy, on account of his failing health and his consequent withdrawal in great measure from the ministerial work which was so dear to his heart; and this volume contains abundant testimony to the warmth of her gratitude and love to teat invaluable friend, and to her appreciation of his noble and holy character.

During their stay in England, Mr. and Mrs. Hinderer frequently received letters from their home in Africa. The first which reached them after Mr. Hinderer's return, brought tidings of the death of Arubo, whom eleven years before they had rescued from starvation, and whom they had brought up in the mission-school; and while at Lowestoft they heard that another lamb had been taken from their little flock to the fold of the Good Shepherd, little Eyila, whom, from the time Mrs. Hinderer had received her as a baby, she had nurtured and cherished with a mother's love. The news of her death brought with it the deepest sorrow. Opening her heart to a friend, she exclaimed: -

"May 15th. — *My sweet, my darling Eyila, has left earth and gone to her Saviour in heaven. She died of smallpox, March 14th. Her last words to her faithful nurse, Abayomi, were, 'Come, let us go home, I am going home, I am going home, but too much thorn in the road, too much thorn.' Sweet little babe, the thorns are passed, and she is at rest and peace with Jesus, who will show me my babe again, my dear Eyila. But I do feel it exceedingly, and so does my husband. We came here to this dear old place last Thursday, and I feel it so sad, so empty, so strange; and now that my little babe is gone, my African home will seem so bereft. Arubo gone, and dear Eyila. 'How grows in Paradise our store!' One of the children wrote me word, 'Baby used to sing so sweetly, "Ogini fun Baba," - the "Gloria Patri' and one day sang part of it when she was ill, and could not get further.'"*

Mrs. Hinderer had parted with this much-loved child just twelve months before, not knowing that she then looked upon her for the last time. The little one could not understand her absence at first, and on the morning after her departure came joyfully into Mr. Hinderer's room, thinking her Iya would be waiting to give her the usual greeting; but when her bright eyes looked for her in vain, she climbed on Mr. Hinderer's knee, and throwing her arms round his neck, sobbed convulsively. She could only explain her grief by leading him to the door, to make another vain search for her Iya on the road by which she had seen her set out. They were to meet again, not on earth but in their Father's courts.

Mrs. Hinderer wrote more calmly,

May 29th: - *"I think much of my little Eyila, and the blank of not meeting her when I get back to Africa but it is indeed well for her, and though I shall sadly miss her, I can be truly thankful she should escape all the sorrows, cares, and sins of life."*

WITH FAMILY IN GERMANY

In June, Mr. and Mrs. Hinderer went to Wurtemberg to visit their relations, and afterwards stayed a month at Heiden, a little village in a beautiful situation overlooking the Lake of Constance. In September they were again in London, where a few weeks were fully occupied in preparation for their return to Africa.

The last Sunday in England, the 20th of October, was spent at Halesowen Rectory. The eagerness and joy with which they were looking forward to a return to their work was observed by all as mo3t remarkable, after the privations and sufferings they bad endured during the years of their seclusion in Ibadan. But to the work of Christ in that town they had given their hearts, and devoted their lives; and now they were animated by the hope of resuming it with renewed strength, and with fresh zeal and vigour of purpose. On that Sunday, Mrs. Hinderer gave a short farewell address to the children in the school, ending by requesting them to do for her what St. Paul asked of the Corinthians, "Ye also helping together by prayer for us

FAITHFUL RETURN TO AFRICA

On the 24th of October they set sail for Africa, in the "*Calabar*," and after an unusually quick passage, arrived at Lagos on the 19th of November. The following letter gives an account of the voyage, and of their reception in Ibadan, which they reached by the road through the Ijebu country, which was open to them through the influence of the Governor of Lagos: -

Anna's letter ...

"*Dec. 29th. — We had a very favoured voyage, and reached Lagos on the 19TH. I had a good share of seasickness, but was not so thoroughly ill as before. It was very sweet to think of you all praying for us, and our gracious God heard and answered. We rested a*

Second Visit to England. Final Years in Ibadan

short time there, and then prepared our things for the interior. About forty Ibadan people came to carry them for us. We slept one night at Ikorodu, and then began our three days' land journey, which was very well accomplished, except that on the second day my husband had an attack of fever, and being worse the next day, was obliged to rest many times, which made us arrive late in Ibadan, to the disappointment of a great many. All the church people had come out some miles on the road, and the children could not eat for excitement. Late as we were, some of them waited, and the shouts and screams, who can describe? As we neared our dwelling, the children burst forth in singing, 'How beautiful upon the mountains;' and as we went up the steps of our house, they sang, 'Welcome home.' It was very pretty of them. Our house was filled for days. I had much to do, for our things had got wet, having been carried up in baskets. In our absence, the white ants took a fancy to our bedroom, and I did not know it. One portmanteau had been covered with tarpaulin, so I knew that it could not be wet, and did not mean to open it for some time, but wanting something out of it, after three days I opened it, and oh, the dismay! You can hardly imagine the scene, my dresses were completely eaten through, and the linen also."

On Thursday, December 27th, Mr. and Mrs. Hinderer gave a feast and presents to the school children, and after morning service, on the first day of the New Year; they provided dinner for the converts.

MORE TRIALS FROM FEVER

The opening of the year 1867 found Mrs. Hinderer already suffering from fever, but at the close of the month she was able to write to friends in England.

"Jan. 30th. —I am but slowly recovering from such a severe attack as I hardly ever experienced. People try to encourage me by saying, having had this, I may expect unusual health. It has been a great trial and disappointment to be so very ill, and still to remain so weak; there seems so much to be done, which only I can do. It was a great comfort to have my husband recovered before my illness began; his hands are more than full, with five classes in a week, beside services, but he is happy if only strength may be given.

"I miss my Konigbagbe sadly; she has a little ugly baby, but as good-tempered as herself and she and her husband go on very well. Mrs. Olubi has her hands full with her four children, and assisting me in the sewing-school. They are all delighted at having us back."

Second Visit to England. Final Years in Ibadan

A letter from Mr. Hinderer, written about this time, introduces the story of a child to whom frequent reference will be found in subsequent quotations, but of whom these particulars are not given in Mrs. Hinderer's own letters.

His letter is dated: -

"Jan. 31st. — My dear wife probably has mentioned the baptism of eighteen adults, three lads, and four children. Most of them have rejoiced my heart on examining them, especially a boy of about eight years of age, whom I wanted to wait till he was a little older, fearing that he was too young to make up his mind as to whom lie would serve. Rut he went to his guardian, a relation of his, who redeemed him from slavery, and is himself a convert, saying, 'You must take me to the 'white man, and beg for me, and tell him I am not too young to serve God; I will not serve the devil; Jesus I want to follow, and I want to be baptized now.' He told his grandmother of his intention, the poor old woman was very angry; whereupon he told her all he knew about Jesus, how He suffered and died for us. The woman was not to be moved. The boy burst out crying, and said, 'How can it be possible for people to hear such good words and not to believe?' Who shall hinder that such should not be baptized? He was baptized by the name of Samuel, which he himself chose."

In the following letters, Mrs. Hinderer continues the story of their life, with its numerous occupations and interests, and gives instances of the various ways in which the Word of God was heard and received by many, who bore witness to the truth of it in their dying hours.

"*Feb. 21st.* —*Thank God, I am now getting into work again. Three of the boys are learning the harmonium; it is a work of patience, in a hot country, only to have to hear it. I have Akielle and Oyebode every morning for lessons, general history, geography, Nicholls' Help, &c., the girls for sewing from twelve to two o'clock, and I am now forming a class of women who live near us, to teach them to sew, once a week. These are some of the regular doings, and the irregular may be called legion; doctoring, mending, housekeeping, receiving visitors. Ogunyomi I use in the house; her temper is her great trial, but we get on, and she has love in her heart which helps through. I give her reading and writing lessons every evening, except Monday and Saturday, with two or three other girls. Olubi has been to Abeokuta, as his mother was in her dying illness. He had the satisfaction of attending and comforting her in her last days upon earth, and seeing her depart in peace, in full faith and trust in her Lord and Saviour.*

"Poor Arubo, they say, when he had seen the last of me, burst into floods of tears, and bye and bye exclaimed, 'I shall never see Iya in Ibadan again;' but I think he did not expect us to return, on account of the great trials we had through the war. We have a good many growing up around us now, and we have many an anxiety concerning them. However, we must work on, waiting for fruit."

"**April 2nd,.** — We have had such a month of awful sickness in the town, death in every house, small-pox quite a pestilence, and no rain. The heat is intense, it is a weariness to look day by day at the cloudless sky, but we had one shower the night before last, which, I trust, will do some good, yet we thirst for more. Two white head-ties, from Dawlish, adorned the heads of two young brides yesterday. Susanna Abayomi was one, the girl who minded my dear little Eyila, so well.

"You might almost hear a pin drop to-day, the town is so quiet. It is the second burial for Bashorun [the head chief] us horse is to be killed on his grave; no market is allowed. At twelve o'clock feasting is to begin, and thousands will go to it. They may steal and do, as they like today without being punished, in honour of Bashorun. Such are their schemes to bury the thought of death; they eat, drink, and fire guns, that death may *not be what it really is after all — a fear and terror to them."*

"April 30th. —' *The Pilgrim's Progress is becoming much appreciated by our people. My class of women on Sunday afternoons are greedy for it; we each read a paragraph, and talk about it; and on the Sunday evenings, after a little Scripture-repeating, and hymn-singing, I read it with my girls, and D. with the boys; they are perfectly charmed. Ogunyomi is suffering fearfully from a whitlow: she said if we could always read Pilgrim she might forget the pain. Their open mouths and exclamations, when the full meaning of something in it presents itself vividly before them, are most entertaining. Many are preparing their money to buy it, and then it will go to farms and houses, and be quite the family book, but it is a little expensive for them; three shillings, or four thousand cowries! and food is very dear, from a scarcity of rain last year, and none yet this year. All the newly-planted corn is dried up, and the yams in a poor condition."*

PAGAN FESTIVALS

"June 20th. — *Our whole town is in an uproar, for seven days making the annual feast for Egungun, so-called spirits from the other world. The eating and* *drinking, dancing, and drumming, are awful. Next will come the worship of the god of the farms, when all will eat new yams; after which we have peaceful nights again for months. In the midst of all this noise and confusion, these dark and evil doings.*

OGUNYOMI'S MOTHER SLEEPS IN JESUS

"*Our dear Lucy Fagbeade, Ogunyomi's mother, fell asleep in Jesus. She was a very sincere woman, who extremely disliked much talking and noise about things in religion. On the third day before her death, some of the Christians gathered round her, and asked what she saw. Poor Lucy was vexed, and spoke roughly, 'I see nothing,' and again, 'I shall see when I have done with earth, and not till then.' Afterwards, when alone with me, she said, 'Oh, Iya, I have no faith in what people say they can see, all my hope is in the blood of Jesus to wash me clean; I can only go behind Jesus, and beg Him to beg God for me,' and she covered her face with her hands, as if she would hide herself then and there. She was conscious to the last minute; within the last quarter of an hour, with great difficulty of speech and breathing, taking my hand, and smiling, she said, 'Iya, thank you, thank you; it is hard, but I am not alone;' and pointed upwards. Tier dear minister's visits to her room were always pleasant to her, and often, in the* night, she would ask for a short prayer, from her husband or daughter; and in suffering, a few verses from 'God's Book' always comforted and soothed her. Eleven years ago we redeemed her from slavery, when she was apparently sick unto death, that her child might nurse her, and soothe her dying hours; and God has spared her eleven years, and redeemed her soul by the precious blood of Christ, and has now taken her to dwell with Him forever. God be praised!

"I have little Bertha Olubi to live with me for the present. I like a little child about the house, it is so cheerful, and she is happy enough and troublesome enough too sometimes. I always think that the trouble of a child is rather good for my nature and disposition. Her little woolly head is the most difficult to keep neat. Their heads, when their mothers cannot do them, are done by regular hairplaiters in the town, which has to last some weeks without being undone; which plan Jib not approve, so I make my girls plait their hair once a week. I do Bertha's after a fashion of my own. You must use a great wooden comb, and drag it through the hair straight upwards! Then I part it down the middle, and three or four places on each side, and then take each little tuft, and drag and plait it as tight as possible, and it hangs down in many short little plaited tails. It would hurt you and me, but their hard heads are used to it, and Bertha often falls asleep while I am doing it!

SPREAD OF CHRISTIANITY

"Many strangers come to church on Sunday, to see if it is true that many of their townspeople have joined the Christian religion. A few Sunday's ago seven persons were baptised. In one we were particularly interested; a blacksmith, who seems to have partaken of the true change, and on whom the Spirit of Life has breathed. Okusehinde, one of our scripture readers, was the means of bringing him into the blessed fold. We have ninety-six communicants; at our last, eighty-eight were pre-. sent, and those absent were ill, or in other towns. So we have much to make us hope, but we are longing to see new ones coming forward to enlist on the Lord's side."

The following account of "A Sunday in Africa" was written by Mrs. Hinderer for the Church Sunday School Magazine: -

"Though our house and church are surrounded by heathen neighbours, some friendly to us, and some not, I always feel there is a good deal of respect shown to us and our day, by these same heathen people. We are very rarely annoyed by any one coming to offer anything to sell on that day; there is far less noise around us than on other days. Some very near to us have given up, of their own accord, using their cloth-dyeing *establishments, and little markets, going to other occupations further aft; and this not from any request on our part, for we did not feel we had the least right to ask it of them. Our quiet orderly services seem of themselves to procure respect—so different from anything of their own, whether heathen or Mohammedan.*

"Our church is very simple, but quite neat, 70 feet by 80, its hard, stony, mud walls straight and smooth, coloured with a pale red wash; containing benches fastened in the ground, neat communion-table, rails, and pulpit, cut and manufactured by Africans, under our superintendence. We also moulded a very pretty font, forming it as well and as neatly as we could with wet clay; we painted it white.

"How very cheering is the sound of our first bell, at half-past eight on Sunday morning, rung so cheerfully and heartily by one of our little African boys! The bell is on the outside of the church at one end, with a neat little roof of boards over it, to protect it from the hot sun and heavy rains; this also takes off the barn-like look our church might otherwise have from its thatched roof. We have plenty of air and light, many windows without glass; the shutters always open, only closed at night and in heavy rains. A heavy tornado does trouble us sometimes; the storm is so furious that prayer or

Second Visit to England. Final Years in Ibadan

preaching has to cease for about a quarter of an hour, as there would be no possibility of a word being heard.

"The first bell rings at half-past eight: from then till a few minutes before nine, when the second bell rings, we can look out and see our people coming, with their nice English bags of coloured print, or their own grass bags, on their heads, containing their books; some with only the Primer, others more advanced in the new art of reading, with various portions of the Word of God; St. Luke, the Psalms, Proverbs, and Genesis, being among the great favourites. Now the whole of the New Testament is complete, and bound in one volume, and our people will, I know, be much delighted with such a volume. We see the people hastening towards us as nine o'clock approaches, for the one hour for school is too precious to be wasted by being five minutes too late. The school consists of men and women, who are most anxiously and diligently reading, and learning to read; men on one side the church, and women on the other. We have to use our more advanced day-scholars as teachers for some classes, and it is very pretty to see the thankfulness and attention of these men and women, some with grey hairs, to their young teachers, and they often bring them presents of honey or fruit, to tempt these children to go on teaching them when the school is over. We have about eight or nine classes of different stages; and a very interesting assembly, at the bottom of

the church, of those who cannot learn to read. We gather these together, and first tell them a short simple Bible story, and let them tell it us again, to see that they remember it, and take it in. Then we teach them a text, or a verse of a hymn, and the last quarter of an hour is always given in all the classes to teaching by repetition some catechism, and sometimes for change we have the whole school together to go over the Creed, the Lord's Prayer, and the Ten Commandments, to make sure they are not forgotten. Oh, what bright, eager, earnest, black, shining faces we have in our African Sunday school!

"*At ten o'clock we have to leave off, to give them opportunity to make ready for service at half-past ten; for the babies come as well as the mothers, and they are allowed the freedom of creeping about, or being nursed by others not much bigger than them-solves, during school-time; but for church they must be packed on their mothers' backs to go to sleep. In that half hour, many of the women and most of the men gather in groups, talking over what they have been reading, or making enquiries and remarks on some things which have struck them in their reading by themselves in their own houses, in the course of the week.*

Second Visit to England. Final Years in Ibadan

Anna's letter...

"At half-past ten service commences; our singing is hearty, our responses very hearty, and the attention to the sermon is also gratifying. We are out by twelve. Our town being so large, many members of our congregation come a distance of between two or three miles; so they bring their dinners with them, spread their mats in our verandahs, take their meal and a little sleep, and a great deal of conversation. At three precisely we meet again for an hour's school, the proceedings much the same as in the morning, except that the last quarter of an hour is generally given to questioning them on the sermon, which shakes up their attention, and always gives us opportunity of explaining some things more particularly. This is followed by service, and all is over by half-past five, when everybody hurries to get back to their houses before dark, as it is always dark by a quarter-past six.

"We have often many heathen visitors; some attracted by the sound of the bell, which they may notice for the first time; others by our hymn-singing, or chanting, which causes them to wonder what is going on inside that large and straight building. A person enters, and finds the white man speaking or praying, and does not take immediate hold of that, feeling it is sure to be in an unknown tongue, as among the Mohammedans; so he amuses himself with looking at the people, then the roof, the smooth straight wall, the benches, the windows, till bye and bye, all at once, he finds the sounds that have been falling on his ear are in his own native tongue; then come the fixed attention, the open mouth, the gazing eye; and different sentences from our beautiful church service find acceptance in his wondering mind; the hands are rubbed as a sign of approbation, with a quiet expression of it in the word 'emo[26]!' – 'wonderful!' When 'all sorts and conditions' of people are prayed for, the 'kindly fruits of the earth' in their season asked for, and so on, he sometimes cannot wait for the response, and does not know that one is to come, but bursts forth with his own hearty 'Amin, Amin!' clapping his hands and his chest; and then perhaps goes away to talk with his heathen companions over what he had heard, and to commend the religion of the white man; wondering greatly at much that he has heard, especially at our praying for our enemies.

"Our evening is spent by the children gathering round us, to whom we can hardly give any attention in the day. They repeat passages of Scripture learned by heart from us, and we sing English and Yoruba hymns, to sweet English tunes, with the harmonium.

---

[26]

"Blessed, happy Sundays! Wearied and tired we often are, and very glad, when the day is done, to lay our poor bodies down to rest in the sweet thought —

'Yet shall there dawn at last a day,
A sun that never sets shall rise,
Night shall not veil its ceaseless ray,
The heavenly Sabbath never dies'

"And there and then shall be gathered a blessed assembly from among all nations, and peoples, and tongues."

MORE TRANSITIONS TO GLORY

"*July 23rd* — *We have nothing of particular interest to communicate this month, except that Antonio has been called to the kingdom above. 'I am going to Jesus, who lived and died for me,' were nearly his last words. He was an emigrant from the Brazils, where he had been carried as a slave, and, on coming back to this country, did not get on with his relations, who treated him very badly; so ten years ago he begged us to let him lodge in a little room in our compound for a few weeks, which came to ten years, though he lived principally on his farm. Living in our compound, he always attended church, and from one and another the good tidings of salvation were set before him. At length the seed sown sank down into his heart, and he became a changed man. He felt himself too old to learn to read Yoruba, and I did not know, till I was leaving for England, that he could read Portuguese; but he never had, any book but the Romish calendar of saints. We sent him a Bible, which has been the greatest pleasure to him; he feasted on the reading of it, and longed to teach me Portuguese, that we might talk about it; but then came his wife's illness, then my illness, then his own, so we shall never talk Portuguese, but we shall be able to speak the language of Canaan, when we meet in that land where there is no more death. His nice wife died on New Year's Day, with the name of Jesus on her dying lips. So heaven's gates are opened to take in some of these poor souls, long living in heathen darkness and in Satan's chains, for whom we pray and labour, and for whom Christ has died. To Him be all honour and glory."*

"I have now his two orphans, his eldest girl Talabi, who has lived with me these ten years, and the little babe of two years, who was given to me by his mother, begging me to nurse him for her. The day she died, some of the heathen relations gave us great trouble; they wanted to get the children, just to become slaves to them, but with quite a battle we maintained our right to them, and God gave us the victory. But this girl is a wonderful trouble, ten Topsies in one; and I have much anxiety, now that

she is growing up. How vain is all our work, all our teaching, until the Spirit of God touches the heart. 'Sow the seed' is the command; we are not told when the reaping-time will come. It is a life of continual struggle, fighting with evil spirits and powers of darkness, but we have seen the presence and blessing of God in our midst. He has given us to see the gathering out of a few souls from heathen darkness, to see them walking in the light, and to see them finish their course with joy.

"*Little Samuel is going on very nicely, and goes to our second day-school. For a time his mother was in the compound in which he resides, but he Las been greatly grieved that she has left it to dwell among the heathen. He cried much, because he hoped she would hear the Word of God; but 'now,' he says, 'she throws salvation away from her.'*"

SALVATION OF MOTHERS

"**Aug. 14th** — *His mother is now redeemed, and has every opportunity of coming to church, but she stoutly refuses, and says her fathers' gods are quite enough for her. But the little fellow told me last Sunday evening, with a feeling of hope, 'Though my mother will not come herself; she says she will not prevent me; that is good, is it not'*"

Lest We Forget

VIOLENCE IN YORUBALAND

The closing months of the year 1867, brought anxiety to the minds of the missionaries in Ibadan. The whole Yoruba country was in a most unsettled state. At Abeokuta the churches were despoiled, and the European missionaries were compelled to make Lagos their refuge. There was a threatening of war, in which it was apprehended that Ibadan would be involved. The thought of being again shut up, and of encountering a recurrence of the privations and trials under which they bad so recently suffered, was sufficiently appalling. To this was added an apprehension that the wild hostility, which had risen up against Europeans and Christianity in Abeokuta, might communicate itself to the heathen people at Ibadan. **But above all these evil things rose the remembrance of past mercies, and the sense of security in committing themselves into their Father's care and keeping. Again and again were the chiefs of Ibadan urged to follow the example of their neighbours, by expelling the white people from the country; but God gave His servants favour in the sight of the heathen rulers, and after a meeting had been held to decide the matter, they were reassured by a promise of protection.** "We have let you do your work, and we have done ours, but you little know how closely we have watched you, and your ways please us. We have not only looked at your mouths but at your hands, and we have no complaint to lay against you. Just go on with your work with a quiet mind; you are our friends, and we are yours.

Finding the Ibadans unwilling to join with them in their cruel design, the Egbas and Ijebus again closed the road to the coast, and the old difficulty of procuring supplies and of sending or receiving letters returned, with all its distressing consequences.

The following letter again tells of sickness: -

"Nov. 19th. — My dear husband has lately had a sharp attack of fever, which is general at the commencement of the hot season; which trying season we have now to look for, through the next six months; but perhaps, before the end of that time, we may, through mercy and love, have reached the rest where storms shall never burst, suns shall never smite, and the inhabitant shall no more say, 'I am sick.' The weight upon us is sometimes very great, and but for the sustaining hand we must sink."

MONETARY CONTRIBUTIONS

In November, Mr. and Mrs. Hinderer were cheered by the hearty response of the converts to an appeal made to them six months previously, to contribute weekly towards the maintenance of their native teachers. The falling off which occurred that year in the income of the

Church Missionary Society was now urged as adding strength to the claim. The people decided that the first year's offerings, gathered in the Apo Oluwa[27], "Bags for the Lord" should be sent to the Society, and the amount remitted was £20 5s 7d.

It was also resolved that the Native Pastorate Fund should be commenced in the following year.

Mrs. Hinderer told of the gathering in of these sums from young and old: -

Anna's letter...

"Nov. 30th — We have had a very busy week collecting cowries. Since our return we have been trying to teach our people to give. Every month we have a prayer-meeting, and now every third month we have united with it a kind of missionary meeting, to give the people an account of the work of God in other lands, and we have advised them to have large pots, with small mouths, in which to put their odd money any day, and once a week to put in it something special. This has been the week to gather them in. Some of them have done exceedingly well, and entered heartily into the

---

[27] **Yoruba** literally 'pocket of God'

Second Visit to England. Final Years in Ibadan

plan; especially the children, who have jumped at many devices for making cowries to drop into the Apo Oluwa. Some have not made much effort, but altogether we are much pleased, considering there is not a rich person among them, that we shall have more than thirty bags of cowries to offer to the Church Missionary Society. As each bag contains 20,000 cowry shells, you may think my business has not been small."

WORN OUT BY SICKNESS

The climate, together with so many years of suffering and privation, had told seriously upon the health of both Mr. and Mrs. Hinderer, and the painful conviction was forcing itself upon their minds that their days of service in Africa were numbered. They longed that younger life and power might be found to carry on their work, but until peace should be restored there was but faint hope of any European missionary being permitted to make his way to Ibadan. The only remaining hope for the mission rested upon the native Christians themselves, and among them there was much to encourage them.

PREPARATIONS TO HAND OVER

In entering upon the new year, 1868, the state and prospects of the Church in Ibadan, were the subjects of their anxious deliberations. They reviewed, and determined to set in order to the utmost of their power, each department of the mission, and Mr. Hinderer thenceforth devoted his best energies to the special preparation of the catechists for ordination, and to the training of some of the younger members of the church for active and efficient service as teachers.

The general work of the mission was making steady progress. More than a hundred baptized Christians assembled for worship in the church at Kudeti, the original and central station, and there were in addition many listeners, of whom there was always hope that some would resolve to confess Christ, and join themselves to the company of believers. Then there was a crude temporary church at Oke Aremo, in which more than ninety gathered together in the name of Christ, and where also many others attended and heard the Gospel preached.

NEW POSTING FOR OLUBI

In the remaining station, that of Oke Ogunpa, the seed which had been sown appeared to be producing little fruit. William Allen, the native catechist who had been labouring there for eight years, was much disheartened. What course was now to be taken? Should the work in that part of the town be given up? Such a thought could hardly be entertained, but it was evident that some new plan must be resorted to. With the earnest hope that a new teacher might be the means of awakening the people out of ignorance and superstition, it was decided that Daniel Olubi should remove to Oke Ogunpa, while his work at Kudeti and Aremo should be transferred to William Allen.

It was a trial to Olubi to leave the mission compound as is shown in the following few but expressive words, which were published in the **Church Missionary Record of 1869.**

> "On removing to this station, though it is in Ibadan, and only two miles from my former home in Kudeti, I must remark it has been a great pain to myself, my wife and children, to go from under the roof of our dear master and mistress. For near nineteen years I have lived in one capacity or other with the Rev. D. Hinderer; and my wife, before I married her, lived with Mrs. Hinderer ever since she came out in 1852, and we have indeed found them not only kind and good, and a faithful master and mistress, but a true father and mother and friends. So no wonder we all feel this parting; but it is for our Master's service. May God long preserve them!"

The rest of the story of this year, with its hopes and encouragements, trials and sufferings, may be told in Mrs. Hinderer's own words, by the following extracts: -

"**Jan. 28th, 1868**. — We are going to lose Olubi; which is a trial; we are so used to him. His wife has been with me more than fifteen years, and their children have been my great pleasure. We are placing him in the third station, about two miles from us, in the north-west part of the town, where Mr. Jeffries died, and Mr. Roper lived in hard times. I am getting through this hot season very fairly, but the last three weeks I have had a cough which is very wearying to me; all, no doubt, the loosening of the pins of the tabernacle in which we 'groan being burdened;' but through mercy we look for a time when we shall serve God without sin, without such infirmities, without sorrow. We have had such strong harmattan[28], which even curled up all the pens! Yet the mornings were fresh and cool, thermometer at 66 degrees, but at noon 93 degrees; it has gone again, and we have only melting heat."

TALES OF ENCOURAGEMENT

"**April 21st** — In our work we are going on with some measure of discouragement, crosses, and toil, but a bright side too is given, one of hope and encouragement ; and we feel that the Lord is owning and blessing his

---

[28] a cold, dry and dusty wind

Second Visit to England. Final Years in Ibadan

work, and gathering out a little company for himself. Last week, we buried a child of fourteen years, after some weeks of great illness. She was the most silent and reserved child I ever met with; I never knew whether she heard any — thing, or not, and could never get, from her more than a 'Yes' or 'No' or 'I don't know' but all at once, in her illness, she was like the dumb man, whose tongue was loosed, and he spake plain. We could only look on and wonder, and give praise to God. Her father is one of the most sincere Christians, her mother only brought into the church by circumstances; her three elder brothers are baptized, and two of them are communicants. She was baptised as a child when four years old. The dear girl poured out her whole heart, saying she had been taught by us all, but never felt the power and blessing of it till she lay on this sick bed, and then God showed her, in her heart and soul, the blessing of salvation, and she laid hold on eternal life. She knew she had a Saviour in the Lord. Jesus Christ.

"She had precious words of comfort for her father and her brothers, but she warned them also telling two of them that she believed they were in earnest, but that she feared another was tempted a little from the straight road when going about trading, and spending much time where God is not worshipped, and Sunday utterly unknown. To her mother, in the most loving way, she said, 'Mother, with your feet you have gone to God's House, not really for the good of your soul but for other purposes ;that is not enough, you must strive with your whole heart after God, and His great salvation through Jesus.' Their heathen relations, and neighbours, who were constantly in and out, were greatly struck by hearing her talk about death, and said, ' This must be a wonderful religion, which could make anyone not afraid to die!'

A short time before her death, worn out by pain and weakness, she exclaimed, 'Oh, for patience but if it pleases God to let me go soon, how glad I shall be. Her heathen aunt, sitting by her, said, 'Where would you go?' 'Oh, go to God, go to Jesus, 'adding, die here, and go to live with God.' The woman was awed by the idea of a child desiring to die, and she came to the burial, and on Sunday to church, for she said she wanted to 'learn how to die, like Moleye.'

STATE OF THE HOME

"I have so much to do at home, I never go beyond the compound except to sick people, unless I am quite obliged. I feel that going out knocks me down more than anything. Some of my girls have married, and some of our boys, after many years of labour for them, have gone after their own ways and pleasures; so there are not that many in and about the house, only seven girls and five boys in the house, and eight in the compound, but we have about thirty six in our day school, and at

Second Visit to England. Final Years in Ibadan

our second station thirty eight, and all have to be attended to and cared for, in different ways.

"My husband's health is far from good, and some times we have feared a thorough break-up; then renewed strength comes again, is so quietly persevering, that he gets through a great deal. He is much interested in instructing the native teachers, and two or three boys who have grown up with us the last fifteen years, and who bid fair to be very useful members of the society; of course they came out of heathen households, and it is a happiness to see them turning out, well. We have been favoured to bring up some to do God's work in their own country, which has ever an aim and object with us. God gives us such comfort in our native teachers, they are so earnest, kind, and affectionate to us, only desiring to relieve, help, and comfort us."

Of some of these teachers, including Olubi, so often mentioned in these pages, Mr. Hinderer wrote about this time: -

Anna's letter...

"We have the comfort of seeing some of our native teachers promise to become efficient ministers of the gospel, and foremost among them is Daniel Olubi. He seems to be increasingly faithful, diligent and pious, and I hope before long, he will be ordained by Bishop Crowther. He was nearly overcome at the thought, when I mentioned my intention of recommending him for ordination: the weight of the responsibility, and the thought of his insufficiency lie heavily upon him,

"Little Samuel has been very ill; I often felt he would go, and dared not ask for his life, there are so many snares and temptations in this dark heathen land, and the child's heart seems so truly in the right way now; but God is raising him up again, may it be for his honour and glory.

"These signs among us of the moving of dead bones, of the shooting forth of tender leaves, in the midst of a more sorrowful side, ought to be enough to make us content and thankful only to be permitted to sow beside all waters, and I often feel ashamed when I have allowed myself to speak of anxieties and discouragements."

BREATHING DIFFICULTIES

"*July 30th*. — Mr. Hinderer has been suffering from congestion of the lungs, which gave him often a severe and cramp-like pain in the heart; he is better, but never well, and is never out of pain. We have many weights

Second Visit to England. Final Years in Ibadan

on our hearts about the mission, but 'the Lord sitteth above the water-flood.'"

"**Sep. 12**th — With a weak and suffering body, D. is getting up a nice church in Aremo, our second station, and a more simple one is now completed in Ogunpa, the third station, where Olubi is. I have been very ill the last six weeks, and have spent all but four or five days of them in much fever and suffering. Now that I am creeping up the hill, I should be glad of many little things to help me, which I should have, if the road were open, but I am getting on without them, and it is almost more trial to my ever kind husband, to be unable to get for me these helps and comforts. Our prospects are no better, we cannot help often fearing we shall break down, before better and more peaceful times come. Last Sunday I was up, but could not go out; many passages in Job were helpful to my spirit: —' He openeth their ear to discipline,' &c. Too often we 'see not the bright light' in the clouds, and are much cast down and discouraged. Truly, the future is very dark, but in the midst of all, we may be sure, 'the bright light is in the cloud,' and it must be for our Master's good purpose, that He has placed and keeps us here so long."

"**Oct. 23rd.**— I am now much better, but recovery seems sadly slow. I am a good deal worn out in body and spirit, and probably I shall never be strong again. I am so tender, I can only sit with pillows round me, and just crawl from one room to another, and I am dreading the thought of the heat which must soon come, but 'sufficient unto the day is the evil thereof.' 'Give us this day our daily bread;' we are not told to ask for tomorrow's bread. My husband is quite wonderful. After all his care and anxiety for me, I feared for him, but now he is so much better than for months before. Oh, how the Father stays the rough wind in the day of the east wind!

DISSAPOINTING FRUIT

"We have had such trial in two of our big boys turning out so wickedly, full of charms and poisons, and determined to do everything with the heathen. Many thorns are in the pillow, but there is another pillow on which to lean the aching heart and head. What should we do without that?

CONVERSIONS ON DEATH BEDS

"As to the work, we try to be hopeful, but it is far below what we want it to be. There is some movement. The heathen talk about the Christian's religion, they ask questions far more than they used to do, and listen to the teaching in the streets, and often drop into church.

Second Visit to England. Final Years in Ibadan

In a remarkable manner, some, on their dying beds, have borne witness to the faithful teaching, and have shown that they believed its truth, and regretted that they had shut their ears to it. About a fortnight ago, a man died: he had only been once to church, but Olubi and Okusehinde[29] had often visited him, and he had heard them in the streets. He was interested, but said it was impossible for such as him to follow our way, yet he could never get it out of his mind; and then he fell ill, and sent for my husband. It was the first time a heathen man had sent for him. He was very weak, but his conversation was such as gives joy to the heart. **He anxiously enquired if there was any help for him, now life was ending, since he had displeased God all his days.** *After some conversation and prayer, he seemed to have a bright glimmer of hope, and folding his hands, said, 'May God have mercy, and if there is such a Saviour as the white man says there is, may He help me.' When they saw him again he could not speak, but put his hands together and lifted them up. Two days after he died. We think that He who took the dying thief in His arms of love and mercy did not turn away from this poor man. Such gleams of hope coming, though rarely, are a wonderful help over the many dark and rough places."*

---

[29] Probably spelt Ogunsehinde

AFRICAN TIME!

"*Oct. 26th.* — *Only last Thursday we received the March mail. An Ijebu man, who has a house in Ibadan, assured the governor he was coming here direct, so he gave him that mail to bring to us; but what is the difference between a day and a year to an African! He stayed six months in Ijebu, but tells us, he took such good care of the parcel, he slept on it every night that no one should take it away.*

"*I am getting on but slowly, and do not feel so well today. I think I am no more what I have been; my rather remarkable rallying power after an illness seems gone; still I may get round again. We have just had such a storm of wind and rain, which has spoiled all my lovely orange-blossoms. The trees have been such a pleasant sight, with an abundance of ripe fruit, though we have gathered, and given away baskets full; at the same time, all the ends of the branches have been so rich in bright fresh young leaves, and those elegant sweet-smelling blossoms; but now the beauty has gone within half an hour. It is so with things of earth; but after this comes the new fruit.*"

Second Visit to England. Final Years in Ibadan

SALVATION OF AN OLD PRINCE

"*Nov. 20th*. — *On Advent Sunday eight adults were admitted, by baptism, into the visible church. One was a very old man, one of the royal family now settled in Oyo, formerly Katunga, which Mungo Park and other travellers visited in its glory. This old man saw all these travellers. He was an heir to the throne, and his name Adeyemi, signifies, 'a crown fits me,' but the earthly crown had indeed failed him. Among the different wars, he has been taken captive by three different tribes, and has undergone many hardships. Five years ago, being old, and nearly useless, he redeemed himself for a few bags of cowries, and reached Ibadan, where he practiced his great medicine and charm knowledge. He found a sister here, who gave him a room in her compound; but, when he was very ill, she put him out in the street to die, as it would be impossible for her to bury one who had been heir to a crown. The poor old man dwelt under a tree, and struggled through his illness, and the passers by, knowing or learning who he was, gave him cowries, or a little food. One of our young schoolmasters who, sixteen years ago, was one of the first African children we took into our house, became much interested in him and, while administering to his bodily needs, would talk to him about his soul. But the old man was greatly enraged, and heaped curses on the youth for daring to speak to him of a way better than his own, stoutly defending the worship of his idols, and only wishing to go to the heaven where they would take him. To the surprise of all, he recovered. Another relation took him in, and our schoolmaster still visited him. At last light broke in upon his poor dark mind, and he now seems to be rejoicing in his Saviour, and the prospect before him.*

"On the day of their baptism, the candidates had been sitting on the front benches in the church, in their white garments, and, as they walked down the aisle to the font, we all sang a hymn, which my husband had composed in Yoruba, on 'Be thou faithful,' to the tune we call 'Halesowen.' It was very touching to see the old man at the font, leaning on his long stay as we might imagine Jacob to have done before Pharaoh, his lips quivering with old age, and his eyes gleaming with pleasure and perfect child-like belief and trust, making the responses, of which he certainly put in some which were not in the book.

OUR JOY AND CROWN

"The others have a history more or less interesting, which gives us every reason to believe that they have laid hold of the hope set before them. This is the bright side of our life in this country, and often such a time has cheered and comforted us, while Passing through many storms and waves. We feel as if we could never give up until we cross to the other side of the river.

OFTEN IN TORMENTS

Anna's letter ...

"We cannot tell you now the darker side of our life, its present and prospective difficulties. It is the burden appointed us to carry, and we shall not be left alone to bear it; yet we do feel it heavy, and often groan under it. But the day hasteth on, the shadows of evening are stretched out, and oh, if infinite mercy and love receive us, we shall then think the heaviest weight, care, and sorrow to have been but light indeed. I am not in a good state of health, and my spirits have undergone such a change; I believe the latter is but the effect of the former. A thorough change would be the best remedy; but when the 'grasshopper is a burden,' the body shrinks from a four days' journey, in this broiling sun, to the coast; yet I dare say it will be accomplished, and in some measure I am making ready for it, putting things to rights, and getting to the end of some of our lesson-books with the boys.

In several of these extracts from the letters of 1868, the health of Mr. and Mrs. Hinderer, which had long taken a sadly prominent place in the history of the mission, presents itself to view more frequently than any other subject. They have been inserted for the purpose of showing that, as the year advanced, the impressions which influenced them at its commencement had deepened, and that, while sometimes they felt that they could "never give up," in calmer moments they regarded the time when their retirement from the mission would be a matter of necessity and duty, as even near at hand.

1869 – THE 17th YEAR

Another year opened, and a little gleam of sunshine brightened its commencement. They were permitted to distinguish it by taking one of those steps of progress which would give the Church of Christ a surer footing in Ibadan.

"On New Year's Day, 1869, the church at Oke Ogunpa station was opened. It is very neat and nice, and stands on a hill. It has a good congregation of about a hundred Christians to begin with; it is an offshoot of our own church. It is remarkable that we get so many converts from that quarter of the town, which is nearly two miles distant from ours. They used to come to us, and bring their dinner. After a while we made a large shed in that quarter, and gave them a service in the afternoon. Now,

for many reasons, we felt it was time they should have a separate church. Some of them were getting into years, and felt it burdensome to come so far to church; and we also felt that having a church there would be a fresh inducement to try and draw others in.

"*All the three congregations assembled at the new church, and they had a cheering and refreshing service. Afterwards some three hundred persons partook of a feast which we make for them every year; having had the children a few days before. It was a very happy day.*

"*Laniyono and Konigbagbe are the schoolmaster and mistress there, and they did work. Koni is so energetic; she had my best powers spent on her, and she is capital. Laniyono is doing well, persevering and industrious*

"*Olubi is working on hard ground, and is first rate. I have groaned and grudged giving him up, but it was right; only we both lost a right hand.*"

DISSAPOINTMENT WITH LANIYONO

In less than two months after this bright and promising beginning, it was found necessary to dismiss Laniyono as a false professor, and a dishonour to the Christian name. Many had been the disappointments and sorrows of Mr. and Mrs. Hinderer in their missionary work, but none, perhaps, was ever more keenly felt than this, when a youth, over whom they had watched with a father's and mother's care and love, from a very early age, who had appeared to give promise that the work of grace wrought in his youthful heart was ripening as he advanced in years, had terribly fallen, at the very time when he was selected to fill a place of trust and usefulness, and that he should have brought dishonour upon the religion of Christ, which was still, in so great a degree, on its trial in the land, and seeking to make its way amongst the people.

Of this sorrow, felt so acutely, Mrs. Hinderer might have written with increased emphasis, what she wrote in a previous time of disappointment of a similar nature, though in some measure less aggravated.

> *"These are deeper and more heart-searching trials than anything from the poor heathen. We often say our dear Saviour's most painful hour on earth was when He could say, 'He that dippeth with rue in the dish hath lifted up his heel against me.'"*

THE GREAT ESCAPE

At Christmas there had been reason to hope that Mrs. Hinderer might be able to go to Lagos, to seek the refreshment and medical treatment which had become so

Second Visit to England. Final Years in Ibadan

needful. But rumours reached Ibadan that a plot had been formed against her life, should she venture upon the journey, arid she bad just given up all thought of moving, when, on New Year's Eve, a messenger arrived, sent by their faithful friend Captain Glover, and instructed to bring them both in safety to the coast. It was impossible for Mr. Hinderer to leave Ibadan in haste, and without commending the native teachers to the protection of the Chiefs, who were all, at this time, with the army in the war. The entire overthrow of the mission might have been the result of so precipitate a movement. But Mrs. Hinderer was in so precarious a state of health that without hesitation it was decided that she should make use of the opportunity offered. She set out Jan. 5th, on this somewhat perilous journey, which she described in a letter from Lagos: -

> "I kept the messenger a few days, to make ready again; and by moonlight one morning, before the plotters would be awake, we set off We came as fast as possible; I was not allowed to put my foot into a house. We slept in the bush; found the Governor's boat, which had been waiting some days in expectation; went rapidly over the lagoon, and in the evening of the third day we landed in Lagos, and I was once more a free woman!

> "Little Dan Olubi is with me, bright and sharp as a needle; Oyebode I have also brought, to learn something of printing,

that we may be able to make use of our press. I can send them home by Abeokuta any day, as that road is open to all but white people."

"**Lagos, Jan. 25th.** —I must write when I can, to be ready for the mail, which seems to come and go in a marvellously short space of time. I cannot yet recover myself, my daily life upset; such a wonderful separation from my husband; I cannot hear from him, nor send to him, as I should like; but I am thankful to have been able to send him, by my carriers, some of the necessaries, if not the comforts, of life. Here there is so much coming and going, I feel bewildered, and do not get settled; and as to my health, I have made no progress as yet. The doctor says I have had a thorough shock to the constitution; **that I am one of a hundred to be in the country at all, and that I must go home. I wish it could have a clear direction, as Moses had, 'Ye have dwelt long enough in this mount; turn you, and take your journey and go.' On the whole, we have had a rough path in our missionary life, but it has been always brightened by hope.** We have been mercifully helped through difficult places, and marvellously favoured to 'carry music in the heart.' The darkest day has always had sunshine in it, and at this moment, in Ibadan, there is much cause for hope in many ways. Never were chiefs and people more kind to us in their way; never were we *more respected than now; and never did people more patiently listen to teaching, though we do not see the fruit of it as much as we should like.*

*"When we look at what is wanted and desired, we may say, what is the result? But on the whole, we have been permitted to see much that makes our hearts glad and thankful. **We came to a town where the name of Jesus had never been heard; that name, and the salvation which He gives, have been proclaimed through the length and breadth of it;** many are thinking and talking of it; a small company have believed and rejoiced in that name, and have died in faith, and trust, and hope; others are walking in the light of it, and others taking first steps in the Christian life. To leave it all is such a sorrow to our hearts, that if we had even bodily strength it must tell upon us. May our God graciously direct our steps! In all probability I shall have to go to England in two or three months, but indeed the to-morrow is very dark. I do not like leaving my husband alone, but we agreed, before parting, to yield to what seems right and best, trusting to be directed b our heavenly Father."*

The much-desired direction came, in an unwelcome way, through an attack of sickness, more severe than ever; and by the next mail she wrote a few hurried lines to prepare her friends in England for her arrival early in the ensuing month.

Anna's letter...

"Feb. 32nd. — There is a mail leaving to-morrow, so I just add a line. I have been very ill, and the doctor and others have wanted to send me off by it; but as I am better, I have pleaded to remain till this time next month that I may send to and hear from my dear husband. He will be quite prepared for the decision. I have just parted with my two boys Dan and Oyebode; it is better to have them back at their own place; **but we have had a sorrowful parting, they cried bitterly.**

"I hope we shall meet before long, but oh, these present moments are rough and thorny, many are the pangs. God comfort, help, lead, and direct. It is so sad to feel I shall never see poor dear Ibadan again, and all my babies. Well, well, there is a land above, 'No seas there shall sever.' You will feel and care for me in the heavy trial of leaving my husband behind, and going home alone."

She wrote by the same mail to another friend:

"Our people's and children's letters are most piteous. It has been the mission and work of our hearts. Pray for poor lonely me, as I shall be on

my voyage when you get this letter; and for my dear husband. 'I will guide thee with Mine eye,' is my resting place. Pray for poor Ibadan, and the little 'garden' there."

It is pleasant to record that early in 1869, Akielle, Mrs. Hinderer's first scholar was appointed master of the school at Kudeti, soon after which he married Ogunyomi, who became a true fellow-helper in his work. About the same time, Oyebode was entrusted with the school at Aremo.

The Church at Ibadan

CHAPTER VIII

Return to England
Close of Life

"O glorious end of life's short day of sadness!
O blessed course so well and nobly run!
O home of true and everlasting gladness!
O crown unfading! And so early won!"

"Though tears will fall, we bless Thee, O our Father, for the dear one for ever with the blest

And wait the Easter dawn when Thou shalt gather Thine own, long parted, to their endless rest."

R. H. BAYNES

THE STORY OF MRS. HINDERER'S voyage and arrival in England is given in a letter to her husband, written on the 7th of April, from Bootle Hall, a week after she had landed in Liverpool.

Lest We Forget

Anna's letter...

"How I wish you could at this moment know how kindly and tenderly I am housed and sheltered in this home of love and comfort. We had a favoured journey over the mighty deep, and reached Liverpool on April 1st, four or five days before the time though we had very rough seas and contrary winds, but mercifully no gale, of which there have been so many. I got on wonderfully, and was never so kindly treated. I was nursed and cared for as if I had been a child. I look forward to recovering now I am at home, but I have had much of illness since we parted in Ibadan; it was a struggle only to get sufficiently better at Lagos to bear the voyage. These dear people, Mr. and Mrs. M., took no end of trouble to get me from the ship. In putting myself and boxes to rights, I got so ill that at times it was a question with me whether I should not suddenly depart. I was thankful when they brought their carriage and took me off; and I have had every luxury and comfort. **If I had been as ill in Ibadan as I have been since I left it, I do not think I should be alive; so we must be thankful I got away when I did.** *Now, if I have rest and care and kindness, all of which I may expect, I think in time I shall be all right again; people are only ready to do too much for me. Fancy poor me, knocking about in the bush the other day, and now*

not allowed to take a first class railway journey without an attendant, and all sorts of luxuries!"

The journey, for which such thoughtful provision had been made, was accomplished on the day after the date of the above letter, and ended at Halesowen Rectory, where she remained with her friends for several weeks. They had the privilege of nursing and tending her through a time of severe suffering, and could not but wonder at the spirit and energy which still continued to animate her as in other days. Often would she take pleasure in telling the story of her last years in Ibadan, sustaining and strengthening the interest which many in that parish had previously taken in the mission. It seemed impossible to restrain her from overtaxing her strength, whenever for a few hours her pain had abated; though there was warning enough from distressing experience, that such efforts would be followed by anguish and exhaustion. **She still yearned after her much-loved work, and she often expressed an earnest longing that it might yet please God to restore her to such a measure of health as would enable her to return to her labours in Africa, for at least a few more years. But those who were with her constantly, and observed her state day by day, were satisfied that such a revival was beyond the reach of hope, and were filled with distressing apprehensions that she might not even survive till her husband's expected and much desired**

arrival in England. Happily, these fears were not realised. God in His mercy heard the petitions of many anxious hearts, and granted her a perceptible return of strength. As soon as she appeared to have been sufficiently revived to bear the fatigue of another journey, she ventured to travel northward as far as Rickerby, near Carlisle, where friends who held her in warm regard were longing to welcome her arrival. There she enjoyed the renewal of early friendship, and was soothed by the kindness which anticipated every want, and ministered considerately to the alleviation of her sufferings. She wrote of the pleasure she derived from the beauty and brightness of the garden, with its rhododendrons in full bloom, and the green park beyond; and having described these, she added: -

"I may take all the pleasant, and all the bright, and all the pretty, — keeping myself prepared for the more usual and commoner every-day life which has to follow."

Soon she had again to tell of serious illness, but her trustful spirit could say: — " *He who appoints the daily lot doeth all things well."*

From Rickerby she went for a few days to London, and thence proceeded to Lowestoft. She could not, as in former years, go in and out among the cottages of the poor. Her time was chiefly spent on the beach, where she

Return to England. Close of Life.

had the full benefit of the fine sea breezes, from which she derived refreshment and strength. But in one of her letters she described a visit she had made to one old friend, whose loving care of her in childhood had secured a place in her affections. **At first the aged woman failed to recognise her, but was at length convinced, and was then overwhelmed with emotion. As soon as she could sufficiently command her feelings, she made the homely and plain-spoken comment, "Well dear, I am Mary still, and I don't hold to deceiving anybody, but my opinion is, dear, that you are booked, and not long for this world."** Mrs. Hinderer told her that she hoped she was "booked" in the better land, but that she fancied she would have to wait a little longer before being called to dwell there.

In September she received the joyful news of Mr. Hinderer's safe arrival in Lagos; and before the end of the month they had the happiness and consolation of meeting again in London. She had been "wearying"' to see him, watching eagerly for the arrival of each mail; and now they were permitted to meet once more, after months of separation, which had been to each of them so full of trouble and suffering; and to sing a new song of thanksgiving to their gracious Father, who had protected and comforted them, and preserved their lives.

Mr. Hinderer had returned to England in sadly impaired health. **During the last six months of his** residence in Ibadan he had repeated attacks of fever, and the native Christians were so fully alive to his critical condition, that, though with heavy hearts, they encouraged his departure before the return of the next hot season, as necessary to the preservation of his life. The wants of the native church were his only anxiety and cause for hesitation, knowing as he did that it was impossible for a European to take his place, until communication with the coast should be re-established. But he believed that he might entrust the mission with confidence to three efficient native agents, who were not only united in the bonds of brotherly love, and anxious to strengthen each other's hands, but also were respected and trusted by the converts, and were making their way among their heathen countrymen. They had received from the chiefs a promise of protection for themselves, and for the Christian congregations. Shortly before his departure from amongst them, Mr. Hinderer had the satisfaction of completing the church at Aremo. Up to the last moment he had cherished a hope of witnessing the ordination of two of his tried and instructed native teachers, to whose care he committed the flock at Ibadan; but this expectation was disappointed, and he had left them still awaiting an opportunity of being ordained.

CALL TO SERVICE FOR OLUBI

On Advent Sunday, 1871, Daniel Olubi was admitted to deacon's orders, at Lagos, by the Right Rev. Henry Cheetham, Bishop of Sierra Leone.

PARTIAL BLINDNESS

Mr. and Mrs. Hinderer were detained for some time in London, **for the benefit of medical treatment in addition to her other bodily afflictions, the sight of Mrs. Hinderer's right eye was impaired, and soon was irrecoverably lost.** The eminent oculist who attended her, attributed this privation to the injurious influences of the climate in Africa. But now, as always, looking upon the mercies which she received as outweighing her trials, she had written of this new calamity, during its progress, in a submissive spirit: —

> *"Perhaps it is only a little weakness, but it goes on and increases, and I am only really comfortable when I shut my eyes. The oculist said, if I had remained in Africa) to get lower than I was, if I had lived I should have gone blind there; so there is much mercy and blessing in everything; and what a favour that my eye has no great pain. A little weakness and weariness and discomfort; truly it is a loss, indeed, but the left eye is quite good,*

and we may hope that with God's blessing it will keep so."

In November they removed to Norwich, and for a short time enjoyed a quiet, happy life, near the Cathedral. A friend, whose recollections of Mrs. Hinderer's trustful anticipations in the prospect of her work in Africa have already been quoted, writes of her at this time: —

"All the years of her perils and sufferings having passed away, once more I remember her, in her last visit to Norwich. She was there with Mr. Hinderer three months, shattered, yet still so bright. I saw much of her at that time; the same characteristics were there, faith, earnestness, brightness, cheerfulness, unselfishness. She told African tales to factory girls, spoke of dangers and toils and triumphs to listeners at a mothers' meeting; took snap-dragon to the patients in a convalescent home; on Christmas eve distributed gifts from a Christmas tree to old and young; paid visits, and cheered many. Yet she was fading. I saw her a day or two before she went to Martham, and then I saw her no more.~'

It was evident to Mr. and Mrs. Hinderer, as well as to their friends, that the thought of a return to the mission could no longer be entertained. But the one desire uppermost in their hearts was that while life was spared, and when some measure of health had been restored, life and strength might be employed in the work and service of their heavenly Master.

NEW VINEYARDS

In January, 1870, she wrote: — *" I do long that it may please God to show us soon what we ought to do, and direct us to a dwelling place;"* and after telling with satisfaction that Mr. Hinderer had been able to take part one Sunday in two services, she added: — *" So I hope we shall soon get into regular work, just enough for us half-worn-out pilgrims to do."*

Before the end of that month the desired opportunity came, in the offer of the curacy of Martham, in Norfolk. This seemed to bring with it the occupation, and the home, which in submission to the will of God they had desired.

Before settling at Martham, they once more spent a few days with their friends at Halesowen. All were then struck by Mrs. Hinderer's vivacity, and her apparent improvement in health. She had left them, but a few months before, thin and worn, and with a look of age far beyond her years, but now her face was full, her complexion clear, and there was something like the appearance of a return to youth. She attended the mothers' meeting, and once more delighted that assembly of poor women by her presence and conversation.

The beginning of March found them settled at Martham. Mrs. Hinderer described the village as "large, with a green, and bright pleasant cottages and houses. There is work enough, with more than 1,200 souls."

May 4th, she wrote:

"We are now getting quite established at Martham. It is so entirely not our doing, and not our particular wish, that we cannot but hope it is the appointment, for the time, of our gracious God, and that He will mercifully accept a work for Him at our hands. We are quite encouraged already, the people welcome us very heartily in our house-to-house visitation, and the Sunday and day schools are much improved. I am hoping to get up two little mothers' meetings in the week, but oh, with everything any of us try to do, how entirely it is nothing without the breath from above, the breath of life. That is what we want; oh, that we may have it!"

Again on the 24th of May: -

"I love to think of you at this sweet time of year at pretty Tirley. You are more lovely than we in Norfolk, I dare say, but I do think just now we are delicious, and

D. and I think we never could live anywhere but in the country, amidst millions of primroses, bright green fields, and the delicious fruit blossoms. Perhaps, being away from them so long makes us more in rapture just now, but certainly it is a glorious season. We like our appointment here, more and more. We are able to work so pleasantly and what we do seems appreciated, which certainly is helpful. My little mothers' meeting is quite a success; we are twenty-five, and I had thought if I got ten or twelve it would be worth while to go on. My second [mothers' meeting] looks hopeful also, in the little outlandish hamlet; but there the women are more in the fields just now. I wish I could have you all know our little abode. You would like a sight of our magnificent church; it certainly is lovely. Then the churchyard is so pleasant now, with its carpet of white and gold, perfectly covered with daisies and buttercups. My eyes have been better, but wind affects them sadly. I see I may not play any tricks with myself. Getting on so bonnily of late, I thought I might venture further, and walked too far yesterday, and had such a night of pain. I must go to my hamlet this afternoon."

LAST BREATH

She was little aware, when writing these words, how near was the end of her trials and her service upon

earth, and how soon that pretty churchyard would be her own last resting-place. The meeting to which she went in that distant hamlet was the last of such gatherings which she attended. They had been a great source of pleasure to her, and a favoured opportunity for the people, who had been had been as much drawn towards her by her loving sympathising spirit, during three short months, as if she had been living and visiting amongst them for years.

She had planned to spend a few hours of the following day, May 25th, at Lowestoft, but she was unwell, and only able to sit up for a few hours. Days of much anguish and acute suffering ensued. Remedies were used without success; and at the end of the first week of this attack of illness, it was too evident that she was rapidly sinking. But while the body was failing, the inner man was renewed day by day. Her mind was fixed on the great change before her, and on the joy of departing to be with Christ. The first prayer she breathed audibly was, "Wash me, and I shall be whiter than snow." Some time after, she asked, "Will He forgive all my sins, and receive me" Without waiting for an answer, the momentary doubt was lost in the blessed assurance, "Yes, He died for me, that I might live." She made an effort to fold her hands, and repeated.

Return to England. Close of Life.

> *"Nothing in my hand I bring;*
> *Simply to Thy cross I cling."*

To Mr. Hinderer's question, "Are you happy?" she replied, "Happy? Yes, in Christ. Bright prospect; yes, bright? And later, seeing him troubled and sorrowful, she asked, "Why are you so unhappy? I am so happy it is nearly finished;" adding to a kind friend who was ministering to her, "It is sweet to die." On waking up from a comfortable quiet sleep, she exclaimed, "A land that I will show thee! Not like that little piece of Canaan!" **She was joyful and peaceful in the midst of severe suffering, and desired that those who were nursing her might rejoice with her in the belief that she was going to be with the Lord. "Are you not glad," she asked, "that I am going home, going to be with the Lord for ever?"** On one of the days, when she was in a state of extreme debility, Mr. Hinderer repeated the hymn

> *"Jesu, lover of my soul."*

She seemed to enjoy it; but when he was about to begin another, she answered, speaking with difficulty, No, that will do—in silence upon my God." For several days she scarcely uttered a word, but on Monday, June 6th, she was roused by the visit of a neighbouring clergyman, who spoke words of peace and refreshment to her soul, and she made an effort to sing: —

*"For ever with the Lord!
Amen, so let it be!"*

During the remaining hours of the day, she could only return a feeble response to any words of Scripture, read or repeated to her. Relief and ease were at length granted, in answer to prayer, and she seemed to be settling into quiet sleep; but it was the sleep of death; and at twenty minutes before nine o'clock her happy spirit entered into rest.

So passed away, in her forty-fourth year, one whose health had been utterly ruined by the pestilential climate of Africa, the dangers of which she had encountered for the love of Christ. She had not held her comforts or her life dear to herself; if only she might do her Lord's work, and bring at least a few hearts to the knowledge of His name. Her desire was granted, she now rests from her labours. Some are gone before, and some shall yet follow, who will be her crown of rejoicing in the presence of our Lord Jesus Christ, at His coming.

It will not be out of place here to give a few extracts from letters written, in English, by members of the native flock in Ibadan, who received the news of their beloved Iya's death on the 16th of July. These are but a small selection out of many tender and touching expressions of love to her, and of sympathy with their bereaved friend and pastor, of deep sorrow that they could neither see her, nor hear from her, again; and of grateful appreciation of the work which she had so affectionately and perseveringly carried on amongst them.

"....The dear Iya's death took us much by surprise. Both ourselves and the Christians, for the whole week, have been deeply sorrowful . . . She has faithfully finished her course, and is now received into glory, to be forever with her Lord and Master, whom she so faithfully served and followed. **Her conjoint labours with you here, in the establishment of Christ's kingdom, upwards of sixteen years, will ever be to her praise.** The sons and daughters she had kindly brought up, and cared for in the Gospel, will ever lament her loss; and her good deeds, as books, will ever be read among us. . . We are fully persuaded that you will remember the living church which God has mercifully gathered here in this place, through your instrumentality. The steady growth, and the faithful teaching in her, by your sons and daughters in the Gospel, will enable you to comfort yourself.

"He has done well, because Iya is now freed from this world of sin and sorrow for a better one, (where there is no more pain, no more trials,) to repay her labours with a crown of glory. Dear Baba, take comfort, Iya shall rise again; by this assurance only we can take comfort and be glad.

Lest We Forget

"'It is the Lord; let Him do what seemeth Him good.' 'In all our affliction He is afflicted,' and what we know not now we shall know hereafter. My whole heart bled for you, my dear Baba, for you are left alone, yet not alone, for Christ is with you. Our dear Iya, though she died, she yet speaketh. Her work in Ibadan will still live, and bear testimony of her, till such time that she will say, 'These are they whom Thou hast given me. Our prayer is, though He smite may He heal, by drawing many unto His fold. We hope the dear and loving friends, who always remember us poor Africans, may still continue their love to us in the absence of Iya."

The preceding extracts are taken from letters written by individual members of the flock. One still remains, which conveyed the outpouring of the hearts of the whole Christian community: —

"OUR DEAR PASTOR, — We are very sorry that our first letter to you is that of sympathy, and that because of our dear and loving white mother in the faith, whose face we are not privileged to see again in the body, but whose image is deeply impressed on us, and whose memory will be lasting. We deeply lament your loss and our loss, but it is the hand of our loving Father; His will must be done. 'Let Him do what seemeth Him good.' 'Blessed be His Name.' Our comfort is that we

shall one day meet in that land where 'sorrow and sighing shall flee away.' You both have brought Jesus with you into our town, but you have left Him among us; for this we are thankful. Having then this Jesus, and being enlightened by His Spirit, our hopes are brightened; and we mourn not, therefore, as those that have no hope. Dear Baba, we commit you, both body and soul, to the kind keeping of the great Jehovah. Mourn not your loss, for it will be joy at the last day. She is gone to her rest, and is now among the redeemed that gather around their Saviour, singing praises to His name. May we all be her boast and rejoicing at the last day. Truly her labours of love will never be forgotten among us. Let us 'work while it is called the day, for the night cometh when no one can work.' And may we walk in faith that we may meet where we shall part no more!

We remain, dear Baba,

"Your sympathizing sons and daughters in the faith,

"The Ibadan Church members."

Lest We Forget

Slave Caravan on the March

STOP PRESS

Rev. Mrs. Oyindamola Amosun is a **'seed'** of the Mele family that donated the portion of land at Kudeti to the Hinderers on which St. David's Church Kudeti was built.

For instance we read in a publication[30] how Hinderer and his wife Anna returned to Ibadan, where they opened a mission at Kudeti on a portion of land given to them by Chief Mele.

She is maternally the grand daughter of the Laosebikan's family, one of the three families that form the Mele-Kanbi family of Kudeti.

Rev. Mrs. Oyindamola Amosun is a practising nurse is actively involved in medical missions with several outreaches to villages and has a great passion for children that are under her medical care.

Above all, she is the dutiful wife of Rev. Victor Amosun, who is the Founding President of Occupy World Outreach Missions (O.W.O.M.) a Missions Agency based in Ibadan.

The **'seed'** of the land donated by the Mele(Mele-Kanbi) no doubt has yielded many fruits! Rev. Mrs. Oyindamola Amosun is one!

Discovered by
Henry Hamilton
International Outreach & Missions Centre (I.O.M.C.), Ibadan.

---

[30] **"The Fearless Evangelists"**, (Goodwill and Congratulatory Messages to the 150th Anniversary of Christianity in Ibadan and its Environs). 150 Years of Christianity in Ibadan, The Untold Story (Anniversary Publication).